£40

9

KEY TEXTS

Classic Studies in the History of Ideas

COMMONPLACE
BOOK
1919-1953

George Edward Moore

Edited by
Casimir Lewy

THOEMMES
PRESS

© Thoemmes Press 1993

Published in 1993 by
Thoemmes Press
85 Park Street
Bristol BS1 5PJ
England

ISBN 1 85506 231 3

This is a reprint of the 1962 Edition

Reprinted by arrangement with Routledge

Publisher's Note

EDITOR'S PREFACE

G. E. Moore expressed a wish that after his death I should go through his philosophical papers and consider the possibility of preparing a selection of them for publication. These papers include nine notebooks, written at various times between 1919 and 1953 and containing his "Commonplace Book". Only the last six notebooks were actually given this name by Moore himself; but the three earlier ones are of exactly the same character and it seemed clearly right to include them.

It was obvious, however, that the notebooks could not be published as they stood, and that it would be necessary to make substantial cuts. My general policy has been to leave out altogether those entries which would have required extensive reconstruction, and to print the others with as few deletions and rearrangements as possible.

There is, however, a feature of the manuscripts which has caused me special difficulty. Moore's main text, in each notebook, is written on the right-hand side pages only; but he also wrote very many remarks (sometimes long passages) on the left-hand side pages. It is not always clear where these remarks should be inserted; and often they are comments on the statements made in the text, qualifying, questioning or contradicting them. In these cases I thought it best to indicate the insertions, and I have enclosed them in pointed brackets. I have also used pointed brackets to enclose short comments which Moore sometimes wrote between the lines of the text itself. Round brackets, on the other hand, are Moore's, except that I have supplied them in those places where he had obviously left them out by oversight. Lastly, square brackets are used for my own insertions and also for my own footnotes.

I have in general retained Moore's contractions of words (except in the titles of entries), and I have not tried to revise systematically his punctuation. More importantly, I have not interfered systematically with his use of quotation marks and italics. This is not uniform, even within single entries; and I have no doubt that he would have revised it had he himself prepared the work for publication. But I did not think that it would be right for me to attempt such a revision.

The order of the entries is the same as in the manuscripts; but I have numbered them for ease of reference.

The notebooks seem to have been written entirely for Moore's private use. In fact when I recall some of the philosophical discussions which I have had with him, I realize that much of this work is an attempt to attack precisely those problems which he had always found especially difficult. I do not know how many of the entries he himself would have approved for publication.

I am very grateful to Mrs G. E. Moore for the help which she gave me on the many occasions on which I have consulted her; to Timothy Moore for reading the entire typescript and drawing my attention to a number of errors which had escaped me; and to the Rockefeller Foundation for financial support.

C. LEWY

Trinity College
Cambridge
April 1962

CONTENTS

NOTEBOOK III (late 1930s to 1940)

NOTEBOOK IV [c. 1941–1942]

NOTEBOOK VIII (Begun at end of 1947)

NOTEBOOK IX [1948–1953]

NOTE ON SYMBOLISM

In a number of entries Moore uses the following symbols and abbreviations:

→ meaning *entails.*

↛ meaning *does not entail.*

⇄ meaning *entails and is entailed by.*

"R." is an abbreviation of "Russell".

"W." (or "Wittg.") is an abbreviation of "Wittgenstein".

NOTEBOOK I

[*c.* 1919]

1

FACTS AND PROPOSITIONS

The *sentences*

"That this is scarlet is a fact"
"That this is scarlet is true"
"The prop. that this is scarlet is true"
"This is scarlet"

are all *equivalent* in meaning; i.e. if what is *meant* by any one of them is true, so is what is meant by any other.

But "The prop. that this is scarlet is a fact" is *not* equivalent to them. Nor is "That this is scarlet is a prop.".

And "The fact that this is scarlet is true" is *meaningless*.

Hence when you assert "That this is scarlet is a fact" *what* you are asserting to be a fact is *not* the prop. that this is scarlet.

If the prop. that this is scarlet is true, *then* this *is* scarlet: is *not* a mere tautology.

What requires proof is that a fact is *not* a true prop.

This is shewn by shewing that "This is scarlet" is equivalent to "That this is scarlet is a fact", but is *not* equivalent to "The prop. that this is scarlet is a fact".

"The prop. that this is scarlet is a fact" is nonsense, which shews that "is a fact" & "is true" are not interchangeable, although the sentences "That this is scarlet is a fact" & "That this is scarlet is true" have the same meaning.

Ramsey's point[1]

"S is believing truly, in believing that my scissors are on my table" is *equivalent* to

"S is believing that my scissors are on my table, & my scissors are on my table."

When you say "The prop. "The moon is larger than the earth" is true, if & only if the moon *is* larger than the earth"

you seem to be saying no more than

"The prop. " "The moon is larger than the earth" is true" entails the prop. "The moon is larger than the earth" & the prop.

[1] [Later addition.]

3

"The moon is larger than the earth" entails the prop. " "The moon is larger than the earth" is true" ".

I.e. to be saying no more than "p is *logically equivalent* to "p is true" ".

"p exists" ⟨Has this any meaning?⟩ does *not* entail p.

2

NECESSITY

Take first sense in which *truths* may be said to be necessary; where "necessary" is opp. to contingent.

Why not say: "p is necess." means "p is an assertion of formal implication, such that if E^1 be substituted for the asserted $\supset$, the prop. so obtained is true"?

Thus to say: pq $\supset$ q is a necessary prop. or a necess. truth: means: pq $\supset$ q is an assertion of formal implication, & pq E q.

And to say: "Every right angle is an angle" is necessary means: $\phi x \supset \psi x$ is an assertion of formal implication & ϕx E ψx.

Thus no prop. is *necessary*, unless it be true; but a prop. wh. is necessary does not *assert* necessity. A prop. wh. asserts necessity, asserts of some other prop. that it is necessary. Thus "Every right angle *must* be an angle" is not itself necessary: it asserts ϕx E ψx, & therefore implies that $\phi x \supset \psi x$ is necessary.

There is another totally different sense of "necessary", when to say P is necessary means merely: There is some true prop. (or fact) from which P follows (or which *causally implies* P).

Thus we can say: This tri. *must* have equal sides (where, e.g., we know that it has equal angs. at the base); or somebody must have been here.

This = "That somebody has been here" is necess.: but you are not saying that the prop. "Somebody has been here" is *apodeictic*. It is, of course, not so.

It bothered me that e.g. similarity seemed to be a necessary relation; & that yet we can't say that, if A is similar to B, then A would necess., in any conceivable Universe, be similar to B; we can't say this, bec. B might not exist.

Also it seems that "A is a part of B" is the same fact as "B has A for a part", & yet that the first is contingent the second necessary.

I think the solution of both puzzles is the same, viz.

(1) when we say similarity is necessary, what we mean is that, if A sim. B, then x = A . y = B : *ent* : x sim. y: i.e. the prop. "x = A . y = B : $\supset$: x sim. y" is not a mere matter of fact, but a necess. truth.

---
[1] [= entails.]

(2) similarly, if it is a fact that A is part of B & therefore also B has A for a part, the first yields us x = A . y = B : ⊃ : x is part of y; the second yields us similarly x = A . y = B : ⊃ : y has x for a part: but whereas it is *not* true that x = A . y = B : *ent* : x is a part of y, it is true that x = A . y = B : *ent* : y has x for part.

3

INFERENCE

"S inferred q from p", can certainly not be identified with "S made a judgment of ⟨or knew⟩ q, which was caused by a judgment of ⟨or knowledge of⟩ p."

Owing to my judgment that p (e.g. that somebody has entered the house), I may go out of the room, & owing to going out of the room I may arrive at q (e.g. that nobody came in), but I certainly have not here inferred q from p.

Or my judgment that p (which I read in the paper) may set me remembering similar things that have happened before, e.g. q; and here my actualised knowledge on this occasion of q is *due* to, caused by, my judgment that p, but is certainly not inferred from it.

In the latter case we may say that the knowing or judging of q was *directly* caused by the knowing or judging of p; but in a sense it seems to be true that what was caused by the knowing of p was only the entry of q into my mind. That my attitude to q was one of judging or knowing was *not* caused by my knowing of p. I didn't *believe* or *know* q, bec. I believed or knew p. In the former case, on the other hand, it was due to my judgment of p not only that q entered my mind, but that I believed or knew it; but the causation is indirect.

Can we say "S *inferred* q from p" means "S's knowing or judging of q was *directly* caused by his knowing or judging of p, & *also* the reason why his attitude to q was one of knowing or judging was because his attitude to p was so"?

I don't at present see any objection to this. But I cannot give any further account of the distinction which it presupposes between: This belief in q was caused by that belief in p: &: That q was *believed* was due to the fact that p was believed. But there undoubtedly *is* here a distinction.

Does inference always involve a judgment: p renders q probable? Is it only when your belief in q is caused by such a judgment, that you can be said to have inferred q from p? I don't think so, but I am not sure. Keynes says so p. 413[1]; but he seems to say so partly through confusion.

[1] [J. N. Keynes, *Formal Logic*, 4th edition (London, 1906).]

7

Is my perception that this (physical object) is further off than that always an inference = arrived at by inference from perceived relations between sense-data?

It is not even certain that it is *caused* by my perception of relations between sense-data: it may be caused by some stimuli wh. cause that perception, but simultaneously. I'm inclined to think that for this reason it is *not* always an inference.

4

MEMORY

There is a sense in which we can only remember p, when we have known p before.

But when I remember that I wrote the last page just now, this does *not* involve that I shall have known p before.

CAUSALITY

What sort of thing do causal laws assert?

R. says: Not merely anything of form $\phi x \supset \psi x$.

Let us take Law of Gravity.

"Any 2 pieces of matter attract one another with a force proportional to the product of their masses divided by the square of their distance."

Whitehead p. 28.[1]

Let A & B be any 2 bodies; let m be mass of A & M mass of B, d the distance between them, & F the force with which they attract one another: then F is *proportional* to $\dfrac{mM}{d^2}$.

Does F is *proportional to*, mean merely: There is *some* number, k, such that, whatever the values of m, M & d may be, $F = k\dfrac{mM}{d^2}$?

If I understand W. rightly, this is so.

If this be so, what the law tells us is not merely:

x has mass 1 lb.. y has mass 2 lb.. x & y are at distance 2 miles . $\supset$. attraction between x & y.

Whitehead p. 39.[1] The weight of a lump of pure gold is a *function* of the weight of the water it displaces (= of an equal volume of water).

Let *the* function be k.

Then if x be a lump of pure gold, & be of weight W, & displaces a volume of water, then it will displace a volume of water of weight kW.

This doesn't merely tell you that if x has the property (golden + of weight 2 lb. + displacing some volume of water) then it has the property of displacing a volume of water of weight k2 lb.

This could be expressed in form $\phi x \supset \psi x$.

What it tells you is something wh. can't be expressed in this form; but from wh. an infinite number of props. of this form follow.

Is this a causal law?

It might seem so, because it tells that any volume of water dis-

[1] [A. N. Whitehead, *An Introduction to Mathematics* (London, 1911).]

placed by a gold lump of weight so & so, will *weigh* so & so, *if weighed.*

But yet it isn't: bec. if it's true of a volume of water that, if it had been displaced by a lump of gold of weight W, it would have weighed kW, it's true of it that it would have weighed kW, even if it hadn't been so displaced.

By no means all functional formulae are *causal*: what distinguishes those wh. are from those wh. aren't?

Can you call a statement which tells you the specific gravity of a certain metal, a statement of a *law*?

The weight of a given volume of water (= *any* piece of water of a given volume) is a *function* of the weight of any equal volume of gold; & the weight of any piece of gold of a given volume is a *function* of the weight of any piece of water of the same volume.

The function wh. it is, is that the gold is 19 times the water.

x is a piece of gold of 1 cubic in. ⊃ x weighs 19 times as much as any piece of water of 1 cub. in.

x is gold of 2 cub. in. & y is water of 2 cub. ins. . ⊃ . x weighs 19 times as much as y.

x has property of being gold & of being of same volume as *this* piece of water . ⊃ . x weighs 19 times as much as *this* piece of water.

But *this* piece of water is not here a constant.

Take a simpler instance.

The weight of any piece of gold is a function of its volume (& vice versa)

= The weight of a piece of gold is *proportional to* or *varies as* (by a constant ratio) its volume.

If you state *what* the function is e.g. f (where f is some constant) this gives you not only

x is gold of volume 1 cub. in. ⊃ x is of weight f lb.

but an infinite number of different props. of this form.

And it is something wh. can't be put itself into this form.

This, R. says, means: the volume of a piece of gold determines its weight; once its volume is known its weight can be calculated.

Is this itself a *causal* law?

It might be a mere coincidence, just as much as "All the books in this shelf are yellow", & if it *were* it wouldn't be a causal law.

That is, *no* functional statement is *itself* a causal law: a causal law must not only make a functional statement, but must also assert that the relation in question is *not* a mere coincidence.

We can, in fact, only *know* that such a statement is true *for all times*, by knowing that it is *not* a mere coincidence.

Though it would *theoretically* be possible to know the one, without knowing the other: = to say it *is* true of all times is not the same thing as to say & does not imply it's not a mere coincidence.

It is the knowledge that in the cases we have met, the weight *depends* on the volume in this way, & does not merely *chance* to have this relation, wh. enables us to know that in *all* other cases the same relation will be found.

And the same knowledge is what enables us to say: If there had been pieces of gold at times or places where there were none, the same would have been true of them.

Thus, though all that is of practical use to us is to know the uniformities, we never could know any useful uniformities, unless there were a kind of dependence (causal dependence) wh. does *not* simply consist in being an example of a uniformity.

It is as with logic. Though all that it's *useful* to know is that $p \cdot p \supset q : \supset : q$, yet we never could know this, unless we saw that $p \cdot p \supset q : E^1 : q$.

[1] [=entails.]

6

CLASSES

McT.[1] says that the class of which the only members are the 4 provinces of Ireland is the same substance as the class of which the only members are the counties of Ireland.

But the two classes can't be the same, because of the one it is true that no county is a member of it, & of the other that every member of it is a county.

What is true is that there is a spatial whole, which is *composed* of the provinces, & also *composed* of the counties.

Composed of means (Whitehead): Each province is a part of it; each province is *separated* from every other province (= no two have any common part); Ireland has no part which is separated from each of the provinces.

We can say: The *extension* of the concept "provinces of Ireland" compose the same whole as the *extension* of the concept "counties of Ireland", but the two extensions are not identical.

The extension of a concept means all the things of which that concept can be truly predicated, & yet, if it can be truly predicated only of *one* thing, *that* thing is not its extension. This is what R. means by saying that where a class has only one member, that member is not identical with the class. The only proof he gives is Frege's that, if you consider a class with many members, that class is the only member of some other class, & yet can't be identical with the class of which it is the only member, bec. that class has only one, whereas *it* has many.

What is the difference (emphasized by Keynes & Mill) between thinking that A is a member of the extension of ϕ, & thinking that ϕ applies to it?

A man may of course know that A is a member of the extension wh. is, in fact, the extension of ϕ, without knowing that ϕ does apply to it.

When *I* say of him: he knows that A is a member of the extension of ϕ, this may be true of him, without his knowing that ϕ applies to A; & R.'s account of classes seems to give a true account

[1] [McTaggart.]

13

of what I know of him, when I know this. I know that there's some concept, having the same extension as ϕ, with regard to wh. he knows that it does apply to A.

But what is the difference between knowing: This has ϕ; &; This is one of the things which have ϕ?

With the ordinary meaning of "class" it is impossible that any class should have only *one* member or none. To say that so & so is a class, is to say that it is the extension of some concept, which applies to at least two different things. Thus there can be no class which is the class of eldest sons of Edward VII.

It is obvious, however, that if we are to talk of *the extension* of a concept which applies to only one thing, the thing in question has not got to the concept in question the same relation which the extension of a concept which applies to several things has to it, & which we assert the extension to have to it when we say it is the extension of that concept. For if we say *men* are the extension of the concept "human being", we imply that the extension is something to which the concept does *not* apply; whereas the Duke of Clarence *was* the eldest son of King Edward, & is not therefore the extension of that concept. This, I think, is a clearer argument then Frege's. And it is certainly a thing worth pointing out; for even those who would say that "eldest son of King Edward" does *not* determine a class, would be inclined to say that the Duke of Clarence was the extension of this concept, & that he was so in the same sense in which men are the extension of the concept human being.

Is there anything which is related to "eldest son of King Edward", in the way in which "men" is related to "human being"? I see no reason to think so; & if so it would follow that R.'s theory of classes is wrong, since, on his theory of what the class "men" is, there would be something related to "eldest son of King Edward" in this way.

In order to get an instance of what Frege's argument requires— a class with several members which is a member of a class with only one—we need, I think, to take as the defining property of the class with only one, some such property as that of being a class which has for members all the red poppies there are & nothing but red poppies. It is obvious that there is only one thing to which this concept applies; & therefore that, *if* a class is defined by it, it is a class which has only one member.

If you are going to say that "$\phi x \equiv_x \psi x$" implies "ϕ & ψ have the same extension", then it follows that ϕ has *an extension* equally whether it applies to several things, or only one, or none.

EXPLANATION

Why was the wall of my staircase so wet on Dec. 27?

Because the wall was much colder than the air in contact with it, & this air was very damp.

This is an *explanation*.

Perhaps it would not be so, unless it were a *law* that the contact of a cold surface with warmer damp air is always *followed by* (or always *causes?*) a condensation of moisture on the surface.

We may still go on to ask: *Why* does the contact of a cold surface with warmer damp air cause a condensation of moisture on the surface?

And the explanation of that would presumably be a more general law of which this was a particular instance.

Why did you go out just now?

Because I wanted to buy some stamps.

This is an explanation.

But it's not true that a desire to buy stamps is always followed by a going out of the person who desires to buy them, or always *causes* it.

8

FUNCTIONS

Is 2^2 a function of 2? or can you only say that x^2 is a function of x?

And if 2^2 is a function of 2, is 4 a function of 2?

Neither R. nor Whitehead explain the meaning of function in such a way as to make the answer to these questions plain.

Frege would certainly deny that either 2^2 or 4 is a function, since he confines the term to the "Sinn"—what is ausgedrückt by—expressions which *need completion*—like R.'s propositional functions.

So far as R. assimilates functions—"descriptive functions"— to propositional functions, it is to be presumed that he agrees with Frege in this.

COLOURS

Among the judgments which I can make with the greatest certainty are such judgments as: This (colour ⟨?⟩) is different in shade from that, but this & that resemble one another in the respect that both of them are shades of blue.

Of many colours I can judge with certainty "This is a shade of blue"; of many with equal certainty "This is not a shade of blue"; but with regard to many I feel a doubt whether they have any tinge of blue in them or not; & moreover, even when I am certain that a shade is bluish—that it has a tinge of blue in it—I should often hesitate to say that it was a shade of blue, or, as we might also say "a blue", or "one of the blues".

Broad says, & Russell commends his opinion, that I can never tell (even with the smallest probability?) that when I judge with certainty that a particular colour is a shade of blue, what I mean by using the words "is a shade of blue" is the same as what anyone else means. This view seems to me to be nonsense. I know not only with great probability but with certainty, that *I* mean by "is a shade of blue" what other people mean by it: though *how* I know this I cannot tell.

But what do I mean by "This is a shade of blue"?

When I judge of 2 colours that they are both shades of blue, I am knowing, of a certain respect, that they resemble one another in *that* respect. But the respect in question is that of being both shades of blue.

I can find no clearer example than this, of what is meant by saying that so & so is an attribute or predicate or property of something else. Each of the 2 shades is a shade of blue; and when I assert this of it, I am asserting it to have a certain property, predicate, attribute or character. And quite clearly I am not asserting it to be *identical* with this character, since I do not assert the 2 shades to be identical, even in quality, & yet I assert both of them to have this character. Of course, identity (see Stout) may, on one interpretation, be involved in my judgment. I may be said to be judging of the character & the shade in question: There is something of wh. it's true *both* that it has this character & that

it's identical with this: there is *a* thing having this character
which is identical with this. Or even: There is one member of the
class "shades of blue", which is identical with this. But ordinarily
when we use such a phrase as "This is *a* shade of blue", we are
not, I think, doing so any more than we are thinking of the class
"men", or of identity, when we say, "That is a man", or of the
class of red things, or of identity, when we use an adjective, e.g.
"This is red". Why we haven't a single word for "red thing", a
noun, e.g. borjum, so that instead of saying This is red, we
should say "This is a borjum"; & why, instead of saying "This
is a man", we haven't a single adjective, e.g. crojous, so that
instead of "This is a man", we should say "This is crojous", I
don't know. I suggest that it is according as, with regard to the
property in question, we want, or don't, often to make such pro-
positions as $(\exists x) : \phi x . \psi x$ (e.g. I met a man); or $(x) . \phi x \supset \psi x$
("All men are mortal"). We don't often want to make props. of
this kind about *all* red things, or some red thing.

This character wh. we express by "is a shade of blue", is, of
course, something which is common to all shades of blue—
something which they have "in common". Some people seem loth
to admit that they have anything "in common". And of course
this character is not "in common" to both of 2 blue shades, in
the sense that it is a part or constituent of both. No part or constituent of a thing is ever *predicable* of it (perhaps). But in any
case to be predicable of is not the same thing as to be a part or
constituent of. If a is a constituent of b, then that b has a for
a part is predicable of b; but obviously it's very rarely, if ever, that
you can predicate of b *both* a & that it has a for a part. Such a
case would occur if you can predicate of the compound adjective
"not blue & hard" that it is not blue.

Obviously this character also is not identical with any shade
which possesses it, nor yet with any other shade of colour that
we *see*. It is not similar in shade to any shade that we *see*. So that,
if it is "seen" at all, it is only in a completely different sense.

10

COLOURS

Let us define "sense-data" as the kind of objects about which I am making my judgment when I say (pointing) "That is a surface of a penny" or "That is an after-image".

About such objects it may perhaps be doubted whether any of them *are* coloured; but it cannot be doubted that many of them *look* coloured.

If, when I touch a surface of a penny, the tactile sense-datum, about which I judge, when I judge "This is a surface of a penny", really is a surface of a penny, then, with regard to this tactual sense-datum I very often do also *judge*: "This is brown", but this tactual sense-datum does not look brown, at the moment, in the same sense, in which, if I am *seeing* the penny, the visual sense-datum, about which I am judging when I judge "This is a surface of a penny", looks brown.

Thus *if* the tactual sense-datum really is identical with the part of the surface of a penny which I am perceiving, *looking* brown is *not* identical with being judged to be brown, since, though it *is* judged to be brown, it does *not* look brown. (This would not prove that looking may not be a *species* of judgment; but if it's ever true, that a thing does *look* so & so, & yet is *not* judged to be so, this would be decisive.)

Let us confine ourselves to what happens when a sense-datum *looks* coloured.

No sense-datum ever *looks* coloured, without looking to be of some particular colour; whenever a sense-datum looks of a particular colour, then there is some particular colour which we can be said to *see*.

Yet when a sense-datum looks blue, it does not follow that we see the colour blue. Whenever a sense-datum *looks* blue, the s.-d. either *is* (= is identical with) some particular shade of blue (which is the view implied by those who say that some sense-data *are* colours) or looks to be *of* some particular shade of blue. This particular shade of colour is the colour which is *seen* when it looks blue; & the colour blue itself is *never* seen in the sense in which this shade is.

All the shades we *see* occupy some position in the colour octahedron; but "blue", in the sense in which many of the shades in the octahedron are "blue", occupies *no* position in it: therefore it is not seen.

All distinguishable shades can be arranged in the form of an octahedron. There *may* be other shades, seen by us, but not distinguishable. But these will either be intermediate between 2 distinguishable ones, or else (as W.[1] suggests to be possible) *outside* the ones wh. form the surface of the octahedron.

[1] [Wittgenstein?]

SUBSTANTIVES AND ADJECTIVES

A word is an adjective, when it is sometimes or always *used as* an adjective. That is to say, the same word may be *both* an adjective *&* a substantive. This is not very common, but occurs, e.g., with names of colours "red", "blue", etc. In "This ball is red" "red" is used as an adjective; in "Red is a colour" it is used as a substantive; & so also in "This is the colour red".

Why people talk as if adjectives & substantives were mutually exclusive classes, is because most words that are substantivally used are never adjectivally used, & vice versa.

The important distinction is between the adjectival & substantival *use* of a word.

So far as English is concerned a word x is substantivally used whenever a complete proposition is expressed by "This is an x" or "This is *the* x". This is *one* mark of substantival use.

A word x is adjectivally used, whenever a complete proposition is expressed by "This is x", *provided* that the meaning of the "is" in that expression is not "This *is identical with* x", but is what it is in "This ball is red". In "This is George", "George" is *not* used adjectivally.

Now the *meaning* of these 2 forms of expression "This is an x" & "This is y" (where y is adjectivally used), is related in a very important manner.

"Bi-ped" is a substantive, & not an adjective; "two-legged" is an adjective & not a substantive. Everybody can see this at once, & similarly in thousands of other cases. But what is the difference expressed by saying that the one is a subst. & the other an adj.? Some difference, certainly, in their *meaning*.

One mark of the difference, *in English*, is that *you can say* "This is a bi-ped" but *cannot* say "This is *a* two-legged" and can say "This is two-legged", but can't say "This is bi-ped"; another that you can use the plural "bi-peds" & cannot use the plural "two-leggeds". But neither of these marks apply to Latin. And are any of these marks universal even in English? (1) A word which is *only* (= always) an adjective, never, I think, has a plural; but do all words wh. are substantives have plurals? "Riches" has none: "willingness" has none. (2) You can't say "A riches". Though you can never say "This is a ϕ", if ϕ be *only* an adjective. (3) You can always say "This is ϕ" if ϕ be an adj.; but you can say "This is virtue" though virtue is *only* a substantive.

But what is the difference in their meaning? What is the difference between Caesar erat homo; &: Caesar erat bonus, which allows us to say that "homo" is a substantive, & "bonus" an adjective?

If you point to something & say "Est homo", you are, as we use the term "naming", naming the thing to wh. you point; whereas if you point to something & say "Est bonus", you are *never* naming it. But what is this difference?

Whatever the difference (if *any*) corresponding to the fact that "homo" is a substant. & bonus an adj., between the meaning of "x est homo" & that of "x est bonus" may be, what "x est homo" means is *logically equivalent to*, even if not identical with, something which *could* be expressed by "x est y" where y should be an adjective (i.e. each *follows* from the other); & similarly "x est bonus" means something *logically equivalent* to what *could* be expressed by "x est y", where y should be a substantive. Let us say that if there were an adjective y such that "x est y" would express something logically equivalent to "x est homo", it would be *the* adj. *corresponding* to the subst. homo; & similarly if there were a subst. y such that "x est y" expressed something exactly logically equivalent to "x est bonus", then y would be the substantive corresponding to bonus. With this use of "corresponding" adj., we have to note that, *as a general rule*,[1] in languages known to me, there is *no* adj. which corresponds to any subst.; & no subst. wh. corresponds to any adj. Thus what "x est humanus" as actually used expresses is by no means exactly logically equivalent to what is expressed by "x est homo"; nor is what is e. by "x is human" to what is e. by "x is a man". What "x is a human being" exp. *is* either identical with or logically equivalent to what "x is a man" exp.; but the phrase "x is human" can't be used to express anything equivalent to what is expressed by "x is a human being". Similarly there is no subst. corresponding to the adjs. "good", "red", "bonus", "rubrum". In Eng. we have to say "This is a good man", "This is a good thing", "This is a

---

[1] ⟨A good example of an exception is "mortal": "x is a mortal" can be used with precisely the same sense as "x is mortal".⟩

red thing" to express what would be expressed by such a subst., if there were one; provided what it would express is really not identical with what is expressed by "This is good", "This is red".

Similarly "All men are mortal" expr. something logically equivalent to what could be expressed by "Whatever is y, is also mortal", where y is an adj.: only neither in English, nor in any other language that I know of, is there an adj. such that this express. *does* express anything logically equivalent to "All men are mortal". And similarly "All men are animals" expresses something logically equivalent to what could be expressed by "Whatever is y, is also z", where both y & z should be adjectives; only there are *no* adjectives which do fulfil this condition.

What the difference is, if any, between what is expressed by "x est homo", & what would be expressed by "x est y", if y were the corresponding adj., I don't know. Nor why it is, that, in some cases, we have words to express only *one* of the equivalent meanings—the substantival one, & in others only to express the other—the adjectival one. The original substantives are, no doubt, names of Mill's "natural kinds", & this may have something to do with it.

Not all substantives are such that they *could* have a corresponding adjective. It is only those which we were taught to call "common nouns", wh. *could* have.[1] *Proper* nouns *cannot* have one: nor can any word, wh. is sometimes used as a *proper* noun, *when* it is so used, even though the same word may sometimes be used as a *common* noun, & then *can* have one. E.g. the same word "red" is *used* in 3 ways (1) as adjective in "This is red" or "seems red", (2) as *proper* noun in "Red is a colour", (3) as common noun in "This is a red" ≡ "one of the reds". Abstract nouns, *when* used as abstract, *can* have no corresponding adjective; but *most* abstract nouns, can *also* be used as common nouns, in which case they *can* have. E.g. in "Virtue is an attribute", "virtue" is used as a proper noun; but in "Benevolence is a virtue" it is used as a common noun.

---

[1] ⟨"Common nouns" = general terms, if general terms be restricted to single words.

"Proper nouns" = singular terms, if singular terms be restricted to single words; the only distinction Keynes seems to make between "singular terms" & "proper names", is that the latter is restricted to single words, while the former includes phrases like "*the* present prime minister". They differ also, in that *some* singular terms, thus defined, have connotation?⟩

12

JUDGMENT AND MULTIPLE RELATIONS

What are you asserting of Z, if you assert: Z is judging that there are matches inside *this* match-box?

Such judgments do occur: but the fact that Z, when he wants to light his pipe, takes up the match-box & looks inside, doesn't prove that he is making one. For (a) he may do so, automatically, without making any judgment at all, if he is absorbed in something else; (b) he may only judge "*Perhaps* there are matches in here".

But cases do occur where you feel very certain that there are; e.g. where you used the box an hour ago & left plenty there, & it's still lying in the same place, & so far as you know nobody has taken them, & somebody asks you for matches, so that your attention is directed to the question whether there are or not.

What are the *objective constituents* to wh. you assert Z to be related?

Let's assume the sense-data Z is seeing are part of the surface of the match-box. He is then judging: There are *matches* having a certain spatial relation (that of being *enclosed* by this side & *the* other sides wh. bear certain spatial relations to this). I.e. he is judging: There are things of wh. it's true that they are *both* matches & inside this.

You can put this in the form: he is asserting with regard to the property of being a match, & the property of being inside *this*, that there are several things to wh. both those properties belong.

This does not give the ultimate analysis because these properties are complex.

E.g. to be "a match", means, to be a fairly rigid thing, much longer than it's broad, but with little difference between its breadth & thickness; & such that it will produce flame when struck on certain kinds of surfaces.

With "inside this box" we've already dealt.

This analysis (due to R.): that the judgment is essentially, *not* about any actual matches, but about the *property of being a match*; & that it asserts essentially, as part of its meaning, that this

25

property belongs to something; is something wh. I don't know that you'll find anywhere pointed out.

You may think it's artificial to talk about "universals" being objects: & universals are, of course, very queer sort of entities: but just consider how "matches" do come in in such a judgment: they *do* come in somehow—you're thinking about them; & yet *not* of any actual match.

Almost (perhaps *all*) our actual judgments, except universal ones, are of this nature that they begin with ($\exists$ x). They're not all "particular" judgments. But what in Logic are called *singular* judgments are nevertheless as a rule of this form.

R. makes things unduly simple by giving as instance "A loves B", & talking as if, when I judge this, both A & B are immediate objects to me, & also as if *loves* were a *simple* relation, *not*, as it certainly is, a *general* one.

If we're to take the account he gave, in defining correspondence, as if every judgment asserts a *relation* between 2 or more terms, we should have, in this instance, to make one of the terms a *universal* (it is not like "This match is inside this box"): & you might say the two terms were then 2 properties, & the relation was that of *both* applying to several different things. (This sort of thing is actually often called a *relation*.)

This, of course, is not the *ultimate* account. You would have to say it really asserts a relation between all the *simple* concepts involved & this surface of a match-box.

But the relation is *equivalent* to this assertion about the 2 complex concepts.

We can say, using Locke's language (wh. is quite natural), that the judgment is certainly about the *idea* of a match: where by "the idea of matches" is meant the predicate wh. we assert of anything when we say "This is a match". It's about the *idea* of a match, *not* about any actual matches.

But now for multiple relations.

Let's treat the concepts "being a match" & "being inside this", as if they were simple.

I said it is evident that the assertion: Z is judging that there are matches in this box" is at least *equivalent* to the assertion of the holding of a certain relation between Z, & ϕ, & ψ, & the notion of applying to.

What *sort* of a relation?

ϕ, ψ, & "applying to" must all be immediate objects to Z; &, with *one* sense of multiple relation, the mere assertion that they are all simultaneously immed. objects to Z, would be the assertion of a multiple relation between them.

That judgment is *not* this must be immed. seen. This merely would not arrange *all* the terms in an order. That it is *not* this is, I think, the most important thing meant by saying that a judgment is a single act—*not* a mere collection of ideas simultaneously present.

You can say of any prop. wh. asserts something or other *about* or *of* more than 2 terms, that what is asserted *of* them must be a multiple relation.

R.'s args. can only shew at most, that there is no single object such that "Z is believing this" is equivalent to saying *merely* that he has a certain relation to that object.

It only shews, therefore, that when you assert Z is judging so & so, you are *asserting* him to have a certain relation to at least 2 objects, & not merely *implying* it, as you would be if you were asserting him to have a relation to one complex object.

It only shews, therefore, that when you assert this you are asserting of at least 3 objects that a certain relation unites them.

But R. includes in his def. another point: viz. that the relation you assert is such that it *can't* be *asserted* between less than 3 (this is implied by "the simplest *prop.* in wh. it occurs") & can't *hold*.

This really asserts something more, bec. though, if it *did* hold between 2, to assert that it did would, *ex hyp.*, not be equivalent to asserting Z is judging; yet it might be the case that, with the same relation, to assert it to hold between 2 things, was *not* equivalent to what is called judging, whereas of 3 it was: that, in fact, in saying Z is judging we were *not* merely asserting him to have a certain kind of relation, but also the number of terms to wh. he had it. Just as seeing asserts *both* a relation & a kind.

And this asserts not only that it doesn't, but that it *can't*.

R. gives no reason for this.

But, I think, in fact we can say a relation wh. never holds between [less than] 3, *can't* [hold] between less.

This doesn't seem so clear in the case of symmetrical relations: e.g. A, B & C are all equal to one another; are all different. This *seems* same as A & B are equal; are different.

But with non-symmetrical it's clearer: e.g. between.

Only here it's *not* clear that: C & D are *both* between A & B, isn't asserting *same* thing of A, B, C & D, as: C is between A & B: is asserting of A, B & C.

R. uses this as an arg. that the relation asserted in asserting that we judge or conceive, must be different from acquaintance.

But now, if it be true that a relation wh. unites 3 terms can never be same as one wh. unites 2, it must also be true that one wh. unites 4 can't be identical with one wh. unites 3, & so on.

But the assertion that so & so believes so & so, is equivalent to assertion with regard to all sorts of different numbers of terms that a certain relation unites them: e.g. that there are black-topped matches, means that more are united than in that there are matches.

It can't therefore be the same specific relation wh. is asserted in all cases.

13

ACQUAINTANCE

An acquaintance with this or that (when this or that is not a proposition) cannot be true or false, qua acquaintance with this or that; which means that the characteristic wh. we attribute to it, when we say it is an acquaintance with A is one in respect of which it cannot be true or false, in the sense in which an idea or judgment *that this* can be true or false, in respect of the character wh. we attribute to it when we say it is an idea or judgment *that this.*

When we say that an idea is false, we always mean that it is a conceiving or affirming or denying of a proposition, & that it is false in respect of this character, in a sense wh. is equivalent to saying that the prop. in question is false.

An idea can only be false in respect of some character wh. it possesses; & the only sort of character in respect of wh. any idea can be false, is one wh. consists in being a conceiving, denying or affirming *that* so & so.

No idea, therefore, can be false in respect of being an acquaintance with A (unless we can be acquainted with prop.), since this character is not one which consists in being a conceiving, affirming or denying *that* so & so.

It can be false in respect of being a judgment *that* this is true of A, but this character is not the same as that of being an acquaintance with A, although what has the first character must also have the second.

An acquaintance with A cannot be false quâ acquaintance with A; although it may be false quâ acquaintance *of this sort* with A, where "of this sort" means quâ idea or judgment that *this* is true of A.

An act cannot be false in respect of being *some sort of a judgment* about A; it can only be false in respect of being a judging of *this* about A.

And similarly an act cannot be false in respect merely of being *a judgment*, but only in respect of being *a judging of this.*

I.e. it is not quâ judgment, but quâ judgment of *this*, that a judgment is false, if it is false.

An act cannot be false, quâ acquaintance with this, but only quâ conceiving of this or judging of this. *If* conceiving of a prop. were identical with acquaintance with it, an act could be false quâ acquaintance with this.

Another way of making it evident that an act can't be false quâ acquaintance with *this*, is to point out that, even if all acquaintance is judging about, it must always be *possible* to be acquainted with A in a true way, i.e. to make a true judgment about it; but if p is a false prop. there is no way of conceiving it in a true way: any conceiving of p *must* be false quâ conceiving of p.

14

PLEASURE, PAIN AND DESIRE

What laws are there, connecting these phenomena?

1. *Generally* when you have a *sensation* that is painful, in any *marked* degree, you also desire to be rid of the *sensation* in question.

Of sensations that are pleasant this is not true.

Here, therefore, is one real difference between the relation of pleasure & that of pain to desire.

Whether the same is true of painful *thoughts*, I doubt. E.g. when the thought of some foolish or awkward thing you have done or said is painful to you, you don't seem to desire to be rid of the *thought*; what you desire (if anything) is that you had not said or done the thing. Again: if you are pained, because someone is angry with you, what you desire is not to get rid of your knowledge that he is angry, but that he should cease to be angry.

Perhaps we can say: When your knowledge that so & so is the case, is in any *marked* degree painful to you, you do generally desire that so & so *should cease to be the case*.

And here again there is a marked contrast between pleasure & pain.

2. *Generally* when you think that a certain kind of *sensation* which you expect, will be painful in any *marked* degree, you desire to avoid it.

The same is certainly not true of a sensation you think will be *pleasant*; but here there is a still further contrast, for here you generally desire to get the sensation.

But if you think it would be pleasant or painful to *know* that so & so is the case, what you desire to have or to avoid is *not* the knowledge that it is so, but *that* it should be so.

PLEASURE AND PAIN

Many organic sensations are distinctly painful, a few are distinctly pleasant. And in their case it almost seems as if the painfulness & the pleasantness were a quality of the sense-datum in the same sense in which yellowness seems to be a quality of some visual sense-data. It certainly seems impossible that anybody should have a sense-datum of the same quality, without its being painful or pleasant to him.

We are here using "organic sensations" to include all sensations *localised* in the body; so as to include e.g. sensations of heat & cold, & also pricks etc., which ought perhaps to be included under touch-sensations. E.g. scratching is often distinctly pleasant.

Tastes & *smells* come nearest to organic sensations, in respect of the fact that it seems as if their pleasantness or unpleasantness (we do not here talk of painfulness) were often a quality of the sense-datum, & as if nobody could have a similar sensation without feeling it pleasant or painful.

But with regard to *sounds* & *visual sense-data*, it seems much more doubtful whether any, *by themselves*, are *distinctly* pleasant or unpleasant. Certainly single sounds are, in some cases, to some degree pleasant: are *any* unpleasant? A very loud noise may be; or the repetition of a piercing whistle.

Combinations of sounds & visual sense-data, certainly are, some much pleasanter than others: e.g. certain melodies, & certain patterns.

But here it does *not* appear (it seems impossible) that the pleasantness should be a *quality* of the combination. Moreover here certainly the same combination may be more pleasant to one than to another; but is it so, *in itself*, apart from associations & thoughts about it? Those who take no pleasure in music, probably do not apprehend the melody: they do not have the same experience; it is not that the same experience which is pleasant to others, is not so to them.

It has been suggested that *why* a melody is pleasant is because it causes pleasant organic sensations; but I think this is certainly untrue: I am much more sure that it does please me, than that I

am having any pleasant organic sensations: there is certainly
nothing which I can localise.

If we go on to other *distinct* (sometimes *intense*) pleasures & pains,
we find a class very different from all the preceding in one respect.
Almost everybody is pleased at being praised or flattered; &
displeased at being blamed or treated with contempt. But here
it is not the same thing which pleases you & me; what pleases you
is that *you* should be praised, what *me* that I should be. Similarly
everybody can be pleased that he is going to see a friend; but what
pleases *me* is that I am going to see a friend of *mine*, what you, that
you are going to see a friend of *yours*. Is this quite similar? In any
case, the feelings wh. each one has about his *self*, differ in some
very radical way from e.g. the pain of tooth-ache, where it is
really the same thing that is painful to you & me. Is my knowledge that you are despising me unpleasant to me in the same
sense in which my tooth-ache is? Certainly here the unpleasantness
is *not* a quality of any sense-datum; it is not even true that the
unpleasantness of the knowledge consists in its causing me unpleasant organic sensations. But can it be a *quality* or "tone" of
my knowledge?

PLEASURE—PAIN

Let's not talk about pleasure & pain, but about *pleasant* & *unpleasant*.

Unpleasant Experiences

1. Physical pains (there are a great variety); & feelings of physical discomfort, e.g. feeling too hot or too cold, or in an uncomfortable position.

The *experience* here is the having a certain kind of *organic* sensation, in the sense of a sensation *localised* in your own body & *not* a visual, auditory, smell or taste sensation. But is the *sense-datum* what is painful or unpleasant?

2. Nasty smells, nasty tastes, overloud noises, discords?, dazzling lights.

3. The sight or touch of certain persons or living things (e.g. spiders, snakes, frogs etc.) & hearing the conversation of certain persons.

4. Being afraid of a certain kind of experience, which you think is certain to or may possibly happen to you.

5. Feeling ashamed of something you have done.

6. Being abused or despised; more accurately, seeing or hearing yourself abused or despised, or anything that is yours which you value; or hearing that you were.

7. The conviction that a certain kind of thing *has happened* or *will happen, does* normally happen: e.g. that someone you love is dead or has suffered a misfortune; or that people have certain vices; that there is no God or future life.

8. Seeing other people or animals in pain.

9. Being bored.

10. Being prevented from attaining something wh. you desire at the moment.

11. Being disappointed of something which you were expecting & looking forward to.

12. Feeling that you are doing wrong.

Pleasant Experiences

1. Physical pleasures (there are not many, that are at all intense: the chief are, certain feelings in the sexual organs when excited, & e.g. the feeling of being scratched, under certain circumstances), & feelings of physical comfort, c.g. the sensation of a warm bath.

Here the experience is certain organic sensations.

2. Pleasant smells or tastes, pleasant simple sounds, & perhaps colours & forms (shapes), pleasant sensations of touch.

3. Pleasant combinations of sounds, or combinations of colour & form.

4. The sight or touch of certain persons or animals in certain conditions, & listening to the conversation of certain persons. E.g. seeing a baby smiling.

5. The hearing or seeing oneself praised (or flattered) or admired or loved; or anything of *yours*.

6. The sight of certain persons or animals enjoying themselves.

7. The feeling proud of something one has done.

8. The conviction that certain things have happened or will happen.

9. The hearing or reading of stories, whether true or fictitious.

10. The appreciation of wit or humour.

DESIRE

Suppose we take one of the most universal desires—the desire to satisfy what arc called the "natural needs"—to empty your bladder or your bowels. Everybody from time to time feels these desires: they *are* desires: they are naturally expressed by "I want to . . .". *Usually* these desires are *caused* by a *slightly* uncomfortable or unpleasant physical sensation: usually, but not always, for you may want to empty your bladder, at a particular time, simply because you think you won't have another chance for a long time. But when they are so caused, it is not true, I think, that you desire to do the action in question *for the sake of* getting rid of the discomfort. Usually you desire the action *for its own sake*. Sometimes, besides desiring it for its own sake, you may desire it *also* for other reasons, e.g. because you think that the omission may injure your health, or that it will keep you in an uncomfortable state, or that it will keep you in an uncomfortable state for a very long time, because you won't have another chance soon. In such cases you do what is called "desiring *as* a means": you desire it *partly* as a means, though also for its own sake. And undoubtedly such considerations may intensify your desire for the action. You desire it *merely* as a means, not at all for its own sake, it would seem, only when, e.g., you desire it bec. you anticipate that you won't have another chance for a long time, without at the present moment feeling any physical discomfort.

We must, I think, retract the statement that in the normal case in which the desire is due to a feeling of physical discomfort, the action is desired for its own sake. What I think is true is that it is not desired at all *as a means*. But we have to imagine that a thing may be desired, not at all as a means, & yet also not *for its own sake*.

NICKY'S DESIRES

When N. makes his first noises in the morn., they certainly express a desire—a desire to see somebody or have some toy presented to him; but this desire is not accompanied by the very least unpleasant feeling.

When he changes to make a complaining noise—the same sort of noise as when he loses a spoon he is playing with—then there is dissatisfaction—unpleasant feeling. And yet it seems that the dissatisfaction is solely due to the non-fulfilment of the desire that was present before & was not fulfilled before.

When he is just going to be fed & is near the breast, the noise he makes then does express some unpleasant feeling & a passionate desire.

Can we say *why* the non-fulfilment of one desire is unpleasant, that of the other not? It is certainly not because in the one case he believes it won't be quickly gratified, in the other that it will.

I don't think it's because the one desire is stronger than the other; for the strongest desires may be unaccompanied by unpleasant feeling.

I think we must say that the mere *continuance* beyond a certain time of an unfulfilled desire, may cause it to be unpleasant; and when it is unpleasant to begin with, delay in the gratification makes it more unpleasant.

What is his state of mind in the first desire? I think he has an image of the sort of thing he wants to see.

GOOD

Does it matter, whether I do this or that, do this or don't do this?
It often doesn't seem to matter, or at least not much.
But sometimes it does seem to matter a good deal.
It matters much only if some distinct *advantage* is to be gained by doing A rather than B or B than A; and the *greater* the advantage the more it matters.
And there are many kinds of things such that their occurrence, or non-occurrence, will, *other things being equal*, be a distinct advantage.
But there are things of two sorts. If by doing A, I shall increase my income, whereas by doing B I shall not, that is an advantage: or if by doing A I shall avoid decreasing it, whereas by doing B I shall decrease it. But what is the advantage of increasing my income? None *in itself*. It is only advantageous, because it enables me to get more goods.
Why shouldn't everybody do just what he likes?
Is it worth while doing this? & why?

EVENTS

As ordinarily used, nothing can be called an "event" or "occurrence", except a change or a series of changes. This use is different from that which I used to adopt when I said mental phenomena were all "events"; different also from that of Johnson, when he says sense-data are all of them "events" (occurrences); & from that of Whitehead when he says the duration of a sense-datum is an event.

Let us try to define the sense of the word "change", by reference to which this sense of event is to be defined. This conception, for which "change" stands, is an extremely fundamental one.

There seem, primâ facie, to be 3 very different kinds of condition, one or other of which must be satisfied, if a change is to be said to have occurred.

Either

(1) Something must at a later time possess a quality, or size, or shape, or intensity, which it did not possess at an earlier, though it then existed: something must undergo a change in quality, size, shape or intensity.

(2) Something must at a later time occupy a different position from that which it occupied at an earlier.

(3) Something must exist at a later time which did not exist at an earlier.

This 3 d. case is clearly distinguishable both from (1) & (2), as e.g. when in a dark field at which I am looking, a small bright light suddenly appears; or when a sound, or a pain suddenly occurs. There are cases of a new thing appearing, & we distinguish them clearly from cases where a thing which was already there changes its quality (etc.) or position.

But what, in such cases, is the change?

It is not the possession by the old thing of the new quality or position, or the existence of the new thing; nor is it the mere existence of the thing at one time with the old quality, or in the old situation, together with its existence at the later time with the new one or in the new one: it is the *transition* from one to the other which is the change.

Our most fundamental kind of perception of change certainly does not consist in our perceiving a thing to have a quality (or size or shape or intensity) & remembering that it formerly had an incompatible one. In such a case I can be said to perceive *that* it has changed; but, if this is all, I have not observed the change in question. Nor in case (2) does it merely consist in our perceiving that A occupies a certain position & remembering that formerly it occupied another: this is what we often do with the hour-hand of a watch; & we then see that it *has* moved, but we *don't* see it moving. So too in case (3).

Can it be that it consists in our perceiving it to be in the new position, & also at the same time perceiving that it was in the old one? Its presence in the old one, does seem to be *perceived*, *when* we are perceiving a change, in a sense in which it is not so, when it is merely remembered. But I do not think a perception of change consists merely in this.

Can it be that even if a perception of a change does not, yet the change itself consists merely in A's being at one time in one position, & at a later time in another, the 2 times being such that there is no interval between the end of the one & the beginning of the other?

21

CHANGE

Let us try to give an account of the chief sorts of changes which occur or appear to occur in the "presentation-continuum".

In the *visual field*.

When my head & my eyes (so far as I can directly tell) are still, & my body also is at rest relatively to the surface of the earth it often happens that some of my visual sense-data *appear to me* to be *moving*, & others appear to me to be at rest.

Russell & Broad would say that those which appear to be moving, really *are* moving; but, if you take seriously the view that movement *is* nothing but change of relative position, they would not be able to assert that *any* of those which appear to be at rest really *are* at rest, since if *one* such sense-datum is moving, *all* those which appear to be at rest *are* changing their position relatively to it.

It is, however, certain that to *appear* to move is not the same thing as to appear to change relative position, since things which don't appear to move certainly do appear to change their relative position. If, therefore, we mean by "move", what these sense-data appear to do, we must say that "move" does *not* mean "change position relatively to *something*".

It remains possible that what we mean by appear to move, is always, relatively to some one particular thing, "appear to change position relatively to *this*."

This kind of movement is a kind of change which appears to occur in parts of the presentation-continuum; since every movement *is* a change.

As a rule, when a visual sense-datum *appears to move*, under these conditions (i.e. when both body, head & eyes are at rest relatively to the surface of the earth), the corresponding physical object really is moving relatively to the surface of the earth. Perhaps *always*? But, that it is *always* moving *absolutely* cannot be safely said, since it is possible that in some cases its movement relatively to the earth's surface might be compensated by the movement of the earth itself on its axis & round the moon, & the movement of the solar system relatively to the fixed stars, &

(perhaps) the movement of the fixed stars relatively to the ether etc. But it is, I think, certain that only a very small proportion of the movements relatively to the earth's surface corresponding to these apparent movements of visual sense-data, can be thus compensated, since they differ from one another so much in velocity & direction. The movements of the earth are, however, sufficient to make the real relative velocities of the movements of the physical objects very different from the apparent relative velocities of the corresponding sense-data.

It is possible that nothing could appear to move in this sense, unless something else simultaneously appears to be at rest or to be moving with a different velocity or in a different direction. But it does not follow that *what* it appears to do is merely to change its position relatively to some such thing.

22

CHANGE

One of the commonest sorts of changes which occurs in my visual field is that which consists in one of my visual sense-data seeming to move relatively to some other.

For A to seem to move relatively to B is not the same thing as for A to seem to change its position relatively to B; for when A seems to change its position relatively to B, B seems also to change its relatively to A, but A can seem to move relatively to B, when B does *not* seem to move relatively to A.

Seeming to move relatively to something else, in this visual sense, is an ultimate notion.

23

LANGUAGE

What is the connection between the word "dog" & dogs, expressed by saying that "dog" is a name for dogs?

For English people in general the use of that kind of sound has a certain kind of causal connection with dogs.

But a sound might be a name for dogs, even if it had this kind of connection for only one person.

What kind of causal connection is it?

It is not merely that the sound is associated with the sight or thought of a dog. A child may associate a sound with a thing without using it as a name for it. E.g. Georgie's counting 1, 2, 3 etc. Certainly 2 was associated with 1; & the whole process with going upstairs.

A child first uses a sound as a *name*, when he expresses by it a judgment on his part that some object he is perceiving is of a particular sort. He uses "dog" as a name for dogs, when by saying "dog" he expresses a judgment that some perceived object has certain properties, which in fact belong to all dogs & only to dogs.

The causal connection is that the use of the sound is *caused* by a judgment, having this connection with dogs that it is a judgment to the effect that a certain thing possesses some property common & peculiar to dogs,—caused in the peculiar way meant by saying that it *expresses* this judgment.

What we need further to do is to say what is meant by saying that a sound or gesture "*expresses*" a mental state.

The sense is the same as that in which a child's cries *express* his feelings or desires or emotions. But these cries are not "words"; they are not used as *names* for anything. A sound is used as a *name* only when it expresses a judgment, & expresses the content of the judgment; & it can then be said to be a name for the property, predicate or attribute (or for anything possessing it) which is such that what it expresses is that the judgment is a predication of that predicate.

But what kind of causal relation is meant when we say a cry *expresses* anger?

I think we might say simply: is a bodily action of the person having the feeling, caused by the fact that he has it; though perhaps we should add also: such that others can infer the feeling from the action: it is because of this possibility of inference that it is said to be *expression*.

The *name* is related to the *content* of the judgment, in the same way as the cry to the *nature* of the feeling.

We must be careful not to suppose that a sound is used as a name only when the user *intends* to use it as a name, or *intends* to express a judgment by it. We can't define expression in terms of intention. A child can express a judgment, just as he can express anger, before he *intends* to express anything. And to intend to express is, if we have defined rightly, different from intending to communicate or convey to others. In fact, however, nobody ever intends to express, in the sense we have defined: never intends his anger to cause a gesture. The only important sense of intending to express is intending to *convey*: and language certainly can be used without any such intention.

What you intend to convey, when you do, is *not* the state of mind expressed, but some fact. In order that a child may intend to convey its anger, it must not only be angry, but *know* that it is: & it is this knowledge, wh., in one sense, the expression then *expresses*. What it intends to convey is not its knowledge, nor its anger, but the fact that it is angry: this means it intends to make others know what it knows.

As for proper names they first express the judgment, with regard to a thing perceived, *not* that it is of a certain kind, but that it is *identical* with something known in the past.

Animals have no language because they never express judgments—only feelings & desires, or perceptions or images. They perceive things as having certain characters; & their cries may express the fact that they are perceiving a thing having that character; but they don't know or judge of any character *that* anything has it. Or, if my seeming view be true, it is that things *seem* to them to have certain characters, & their cries express the fact that they so seem. The fact that a thing they perceive has a certain character can't have any effect upon their movements, when the character also is, in some sense, perceived. Seeming is confined to those qualities which are *infimae species*: a thing can't seem green; it can only seem to be of this particular shade of green. But an animal may be affected in the same way by a perception of 2 different infimae species, the effect being due to some common quality, though he does not know or judge *that* they share this quality.

What do I know when I know that my baby's *name* is Nicholas? or, what is much more fundamental, that *I call* him Nicky?

It seems what I know is that *I use* the sound "Nicky" to express my judgments about him.

But that I *use to* express is not essential; for this means that when I *want* to express a judgment, I use the sound.

All that is essential is that I *do* express judgments about him, by using the sound; whether or not I use it *for the purpose of* expressing them.

But more accurately my use of the sound, *in certain combinations with others*, expresses the fact that I am making a judgment about him.

The expression "Nicky" *stands for* him seems to embody Russell's view, which is essentially that to say it is his *name* means that it acts as a *substitute* for him in certain conditions.

Words generally can, for certain purposes, act as substitutes for what they stand for; but this is not what is meant by saying they stand for them: what is meant is that they *express* judgments about them.

In knowing that I call him "Nicky", I am certainly not merely knowing that that sound is associated, in my mind, with him, in such a way that the sight or thought of him makes me utter the sound, or that the hearing of the *sound* makes me think of him.

When a dog barks because he sees his master, he is not using that sound as a name for his master; *is* he expressing his sight of his master by means of it? He *is* expressing joy by means of it.

It seems plausible to say that the use of a general name involves recognition of a character, just as the use of a proper name involves recognition of an individual.

Animals can recognise individuals, but *not* characters.

But what *is* recognition of a character?

Can we say: I am *calling* the baby "Nicky", when & only when I often *intend* by my use of the sound to make other people think of him?

Thus "meaning" as applied to words would be derived from that sense of "mean" in which mean = intend.

24

LANGUAGE

A sound has meaning, in the sense in wh. words have = is a *name*, whenever & only when somebody actually uses it in a certain way = makes it under certain conditions.

The cry of a child certainly has *not* meaning in this sense: it is not a name for the pain or discomfort he feels: although it does express it, is a sign of it, & actually conveys to other people the fact that the child is feeling so & so.

The question is: What conditions must the making of a sound satisfy, *besides* that of expressing something, in order that it may truly be said to be being used as a name?

It does seem to be an essential thing about language, that it is sounds made *in order to* produce a certain state of mind in some-one else. But is it really essential that sounds should be made with a certain *intention* to be names? & is this sufficient?

A dog which barks to collect sheep may do this for the purpose of having a certain effect on them (though scarcely on their minds), & so when I say "Shoo" to a cat, or call out "Hullo" to attract a friend's attention. These are not names.

The whole point really is about universals.

And there are 2: proper names & general names.

A dog recognises men, & he also recognises his master: these are quite different things.

He has no *name* either for men or for his master.

To say that I call Nicky "Nicky"—that I use this sound as a name for him—seems equivalent to saying that that is the sound I use in order to make other people think of him.

Similarly to say that I *call* flowers "flowers"—that I use this sound as a name for flowers—seems equivalent to saying that that is the sound I use in order to make other people think of the universal "flower".

But when a dog barks, in order to get the door open, can we say that he uses that sound as a name for the universal "opening of the door"? We *can* say, apparently, that he uses it in order to make people think of opening the door—but not of the *universal* "opening of this door"? Yes, of the universal: for it is not of any particular opening that he wants to make you think, but just of *some* opening. To think of a *future* opening is only possible by means of a universal; of a past or present *not*.

The mere fact that the dog uses the same sound to make people think of many other quite different universals on other occasions is no reason for denying that he does use it as a name for this one, for I myself use the same sound "flower" also as a name for flour.

The origin of language is, perhaps, not like the first use of language by the child, to name things which the person addressed can see as well as the person addressing; but to warn the person addressed of things which he can not see. As when a savage has discovered enemies approaching, & runs to warn the tribe of their approach; or has discovered a herd of deer, & runs to fetch the tribe to hunt; or has left his chief wounded, & runs to fetch help. Thus its prototype would be the warning bark of a dog. Nothing, can we say? would get a name, unless there were occasion to refer to it in its absence? or at least in its absence to the person addressed, in the sense of not being perceived by him.

25

SENSE-DATA

In the case of *sounds* it is, I think, impossible to take the "seeming" view. It seems to me imposs. that what is now immediately given to me, when I hear the sound of the wind in the trees, should really be the air-vibrations which physics takes this sound to be; & that it should be these vibrations which *seem* to have the sense-given quality, which I discriminate so easily. What is immediately given seems to be just as much a thing, as in the case of a visual sense-datum; only that in this particular case it is constantly changing, e.g. in intensity.

What is immediately given, in this case, surely really *has* the qualities it seems to have.

It certainly seems to be (1) at a distance from me (2) in a certain direction from me (3) to have intensity; but *not* to have shape.

On the other hand I see no reason to think it an experience of my own. I can quite easily imagine it existing out of all relation to me. For the matter of that so I can with my tooth-ache, or any bodily pain.

What *is* this thing—the sense-datum—of which I am immediately aware?

It *has* certain sense-given qualities, & *cannot* have others e.g. *cannot* be coloured. Is it a quality—an infima species? The only reason for saying so is that it seems doubtful whether it *can* have any other infima quality except the one it is given as having. There seems no meaning in asking *what* it is other than this quality. The reason for saying that it is *not*, is that you may have 2 sounds immediately succeeding one another, which seem quite indistinguishable in quality, & yet are plainly 2: we cannot say that each *is* the same quality in different places or at different times.

What infima quality a material object possesses we cannot say. Yet it seems everything must have some. And if no infima quality, then none other; because *other* qualities, what are usually called such, are all derived from them.

26

UNIVERSALS

There are 2 different sorts of universals, known to us in quite different ways. The first sort are known without abstraction, & cannot be abstracted; the second only by abstraction.

This is a distinction to which I have never seen any allusion, & is bound up with several very fundamental questions.

Let us begin with *qualities*, in the narrowest sense, e.g. shades of colour.

The universals "red", "blue", "scarlet", "primrose-yellow" certainly never are *presented* to me in the same sense in which particular shades, all of which are nameless, & which are species, of which these are genera, are presented to me. Whenever anything is presented to me, which is perceived by me (or seems to me) to be primrose-yellow, it always also is of some particular shade of primrose-yellow; & this shade is *given* to me, in a sense in which the generic universal "primrose-yellow" is not given, & the thing is *perceived as having* (or seems to have) that shade of colour. Such shades are species of primrose-yellow, in the sense that, in the case of each, the things which have it form a sub-class included in the class "primrose-yellow things". *They* (the universals) are species only in the sense in which "human", "monkeyish", "bearish" (if we may use these terms) are species of the genus "animalish". When we talk of species & genus, we usu. use both terms for a *class*, & mean by a species a sub-class included in the genus. The sense in which I have been using species & genus above, on the other hand, is that in which, if *a* is a class which includes *b*, then any defining predicate of *b* is a species of wh. any defining pred. of *a* is a genus. I do not know what name, or whether any, is in common use for this relation between universals—that which subsists between ϕ & χ, when & when only all χ's are ϕ's, but not all ϕ's are χ's. Can χ be said to be *subordinate* to ϕ?

But in our case it is not only that everything which is χ is also ϕ: it is also the case that everything which is χ must (at the time when it is so) be ϕ. What is of any of the shades, which are varieties of primrose-yellow, *must* be primrose-yellow. And I think perhaps the names species & genus are commonly confined to classes, such that not only *is* the species included in the genus, but the species *must* be so included. E.g. man & horse, seem to be so related to animal, & to vertebrate. We should not say husbands were a species of men, although they are a sub-class included in men. We might say that men & women are two different species of human beings.

But further the kind of universals I am talking of are distinguished from the others in that they are (or determine) *infimae species*. There are no qualities which are subordinate to them in the sense in wh. they are subordinate, some to red, some to primrose-yellow etc.; & in wh. primrose-yellow is subordinate to yellow. Not only *are* there none, but there *can* be none. "Of *this* shade & round" is, of course, subordinate to "of *this* shade"; but its relation to "of this shade" is different *somehow* from that of "of *this* shade" to "red". How exactly? "Of *this* shade & round" is, of course, *not* a quality; & it is not a *simple* predicate or attribute, whereas those we are talking of are so. But is this the whole difference? I think Johnson would express this property which does belong to our first sort of universals, by saying that they are *absolutely* determinate. But perhaps he would deny that any absolutely determinate quality is given to us?

Let us leave *qualities*, & consider *shapes* & *sizes*. "Round" is a name for an indeterminate shape. But "circular", strictly used, would seem to be a name for an absolutely determinate one. In this case, therefore, we seem to have a name for an absolutely determinate attribute, whereas with qualities we never have any. Why's this & what is the difference? "Circularity" is perhaps given, but we can never tell that a thing is circular, as we can tell that it is round; just as we can never tell that a thing is of *this* precise shade.

Our name "circular", when strictly used, is not a name for any presented shape, but for a *negative* attribute, which does no doubt belong to a certain presented shape & to that only, but is not identical with it. In the case of particular shades of colour, there is no similar attribute which belongs always & only to any one shade. The negative attribute is that of being the shape of something which encloses a point such that every point of the circumference is at an equal distance from that point. And "equal" as applied to lengths or distances is a negative conception: it means "*not* differing in magnitude". Difference in magnitude is, in a sense, presented; but equality never. We can say for certain, in many cases: This is longer or larger than that; but in none: This is *not* larger or longer than that; though we can say: This is not perceptibly so.

I have implied that circularity, as a presented shape, cannot be abstracted, & cannot therefore be named. This seems a contradiction; but it is not, as may be seen, if it is remembered that in this prop. we mean by circularity *the* presented shape, wh. is such that everything & only those things wh. have it possess the negative attribute above defined.

What exactly is meant by saying that such particular shapes & shades cannot be abstracted? (1) It is impossible to recognise or identify such a shape or shade; that is to say, it is imposs. to say for certain *this* shade is not *perceptibly* different from that I saw just now, & now remember: whereas it is possible to say for certain, This is red & so was that. (2) Even when 2 shapes or 2 things having a shape are simultaneously presented, it is impossible to say for certain that there is *no* difference in the shape, though possible to say there is no *perceptible* difference. This is what Stumpf's argument proves.

A thing can't look red, without looking of some particular shade of red.

But it isn't true that a thing can't look of a particular shade, without looking of some particular shade of that shade: otherwise there would be an infinite regress.

Of *some* so-called "shades" this is true; e.g. a thing can't look "scarlet" without looking of some particular shade of scarlet.

But there are shades such that a thing can look of that shade, without looking of any particular shade of it.

Let's call such shades "infimae species" or absolutely particular universals or absolutely determinate universals.

I *think* it is true of such that there *can* be no shades which are shades of them, i.e. no universals which are related to them as shades of red are to red. But is this quite certain? (Proof on next page.)[1]

To say that O looks red to A, *means* that O looks of some

---

[1] [I.e. next paragraph but one.]

particular shade of red to A; that is, "looks" in the first sentence has a meaning different from & only definable in terms of that which it bears in the second. In order that I may judge of A that O looks red to him, or of myself that O looks red to me, it is necessary that I should apprehend the universal "red": but in order that O should look red to A, it is *not* necessary that he should apprehend the universal "red"; all that is necessary is that O shd. look, to A, of some particular shade, which is, *in fact*, a shade of red.

All shades which a thing can "look" in the fundamental sense are, I think, obviously of the same order; none is a shade *of* another. But if there were shades which were shades *of* any of these, it would be possible that a thing should "look" *of* one of these subordinate shades; hence that 2 shades wh. a thing could "look" (in the fundamental sense) were *not* of the same order— that one was a species of the other.

To say that A looks different from B *means* that some absolutely particular character wh. A looks to have (in fund. sense) is *perceived to be* different from some absolutely particular character which B looks to have, the 2 characters being incompatible. We cannot say merely that "looks different" means looks to have some character, wh. is *in fact* different from any wh. B looks to have, since, if Stumpf is right, this may happen, where A & B do *not* look different: for they don't look different, if there is no perceptible difference between them. Or should we perhaps say that it means: is, to the subject in question, *perceptibly* different? since it does not seem that any part of my field of view which looks different from another part is, in fact, *perceived* by me to be different from it. Parts of a dog's visual field *look* different to him from other parts, but yet it may be doubted, whether he ever *perceives* 2 to *be* different. But then, if we say *looks different* to the dog, means, are to him perceptibly different, we can hardly interpret this as meaning that he *could* perceive them to be different; since he may not be capable of such perceptions at all.

We cannot say that, in order that A may look red, there must be some one particular shade of red, such that A looks of that shade; since A may look red, even when different parts of it look of different particular shades.

What we can say is that, in order that A may look red, there must be *a* set of parts which constitute it (in Whitehead's sense), such that each of these looks to be of some particular shade of red. But this is not enough; since every *perceptible* part must look red. Is it enough to say: *a* set of perceptible parts, constituting it, such that each of these looks of some particular shade?

But we want to know what it is we know, when we know that a particular shade is a shade of *red*.

James says that if all red things were round, & all round things red, we should find it much more difficult than we do to discriminate round from red.

This is what Johnson calls discernment, as distinguished from discrimination. He seems to confine *discrimination* to incompatible characters, i.e. characters which can't both belong to the same thing at the same time, or can't *look* to. And obviously James' explanation of how we come to discriminate will only apply to *compatible* characters, i.e. to discernment. But it may apply to our discernment of red from a particular shade of red.

What exactly is the explanation?

Practically he says: if only one shade of red were ever presented to us, we should never discern red from that shade. I.e. our discernment of red is only to be explained by the fact that different shades are presented to us all of which are red. What is the supposed process of discernment? We must apparently somehow see that A & B both have a property, wh. some third thing C has not got (wh. is perhaps blue), & we must also see that the particular shade possessed by A is not possessed by B.

Let us, for the sake of brevity, call characters, which are such that, in order that a thing may look to have them, it must look to have some character related to them as a particular shade of red is to red (we may say "some particular *variety* of that character") "*general* characters", & characters which are *not* of this nature "specific characters". (Better names are "generic" & "non-generic".)

To *look*: corresponds: that *feels* hot, *smells* sweet, *feels* hard, *sounds* loud.

Now we say, first, that I am acquainted with a sense-datum, only when I am acquainted with some *specific* character which belongs (or seems to belong) to it. We can say: it is always given to me *as having* some specific character.

Let us say a specific character is *presented* to me, when some sense-datum is given as having that character.

Now, in order to *distinguish* a general character, it is necessary both (1) that some specific character incompatible with it should have been presented to me & (2) that at least 2 different specific characters, which are varieties of it, should have been presented to me.

RECOGNITION

There is a clear distinction between recognising an individual thing, & recognising a *kind* of thing.

As regards individual things, there is no doubt whatever that the having seen it *often* makes it easier to recognise—why, is another question. If you have seen a man only once or twice, & for short periods, you will be much more likely, in general, to take another man, whom you see, for him, or, when you see him or another man, not to feel sure whether it is him or not, than if you have seen him often.

What does recognising an individual thing mean?

Generally, the judging (truly) with regard to it: This is *the* thing which I saw on that or those occasions; or *the* thing which I have often heard referred to by the proper name "Smith" etc.

But when we say that a baby recognises its mother, it is doubtful whether we mean this. We mean rather that the sight of her, owing to past experiences of her, produces effects which the sight of no-one else does produce. So long as the sight of any other woman will produce on him the same effects as will the sight of his mother, we should say he does not recognise her. But what sort of effects are meant? It must be a mere feeling of familiarity; since his nurse also may produce this.

As for *kinds* of things, the first kinds of things we recognise seem to be complexes, not simple qualities. These seem to be the first we name. Dogs, flowers, horses, men.

Here familiarity does not seem to play so great a part as in recognition of individuals, because, in many more cases, the difference between one kind & *all* ⟨or presented?⟩ other kinds is much more striking.

What does recognising a thing as a horse, consist in?

Certainly not that the sight of a horse produces a feeling of familiarity.

28

SHAPE

Those only among visual sense-data are *given as having* a specific shape which are such that all round their boundaries there is a *discontinuity* between the specific colour which that part of them is given as having & the specific colour which the outside sense-datum adjoining the boundary is given as having.

And very often, in talking of visual sense-data, we confine the term to those which are given as having a specific shape.

If, however, we do so, we certainly cannot maintain that all the given parts of a visual sense-datum are themselves sense-data; or that an extended visual sense-datum always has parts which are themselves sense-data to the same person.

It seems evident that every extended part must *have* a shape; but it certainly need not be *given as having one*; &, therefore, if the "seeming" view be true need not seem to have one.

It is certainly the case that, with a continuously coloured surface, you cannot *single out* clearly *any* parts. *Are* the parts in that case given?

O Here I can single out the black line, & each of the white spaces into which the black line divides the area. But I cannot clearly single out any parts within the spaces. Can all or any of their parts be said to be given to me? On the "seeming" view it is necessary that some should, bec. on that view the thing *has* parts, which are certainly not given.

COLOUR

Take 2 shades of colour on the circle of spectrum colours, which are at an equal distance from pure red, one about a third of the way towards pure yellow, & the other about a third of the way towards pure blue.

These two shades are *both red*. But if, starting from one of them you take 2 shades at the *same* distance (as they are from pure red) on either side of that one, these 2 are not both of any colour.

This, I think, puts in a clearer way what is meant by saying that at pure red, pure yellow, pure blue & pure green, there is a *change* in direction.

Moreover, if true, it shews clearly that "red" does not *mean* at such & such a distance from pure red; since our second 2 shades are at an equal distance from the one we started from; & hence if being at such & such a distance from pure red were a quality, being at such & such a distance from this one would be so also, & hence they both would be of a certain colour.

Hence for 2 things to have a common quality is not the same thing as for them to have a certain degree of likeness. Two shades wh. have no common quality may be just as like as or more like than 2 others which have one. Hence likeness, in the sense in wh. we talk of more or less like between simple qualities, does not consist in possession of a common quality. But there is another sense of likeness, in which to say that 2 things have a common quality is to say they are alike.

What do we mean by "red"?

The same thing may be both red & scarlet; & it can't be maintained that every one who sees 2 shades that are both also sees both that they are red & that they are scarlet.

Of 3 shades, a, b & c, of which b is intermediate between a & c in respect of shade, it may be the case that there is no quality such that c has it in a greater degree than b, & b than a.

Take first 3 reds that lie on the saturated line between orange & pure red. Here b will be *redder* than a, & c than b. But if you take 3 reds one of which is on the blue side of pure red, & the other on the yellow, & the third between the two, it will not necessarily be the case that both c will be redder than b & b than a, though it may be. All that here will necessarily be the case is that c will be *darker* than b, & b than a.

But even this difference in darkness can be avoided by taking 3 reds sufficiently high up towards white. Take a whitish red on the line between pure red & white (b), a yellowish red on the line between a saturated yellowish red & white (a), & a bluish red on the line between a saturated bluish red & white (c); let the 2nd be so far from white that it is as *dark* as the first, & the 3rd so near to white that it is as *light* as the first; & let them be so chosen also that all are equally red (this can be done by taking your saturated yellowish & bluish reds at suitable distances from pure red). It will still be the case that a is, in a certain respect, more like b than b is like c, i.e. that b is intermediate between a & c; & yet will there be any quality such that both c is more of that than b, & b than a? Only if we can say that a is *whiter* than b & b than c, in spite of the fact that it is *not* lighter. *Perhaps* we can say this. We certainly can if of no 2 saturated reds it can be said that one is *whiter* than the other.

But in any case, this is not, I think, to the point; for we can, I think, say that *the* difference between a & c is greater than that between either & b; and a difference in respect of whiteness could not be *the* difference between them.

Similarly *the* difference between 2 saturated reds a & b, of which b is redder than a, may be no greater than *the* difference between b & c, where c is *not* redder than b, although b is redder than a *as well as* darker, & c is *only* darker than b & not redder.

Pure reds are the reddest reds, including therefore some that are *not* saturated. How is saturated to be defined? Does it mean the reddest red, the bluest blue, the greenest green & yellowest yellow, & all those shades which are intermediate between any 2 of these, *going by the shortest route*, i.e. by the route which involves the smallest number of shades where difference is just perceptible?

To refute Russell's theory of universals, it is sufficient to ask what is meant by the prop. "Yellow is lighter than red".

The use by psychologists of the word "bright", with reference to colours is misleading. What they mean is what is most properly expressed in English by "light" as opposed to "dark": which also means the same as "pale". We do not use "bright" for this; though the Germans use "hell" *both* for "light" & for "bright". "Bright" suggests a quality which can be most unambiguously named "shining"; and this is certainly different from "light". For a red light may *shine* more than a white surface, & yet *not* be of so light a colour.

What is meant by saying that one shade, b, is *between* 2 others a & c? e.g. a shade of orange between a shade of yellow & a shade of red.

It is *meant*, I think, that *the* difference between a & c is greater both than that between a & b & that between b & c.

But how define what is meant by saying that b is not only between a & c, but directly between them or between them *on the shortest line*?

I can see no way but by saying that of all those shades intermediate between a & b, which are such that the proportion between their difference from b & their difference from a is the same as that of this one, it is the one whose difference from a is smallest (& therefore also its difference from b).

Taking a certain degree of difference in shades, we can, starting from any shade whatever, form a group of all those shades which differ from it by no more than the difference in question. But in the case of *some* groups of this nature, all the members of it will be also distinguished by having more of a certain quality than any shades not included in the group; while in the case of others, they will not. E.g. if we fix our difference at such a degree that any shade which differs from the purest red by no more than that amount is distinctly red, then the members of the group which differ no more than that amount from the purest red, will all be *redder* than any shades not included in it, whatever distance we take conforming to the condition laid down. But for each such distance there will be an immense number of groups, starting from red shades other than the purest red, of which we cannot say that the members have more of any quality whatever than shades not included in the group. There are thus many groups (but such that of any 2, one must include the other), of each of which all the members are redder, many of each of which all are greener, many of each of which all are yellower, many of each of which all are bluer, many of each of which all are whiter, & many of each of which all are *blacker*, than any shades not included in the group. But are there not also others? Are there not a set of shades each of which is more scarlet, a set each of which is more orange, a set each of which is more crimson, etc.? I am not sure. It all depends on whether there is any one shade that is more orange than all others, more scarlet, or more crimson.

To say that a is redder than b, means that there is some shade, which is not red at all, to which b is *nearer* than a is to any shade which is not red at all. In the case of some pairs of reds we can see immediately that one of the two is in this sense redder than the other; but in the case of many we cannot.

Nor can we by any means always in comparing 2 pairs of shades, tell immediately whether the distance between the first pair is or is not greater than that between the second.

Where we cannot tell immediately the only way of discovering seems to be by comparing the number of just perceptibly different shades intermediate between a & b, with the number intermediate between c & d. But then it must be of those intermediate by *the shortest route*. And how are we to tell which is the shortest route?

If we compare a very light red with (1) a very light blue & (2) a nearly pure red, it seems natural to say that, in respect of lightness, it is more like (1) than it is like (2), but that in respect of *hue* it is more like (2) than it is like (1).

b may come between a & c in respect of lightness without coming between a & c in respect of hue. But it cannot come between a & c in respect of hue, without also coming between them in respect of lightness.

This seems to be one difference between colours & sounds. b may come between a & c in respect of loudness without coming between them in respect of pitch; but it may also come between in respect of pitch without coming between in respect of loudness. Loudness & pitch are (*within limits*, for a very high sound cannot be *so* loud as a low one) mutually independent; whereas though lightness is independent of hue, hue is not independent of lightness?

Two shades can't differ in lightness without differing in hue; & they also can't differ in hue without differing in lightness.

But 2 sounds can differ in loudness without differing in pitch; & they can also differ in pitch without differing in loudness.

You can say with certainty of one shade that it is red, & of another that it is not, in spite of the fact that there is a continuous passage from one to the other.

Similarly, I suppose, there might be intermediate gradations between acquaintance & judgment, or between sense & thought, in spite of the fact that you could say quite definitely this is acquaintance & not judgment, or this is judgment & not acquaintance, or this is sense & not thought, or this is thought & not sense.

30

DISCRIMINATION

What is it?

To discriminate = to distinguish: the only reason why the word "discrimination" has been used by psychologists, is because "distinction" can't be used unambiguously for the act (or power) of distinguishing.

J.[1] says we must rigorously distinguish 3 acts: (1) that which he calls "separation", & which is such that only *substantives* can be separated from one another (including "experiences", which are a class of "occurrences" among substantives). To separate A from B, is not (he says, p. 11)[2] to think about A "as being distinct" from B. Nor does separation of A from B involve an "apprehension of the relation of otherness". This, however, *is* involved in a *combined attention* to A & B, *if* we have *previously* both separated A, & also (subsequently) separated B. He implies that you can't separate A, without *thinking about* A; &, acc. to his doctrine, you can't apparently think about A without characterising it. *Apparently* also you can only separate A if A is *given*. (2) that which he calls "discrimination", & which is such that only "characters" or "adjectives" can be discriminated from one another, & apparently also only what he calls "comparable" characters, which is the same (I think) as *incompatible* ones. (3) that which he calls "discernment", which is again such that only "characters" can be discerned: but apparently characters which can be discriminated can't be discerned, & vice versa; & no characters can be discerned, except such as are *fused*, which involves that they should all characterise the same substantive. App. also in order to discern 2 characters we must apprehend them *as characterising* the same substantive, i.e. they must not only do so, but we must apprehend them as doing so.

Certainly psychologists, in general, talk of both (2) & (3) as cases of discrimination; & also include under that term some process such that 2 substantives may be discriminated from one another.

How is "discrimination" actually used?

[1] [W. E. Johnson.]
[2] ["Analysis of Thinking", *Mind*, vol. XXVII, 1918.]

When, as in experiments on Weber's law, we definitely *try to discover* with regard to 2 visual sense-data, or 2 sounds, or 2 impressions of weight, *is* the shade of this different from the shade of that, is this higher than that or louder than that (or do they *differ* in pitch or loudness), do these 2 impressions feel different in respect of heaviness, we are said to be able to discriminate them, when we can judge with certainty this *does* differ in character from that. And A's discriminative sensibility would be said to be greater than B's, if in the case of the sensations produced by 2 stimuli, under the same circumstances, A can be certain "This is different from that", when B cannot. But it is here uncertain whether B's sensations do really differ as much as A's. Some people would say: If B, when expressly comparing them with a view to discover whether they are different in a certain respect or not, cannot see that they are, then they are not: i.e. if they are not perceptibly (to B) different, they are not different at all. But it is well to realise what this view implies. The *infima* shade which, ex hypothesi, both the sensations, a & b, are presented as having to B, will either be identical with one of the 2 different shades, which a' & b' are presented as having to A, or some shade intermediate between the 2, or at least some shade belonging to the series to which these belong. That is to say, the hypothesis that B has less differentiated sensations, means that out of the whole series of shades presented to A, some only are presented to B, & those really *more* different from one another than the intermediate ones presented to A: the smallest difference perceptible to B is a *greater* difference than the smallest perceptible to A (this is so on either hypothesis). It cannot be that the shades B perceives are e.g. identical with red, or blue, or scarlet: for, since I can distinguish several different shades all of which are shades of scarlet, scarlet itself is not identical with any one of them, nor intermediate between any 2 of them.

Take 2 sounds. I constantly cannot tell whether 2 are different in pitch or not, where a piano-tuner can tell not only that they certainly are, but which is the higher. Here it seems pretty certain that it is *not* the case that the pitch wh. a is presented to me as having, & the pitch wh. b is presented to me as having, are in fact identical or less different than those wh. the tuner's a' & b' are presented to him as having; but simply that I cannot perceive the difference of 2 of wh. he *can* perceive it.

Because one can be in doubt whether they are different or not, it seems imposs. to hold that where 2 are different, it must always be possible, if you attend, to see that they are.

Here discrimination seems to mean merely *noticing* that 2 are different. But it seems to me as if there were something intermediate between *noticing* that 2 characters are different, & merely *having* 2 characters presented wh. are in fact different: something which I don't know how to express except by saying they produce an *impression of difference*. Where the difference is slight, they may not, I think, produce an impression of difference, even where, if your attention was directed to the point, you could notice that they were different. But where the difference is great, you do I think normally have an impression of difference, even where you don't notice it.

Another point is of importance. You may notice: There *are* things which differ in colour *in this region*, without noticing *this* is different in colour from *that*; simply bec. you can't single out this & that. This happens where you have a single surface with differences of colour, not marked off by a sharp outline; & also I think with regard to your whole visual field at any one time. Similarly when you hear a confused variety of sounds at any one time. You notice that there are many different sounds, without singling out all or any of them. And so too with *impressions* of difference.

What you notice here is not, obviously, simply: There *are* different sounds *in* the Universe. Nor does it seem to mean: There are different sounds *presented* to me: you may have no consciousness of yourself. It seems to be merely: There are *in this region*: & what this means except round about *this*, where *this* is something which *is* singled out, I can't see. Yet I'm not sure that there always need be *anything* singled out.

I think we must say that a whole can be a *this* to you without having (so to speak) definite outlines—that is to say, it is not *given as having* definite outlines. In other words you can *single out* a vague whole, so as to be able to know: *Within* this whole there are parts different in colour, in pitch etc.

Whatever *substantive* you *single out*, & only what you single out, is a *this* substantive to you; & within what you single out, there are very often parts which you simply *can't* (not only *don't*) single out.

I suppose what I call "single out", is the same as what J. calls "separate".

I do not think that the *whole* of what is presented to you at any one time is ever a *this* to you. If it were, then "singling out" could not mean singling out from *other* things presented to you.

You can never *tell* that the shade or length or pitch or shape which *this* is presented as having is the *same* as the shade or length or pitch which *that* is presented as having: they *may* always be slightly different. Yet you *can* tell that this & that are *both* red, *both* long, *both* high. That is to say, of an absolutely particular character, you can never say: *This* belongs both to this & that; whereas of a *general* character you can. You can identify *a* character of this with *a* character of that, but never *the* character of this with *the* character of that.

In the case of every *substantive* which is given to you at all, there is *either* at least one *absolutely particular character* such that it is given to you as having that character, or there is a *set* of parts of it (defined as parts wh. make it up in Whitehead's sense), in the case of each of which there is at least one absolutely particular character which that part is given to you as having.

A number of substantives that are given to you can give you the impression that there are substantives of different character among them, even when you have not singled out any one of them.

Take as the first meaning of discrimination, the *singling out* of a substantive: when one is singled out it becomes a "this" to you.

By no means every substantive that is *given* is singled out, or is, therefore, a this to you.

This appears in 2 ways.

(1) In the case of a substantive which *is* singled out, you can sometimes see that it has parts given to you, wh. simply can't be singled out even vaguely: e.g. the appearance of a cloud.

(2) You can also sometimes see that it has parts which *could* be singled out, but which you haven't singled out?

By no means every substantive that is *given* to you is a "this" to you.

Any given substantive to which you are attending is a "this" to you.

Very often, perhaps most commonly, a substantive which is a "this" to you has substantive parts, which are also given to you, & which are such that the *ultimate* characters which some are given as having are different from those which others are given as having; & by no means all of these parts are "thises" to you, when the whole is.

31

[NO TITLE]

When a thing looks red to me, it always also looks of some particular shade of red. I can discern this, because in each case I can think of a shade *other than* that which it looks to be of, which is yet such that if it had looked to be of that shade it would have looked red.

I think we can say that "x looks red" means "x looks (in another and more fundamental sense) of some particular shade, which is of *this* character".

If, however, I know or judge "*This* looks red to me" or "There is something there which looks red to me" I am not merely knowing or judging with regard to some particular shade, wh. has in fact the character in question, that This looks to be of that shade: on the contrary the universal "red" enters as a constituent into such an act of knowing or judging in a way in which it does not enter into a state of mind which is merely a case of its looking red to me. A thing can look red to me, without my apprehending the universal red at all; but I cannot know that it looks red to me, without apprehending that universal.

But when I said: if it looks red to me, it always looks of some particular shade, I was not quite accurate. For it may be that there are several different particular shades, such that some parts of it look of one of these & others of others. In such cases there is no particular shade, such that it, as a whole, looks of that shade.

I can often tell at once with certainty: When that looked red to me, different parts of it did look of different shades. But in other cases, I find it difficult to be sure, whether different parts of it are looking or were looking of different shades or not. If I concentrate my attention on the question, in order to try to make sure, I am sometimes still not sure. And moreover sometimes when I am sure that, now that my attention is concentrated, different parts *do* look of different shades, I do not feel sure whether, *before* my attention was concentrated, they did.

But how can I distinguish between looking of different shades in different parts, & looking of some one shade all over? The first notion is a clear one: I know that, when a thing looks red, it does sometimes look of different shades in different parts. But do I ever know that it does *not*? I know that I sometimes cannot tell that it *does*. But we have *defined* the looking of different shades in different parts, as if it involved that certain parts should look of some one shade *all over*. Am I in fact sure that anything ever does look of the same *ultimate* shade all over? Yet can a thing look of different ultimate shades in different parts, without there being any part which looks of any one particular ultimate shade? I think, perhaps, it can.

We had better, therefore, *define*: Looking of one particular ultimate shade as meaning: *Either* looking of several different ultimate shades in different parts *or* looking of the same all over (not being sure whether the latter is ever realised).

With this definition we can stick to our original statement about red, & can say that the same holds of any *named* colour.

Similarly for a thing to look round, means that it looks of some particular shape, wh. is a round shape; for it to look big, that it looks of some particular size, wh. is a big size.

But does "look circular" mean "look of some particular shape, wh. is a circular shape"? I cannot say here for certain that I know of any other shapes which I can see to be [circular].

32

LOOKING

"Looking" is very ambiguous.

When I see the side of a house through a window, it does in one sense "look" *continuous* with the window-frame, whereas in another it *looks* as if it were at a considerable distance from it (it is not *merely judged* to be so).

And the same seems to be equally true of the corresponding sense-data, even if these are not identical with the side of the house & the window-frame.

Moreover if we take a picture of a side of a house seen through a window-frame we have 3 senses of look (1) they look continuous (2) it does *not* look at a distance from it, in the sense in which the real house does; yet (3) if the perspective is good, it *does* look at a distance from it in a 3d. sense: it gives a "sense" of depth or distance.

The difference between (2) & (3) is that, if I had (2), in a case in which the 2 were *not* really distant, I should be having an illusion; whereas in (3) they are not distant, yet I am having no illusion (though we do say, speaking loosely, the picture produces "the illusion" of distance).

Perhaps the difference between (2) & (3) is solely that (2) means *both* looks in sense (3) *&* is judged to be. If so, when we speak of an illusion still persisting in spite of a judgment to the contrary, we shall be using illusion in a sense in wh. (3) really is an illusion.

We must also distinguish 2 different senses in which the same physical thing may be said to *look different* at different times. This may mean (1) that it seems to have undergone a visible change or (2) merely that the ultimate characters which it is presented as having are different (*and* are felt to be so?)

⟨It is quite sensible to say: There is a change in the appearance of that, but it doesn't look as if it had changed itself: there is no change in appearance, of the kind that indicates real change.⟩

When I say that the penny, turned round to be seen obliquely, does, to every one, *look* different in shape; I think I mean only that the ultimate character which it is presented as having *is* different; and this may certainly happen without its seeming to have undergone a visible change in shape. But does this latter mean only that, besides the ultimate character wh. it is presented as having *being* different, it is also *judged* that it really has at the 2 times these different ultimate characters? Not *merely*; bec. the change of shape which it is judged to have undergone may not consist in its having at either time the ultimate character it is presented as having. In order that I may see that this has changed in shape, it is necessary that the ultimate shape-character wh. it is presented as having should be different from what it was, but it is not necessary that I should know that it now has the ultimate shape wh. it is presented as having.

When we say the moon *looks* larger, we mean both (1) that the magnitude which it is presented as having *is* larger & (2) that it is seen to be so.

33

LANGUAGE

A dog's bark may express the fact that an ultimate character (a complex one), which is *in fact* of a certain kind, is presented to him; but it does not express the fact that he knows or judges the ultimate character to be of that kind.

But when an individual *calls* an object "box", "flower", "dog" etc., his making of the sound expresses the fact that he knows or judges an ultimate character which is presented to him to be of a certain kind.

This, I think, is the ultimate difference between the use of sounds to *call* a thing by a general name; & a use of expressive sounds which are not used as names at all.

But there is still a difficulty in defining what is meant by using a sound as a *proper* name. Can the bark of a dog ever be a proper name, &, if not, why not?

To *use* a sound *as* a person's or animal's name, & to know that it is his name are different things; but to know that it is his name is to know that it is used as a name for him.

When *is* a sound used as a name for a person?

Certainly when it is used to convey to another person (whether the one in question or not) that you are thinking of him. But it seems it *can* be used as a name, without being used for this purpose: e.g. when you call a dog by its name?

Can we say: When it is used in order to make someone else think of that person? This also is not sufficient, if you are using "Fido" as a name, when you call "Fido".

Moreover, when a baby first uses "Dadda" as a name for its father, it does not seem necessarily to have either of these purposes. Or perhaps, does it *not* use "Dadda" as a name, until it uses it for these purposes, even when it says "Dadda" when & only when it sees its father?

That its use of "Dadda" should express the fact that it is seeing or thinking of its father, is certainly not enough; since otherwise a joyful bark might be a dog's name for its master.

34

SENSE-DATA AND PHYSICAL OBJECTS

As I look out of my window, I see a piece of the roof of St. Giles'
cut off by the window-frame.

I *know: That* is a part of the roof of S. Giles'; *and: This* is a
part of the frame of one of my windows.

"That" & "this", in these expressions, are names for visual
sense-data given to me at the moment.

"That" is *given* to me *as* being, in most of its parts, of a bluish-
greenish-grey, though there are particles of a darker colour in it;
"this" is *given* to me *as* being of a whitish-yellowish grey, darker
than the other (the window-frame is of the common dull-white
Cambridge brick), but by no means uniform in colour.

When I say "that" is *given as* of a bluish-greenish-grey, I do not
mean to assert that there is any *one* particular shade of this kind,
such that all the parts wh. are given to me as of a shade of that
kind, are given as of *that* shade. For all I can tell the shade as
being of which any 2 different parts are given is, in every case,
slightly different; though I cannot with the best attention see that
this is the case: some extended parts of it *look* of a uniform
colour, in the sense that I cannot *see* that there are any different
shades which they are given as being of, as regards part of their
extent. But this that they *look* of a uniform colour, must not be
understood to mean that they are not, in fact, given as of different
shades in different parts.

Moreover when I say that "that" is *given as* of different colours
in different parts, this must not be understood to mean that I
notice that it is of different colours. I do, in fact, notice it. But a
thing may be *given as* of different colours, without your noticing
that it is.

N.B. also that when I say parts are *given as* of *a* bluish-greenish-
grey, I am not saying that they are *given as* bluish, in the same
sense as that in which they are given as of one or several bluish
shades. *The* colour "bluish" is not identical with any one particular bluish shade; & when we say a thing is given as "bluish",
what we mean is that it is *given as* (in a more fundamental sense)
of some one or several shades, which is or are in fact bluish.

73

Nothing is or can be *given as* bluish, in the sense in wh. it is given
as of a particular bluish shade. There may be a temptation to use
the phrase "given as bluish", in such a way that in order that a
thing may be given to you as bluish, you must apprehend the
universal bluish. But this is not how the phrase is in fact generally
used. To say that a thing is given as bluish, means only: There is
one (or several) bluish shades such that the thing is given as
of that or those. In order that this may happen, the universals
which are these shades must be apprehended, but the universal
"bluish" need not be.

"That" is also *given as continuous* with "this".

Now when I say that "that" & "this" are names for visual
sense-data given to me at the moment, I do not mean to assert
that when I know "That is a part of the roof of S. Giles' ", I am
knowing of my visual sense-datum that *it* is a part of a roof. It
can, at most, be part of a roof, in the sense that it is part of *one
surface* of a roof.

But is it even this?

(1) Russell & Broad would say that whatever it is *given as* being,
it *is*; & that hence "that" really is continuous with "this".

Now I know that no part of the surface of the roof of S. Giles'
is continuous with the frame of my window *in physical space*.

It is, no doubt, possible that they are continuous in some *other*
space—e.g. my private space at this moment; & hence even if
"this" & "that" really are continuous, it is possible that they are
parts of the surface of a roof & of the surface of my window-
frame. But I think this is a possibility scarcely worth considering.

(2) I know that that part of the surface of the roof is in physical
space at a considerable distance from this part of my window-
frame.

If, therefore, my sense-data really are identical with these
surfaces, I know that they are *not* continuous in physical space,
but *are in* physical space.

But I do not know that the thing wh. is given to me as of that
greenish-blue colour, & as continuous with the thing given to me
as of this whitish-grey colour, is identical with that part of the
roof's surface. That is to say I do not know that the 2 descriptions
apply to the same thing.

In *that* sense I do not know that my sense-data are identical
with the surface of the roof & of my window-frame; & similarly

I do not know that my sense-data, described as *the* things given to me *as* of these colours & continuous are in physical space at all.

(3) I know that the 2 surfaces existed before I saw them; but of the sense-data, described as the things given to me as having these characters, I do *not* know that this is so.

(4) I know that *you* can see the 2 surfaces, but of the sense-data described as above, I do *not* know that this is so.

(5) 4 hrs. have gone by since I wrote the above. Yet I know of 2 sense-data I am now seeing, that *that* roof is at least partially the same as the one I saw this morning, & that *this* brick window-frame is also the same.

I can see that the blue-grey shade which *that* is now *given* to me *as* being of is darker relatively to the whitish-grey of *this*, than was this morning's blue-grey shade: I suppose this is because the sun is now shining on the opposite side of the roof, so that this side is in shade. The *appearance*, then, either of the roof, or of the window-frame or of both has certainly changed; yet I cannot *see* that either the roof or the window-frame has changed. Very likely they have; but I cannot see that they have, as I *can* see that the surface of this paper has changed, by the presence of the black marks I have made on it. We must therefore distinguish between a *seen* change in a physical object, & a change in its visual appearance. I know that there has been a change in the visual appearance to me of one or both of these 2 objects; but I know also that I do not *see* any change in either.

Can it be that both "that" & "this" are the *same* "that" & "this" which I saw this morning, in spite of the fact that one or both of them is given as having a different colour, from the that & this of the morning?

Yes; for one of either reason (1) because they may be the same in spite of having changed, & (2) because they may not really have had the colours, either then or now, which they were given as having.

But it is *only* on hypothesis (2), that they can be identical respectively the present this & that with the surface of the window-frame & of the roof, *as they are now*, & the past this & that with those surfaces as they were then, because of these 2 surfaces I do *not* see that they have changed relatively to one another, whereas I *do* see that there is a difference between the relations of the colours which the present this & that are given as having, & those which the past this & that were given as having.

This notion of "*given as*" having certain ultimate characters, or given as having certain relations to other given things, is *one* of the ultimate psychological notions. I have chosen the term, because it does not necessarily imply that what is *given as* having a character necessarily has it. It is also clearer than looking or seeming, because we can truly say that this does *not* look continuous with that, whereas it certainly is *given as* continuous with it.

It is probably identical with what R. has meant when he has spoken of acquaintance with sense-data; for certainly whenever we are acquainted with a sense-datum, it is *given as* having certain ultimate characters. In that case, this sort of acquaintance is *not* a dual relation.

In the case of memory the thing remembered is never *given as having any* ultimate character which it *was* given as having when perceived. And unless the thing remembered is identical with some memory-image, it is not *given as having* any ultimate character whatever: it is only known *to have had* some *general* character.

What are the objections to supposing that those of our visual sense-data, of which we can truly say: That is a "so-&-so" (being a kind of physical object), are identical with surfaces of the object in question?

(1) That it is difficult not to think that our sense-data really have all the characters which they are given as having.

And, if they have, then

(a) I often do *not* see that the surface which "this" is & "that" was has changed, when I do see that "this" is given as having a character incompatible with that which "that" was given as having.

(b) I often know that this surface is *not* continuous with that, when "this" is given as being continuous with "that". (This *might* be got over by saying that it is *in* different spaces that the things in question are & are not continuous.)

(c) I often know that this surface is being seen by you too, whereas I have ample reason to believe that the thing given to you, which is either identical with this surface, or, if not so, stands in the same relation to this surface, as "this" that is given to me does, is given to you as having a character incompatible with that which this is given to me as having.

In saying: This surface is seen by you too: I am saying *either*: *This* is given to you as having certain visual characters; *or*: Something is given to you as having certain visual characters, which is a *manifestation* of this surface ("manifestation" being a name for the relation R, whatever it is, which is such that when I say "this surface" I mean "the thing to which "this" has R"); i.e. I am saying: Something is given to you which has R to that to which "this" has R.

(d) It is difficult not to think that some of the characters which tactual sense-data are given as having are incompatible with colours; & if so, then we have new arguments of types (a) & (c).

(2) It is often claimed that my sense-data are experiences of my own ("sensations" of mine), & that I know they cease to exist, at times when the corresponding surfaces certainly don't.

(3) That even if (1) & (2) can be got over, it is difficult to see how we can ever know that our sense-data have not got the characters they are given as having & have got others incompatible with these.

E.g. how do I know that that roof is *really* at a considerable distance from this window-frame; that this sense-datum (of a penny) which is given as elliptical, is really circular?

35

SENSE-DATA AND PHYSICAL OBJECTS

Double images have convinced me that the sense-datum of which I am speaking when I say "That's a sofa" is *not* identical with any part of the surface of the sofa.

For I cannot doubt that the two images are two different *things*: it cannot be that each of those 2 images of my finger *was* my finger (or a part of its surface), & that it merely *appeared* to be in 2 different places at once—to be outside itself, & both to the right of & to the left of itself.

If A is *given as* to the right of B, A must *be* to the right of B, & if A is to the right of B, A is other than B.

Nor can it be that one of the two is the surface of my finger, & the other something else, not identical with any physical object.

At the same time I do not pretend to be sure in all cases where something is given to me as having a certain character, & something as having another character, whether that which has the one is or is not identical with that which has the other. E.g. when I press against a cold surface, something is given as cold & something is given as having a pressure-character, but whether it is the same thing that is given as both, or one thing given as the one, & another as the other, I cannot tell. If the thing that is given as cold were given as *in a different place from* the thing that is given as having the pressure-character or as smooth, I should have no doubt that they were different; but when that is not the case, I don't see how to tell. Similarly when I hear a chord, & can distinguish that something is given of a low pitch, & something of a high, is it the whole sound which is given as having both characters, or is there a *part* of it given as having one, & a part given as having the other? I think it is clear here that the *whole chord* does not sound high nor low, & that therefore we have here to do with 2 different *things*—*parts* of the chord—of which one is high, the other low.

To return to the double images: The real point is, I think, that the images are a "this" & a "that", & that it is really nonsense to suggest (if one could see it) that a "this" ever is identical with a "that". *Two* things can't be identical with one another; & where it appears as if there were a possibility that 2 things are, the possibility is always only *really* that "this" is identical with *the* thing which has *this* character, or that "the thing wh. has this character" is identical with the thing which has that. When I judge of the one: This is of these two the right hand one (or the one which looks so), I am quite certainly *not* judging of the other: *This* is of these two the right hand one.

Let us try to apply this test to other difficult cases of identity.

(1) As to identity of successive sense-data. When a sense-datum has a certain duration, is this analogous to its having a certain size, in the respect that it has temporal parts, which are identical neither with it nor with one another?

What we call *"a sound"* certainly may have temporal parts; e.g. a clap of thunder, or the sound of a motor bicycle going past. We can say: it began comparatively faint—its *earlier part* was comparatively faint—became very loud, in its middle part, & ended faint again.

Similarly a movement (or other change, e.g. a change in a light) may have temporal parts; but for some reason or other it seems to me wholly unnatural to talk of a visual sense-datum, like that of this jug, as having temporal parts. Yet I don't see how it differs from a *uniform* sound.

All this is connected with the question whether sense-data continue to exist when we don't see them. The sound *I hear*, when a motor-bic. passes, which begins faint & ends faint, certainly doesn't so continue; though I know it goes on making a similar sound, only it moves away from me so that I can't hear it: moreover it's *making just as much noise*, when the noise *I hear* is faint, as when it's loud. Similarly a visual movement *which I see* begins when I begin to see it, & ends when I cease to see it, though the corresponding physical movement may be merely a part of a movement which goes on. But somehow this sense-datum of the jug does *not* seem to me like that. The cessation of *my seeing it*, when I close my eyes, or turn my head, does not seem quite like the cessation of a sound, when a door is shut or I stop my ears: the latter seems to be not merely a cessation of my hearing it, but of *the sound* I hear; the former seems only a cessation of my seeing it, *not* of the coloured thing I saw.

D *Commonplace Book*

A temporal whole of this sort, which is *given*, no more *consists* of its parts than Whitehead's spatial whole. It is given as a whole, & is given as having characters wh. the parts have not got, just as a spatial whole.

NOTEBOOK II

[c. 1926]

1

WHITEHEAD'S "PRINCIPLES OF NATURAL KNOWLEDGE"

What is a "duration"? pp. 68–9, pp. 110–11[1].

An event which is simultaneous with certain other events & contains every event with which it is simultaneous.

I think so.

That is: take any ordinary (= other than a duration) event you like; there will be one & only one event which contains both it & every event simultaneous with it, & which is *also* simultaneous with it; & this event will be a duration.

Are there any durations, with this meaning? I don't know how it can be proved that there are. I suppose W. must be assuming that a set of simultaneous events always are parts of one event; & this seems plausible.

But what is meant by the hypothesis that there are different time-systems, & that each duration belongs only to one such system? p. 81, p. 112, p. 114.

It is involved, I think, that 2 events x & y may both be simultaneous with a third w, without being sim. with one another.

What is a "moment"?

It is (p. 110) any set of events, which are the members of the absolute antiprimes which cover some one assigned absolute antiprime.

Absolute antiprime = abstractive class which covers every abstractive class which covers it (p. 110).

Abstractive class = class of events such that (1) of any 2 of its members one contains the other (2) there is no event which is contained in every event of the class (p. 104).

And to say that α "covers" β means, that *every* member of α contains *some* member of β.

To say that there are abstractive classes of events seems a

---

[1] [A. N. Whitehead, *An Enquiry concerning the Principles of Natural Knowledge* (Cambridge, 1919).]

doubtful assumption. For though there certainly are classes of events wh. satisfy condition (1), it seems doubtful whether they may not all of them be classes which do *not* satisfy (2). (2) seems equivalent to saying that every event in the class *contains* some other event that is in the class.

2

EVENTS

What is an event, & how does it differ from a thing?

We start from knowing that what certain names stand for certainly are events, & what others stand for certainly are *not* & are things.

The battle of Waterloo, *this* movement of my arm, my present perception of these visual sense-data are events: Napoleon, my arm, this desk are *not* events but things.

Johnson uses the term "occurrence": perhaps this means something slightly different from "event"; but I can see no difference. Everything that is an "event" is an "occurrence" so far as I can see, & vice versa.

"Events" occur or happen; things do *not*.

Most events that we distinguish & talk of are obviously complex, in the sense that they contain or include subordinate *events*, & that in 2 ways. They include events which happened at different times, & also different simultaneous events. Thus the battle of Waterloo passed through many different stages, each of which was an event; & also each stage included many different events happening in different places—in different parts of the field. Even my present perception of *this* lasts a little time, and any part of it which occupies only part of that time, is an event included in it. Whether it contains any 2 events, which are simultaneous with one another, may be doubted.

Can it be that events, which contain other events, are mere collections of events?

It is quite certain that not all collections of events are themselves events; since 2 events separated by an interval of time are certainly not an event, though they may both be parts of one.

It is only, therefore, collections of events, such that all the members of the collection are related in a certain way, which could possibly be themselves events. That is to say by "This is an event" we certainly don't *mean* "This is a collection of events"; but it might be the case that some events *are* collections of others.

But now many events which are parts of other events, themselves have parts. And in this case the event which contains these subordinate events is certainly not the collection of *all* its parts. Suppose this movement of my arm lasts a second. It has for parts (1) that part of the movement which occupied the first half of that second, & (2) that part which occupied the second half; it has (3) that part wh. occupied the first 3rd, (4) that which occupied the 2nd 3rd, (5) & that which occupied the 3^d 3^d: etc. etc. And by the whole movement we certainly do not mean any collection of which all these 5 are members. (3) is a part of (1) & (5) is a part of (2).

It is not true, therefore, that all the events which are parts of an event are *members* of that event. Those of them which themselves have parts are, if the event is a class at all, certainly sub-classes of it & *not* members: they have to it the relation $\subset$, not ϵ.

For this reason, if such an event is a collection of events at all, it must be a collection of events, which have no other events as parts. But are there any events which have no events as parts?

The beginning or the ending of an event is an event, & one which has no events as parts. But no event which has a beginning & an ending is composed of beginnings & endings. The kind of events we are talking of all have beginnings & endings; & hence if they are collections of events at all they are collections of events which both (1) are not beginnings or endings & (2) have neither beginnings nor endings.

There may perhaps *be* such events, but it is impossible to point any out.

The relation of a subordinate complex event to an including event, which we call being a *part* of it, is therefore (a) certainly not that of member to class (b) can only be that of sub-class to class, if there are events having this peculiar property.

But every event which is part of another seems to be so in the same sense. We cannot distinguish some which are members, & others which are sub-classes: but if *any* are sub-classes, there must be some wh. are members. I think, therefore, the probability is that none are sub-classes; that therefore no event is a collection; & that the relation of whole to part is an 'timate relation— Whitehead's "extending over"—except that .emporally extending over" is a different relation from "extending over" of 2 simultaneous events.

Some events, therefore, certainly have duration.

3

THE PRESENT

A judgment that an event *is* happening is never true unless the event in question is simultaneous with the judgment in question: not only *is* not, but *cannot* be.

Of any event A it can be truly said, *at one time*, A *is* happening, at another, A *was* happening, at another A *will* happen.

Let t′ be a time at which it cannot be truly said of A "A is happening", but only "A has happened".

Why cannot "A is happening" be truly said of A at t′?

One reason is that the words "x is happening" imply (though I think they cannot assert) that x is simultaneous with the use of them: a use of the words "A is happening" will therefore never be true (will not *correctly* express something true), unless A is simultaneous with that use.

For "A is *not* present" to be true, it seems, therefore, sufficient that A should not be simultaneous with the use of these words which is in question: & for "A *did* happen" that A should be *before* the use of the words in question.

When I judge, at one time, "A is happening", e.g. "This *is* near this", & at another, "B is happening", e.g. "That *is* near that", there is some similarity in the *contents* of the judgments, which is expressed by saying that each is a judgment *of the form* "x is happening".

An event which *was* present, *is* past. Yet the event itself has not changed, i.e. it has not changed intrinsically. Nor has it changed its relations to anything. If you can say "A is simultaneous with B", without using "is" in a temporal sense, & similarly with "before" & "after", [then] it can truly be said *now* to be simultaneous with everything with which it could truly be said *then* to be simultaneous, & can truly be said *now* to be before & after everything which it could truly be said *then* to be before & after. All that has happened is that one of the events which it was then before & is now before, was then future & is now present. But this change is of exactly the same nature. The event which was future & is present has neither changed its nature nor any of its relations.

This, I think, puts the difficulty about past, present & future. It seems as if, in order that any property ϕ may be true of A at one time & not at another, either A must have changed intrinsically (if this is possible) i.e. it must be intrinsically different at the one time from what it is at the other, *or* it must have a relation to something at the one time wh. it hasn't at the other. But "present" seems to be a property. Yet we have a thing at one time present, at another not, *without* its being true that it is intrinsically different at the 2 times, nor yet that it has any relations at the one wh. it has not at the other.

In answer to this, it may be said, first, that in order that a thing may properly be said to have an intrinsic property at one time & not to have it at another, it must *be* at both times; whereas a past event simply *is* not at a time at which it is past. When we say of an event A & a time t', that A is *not* present at t', we are not asserting of it either that it has *not* a certain intrinsic property at that time, nor yet that it has not certain relations at it; but something wh. falls under *neither* of these heads.

What are we asserting of it?

So far as this goes, it might be simply that it is not simultaneous with *this* (this being something wh. is in fact at time t'), where "is" is to be understood in a non-temporal sense.

But when we say of A "A *is* not present" it seems imposs. we shd. mean simply "A is not sim. with this"; since that is something wh. might have been truly said of A, even when it could be truly said "A *is* present".

An event, *when* it is present, has some special character, which it has at no other time. *Every* event, when it is present, has that character. What can the character be?

It may be remarked, first of all, that no event has any character whatever except when it is present. It may be truly judged of it, at another time, e.g. that it is past; but this does not mean that at that other time it possesses any character whatever. It only means that if there were a judgment that it is past among the group containing a given event & all those sim. with it, which defines that other time, that judgment would be true; & (what is a condition for this) that it precedes all the members of that group.

But further it may be doubted whether any event possesses any character at *any* time. For to say that a thing possesses a character *at* a time, seems to mean that its possession of the character is an event wh. is a member of the group that defines that time. And though events do possess characters, it does not seem that the possession of a character by an event is ever itself an event.

Another way *of stating* the difficulty.

It seems, at first sight, obvious that, if you have a number of judgments with the same content, if one is true the rest must be.

But if you take a set of judgments with regard to a given event A, either that it is happening, or that it is past, or that it is future, some of each set will be true, & some false; which are true & wh. false depending on the time when the judgment is made.

It seems a sufficient answer to this to say that a judgment "A is happening" made at one time never has the same content as the judgment "A is happening" made at another.

4

NUMBER

"There are 2 pennies in my pocket" asserts a certain property to belong to the property "is a penny now in my pocket" ($= \phi$).

What it asserts is: $(\exists\, x, y) :. \phi x . \phi y . x \neq y : (z) : z \neq y . z \neq x : \supset : \sim \phi z$. I.e. it asserts a certain *logical property* to belong to ϕ.

But is this *logical* property *the* number 2? If so, what is meant by saying that it is "a number"?

Can we say it is a property such that the classes defined by all properties wh. possess it *must* be all similar to one another? & that this is what is meant by saying it is a number? I.e. that any property of a property wh. is such that all properties possessing it *must* define similar classes, is a number?

α has the same number as β . $\equiv$. α is similar to β.

I think *perhaps* the true view is that nothing is *the* number 2 & that nothing is *a number*: nay more that "is a number" does not stand for any property whatever, though "2 is a number" is true. What is meant by "2 is a number" is that the logical property above defined is such that all properties wh. possess it *must* define similar classes; although 2 is not the property in question, nor is the property possessed by the logical property "is a number". Just as "Red things exist" means $(\exists\, x) . x$ is red.

5

ABSOLUTE AND RELATIVE TIME

What is *a* time = a period of time?

E.g. analyse the proposition "There was a time at which I was seeing St. Paul's".

The natural analysis is that it is asserting of a property ϕ : ($\exists$ x) : ϕx . I was seeing St. Paul's *at* x.

Just as: "There is a red thing near me" asserts of the property red: ($\exists$ x) : x is red . x is near me.

The absolute theory asserts that this analysis is correct; the relative denies it.

I.e. the relative denies that there is any *property* such that the proposition can be analysed in this way; not merely that there is nothing of wh. it can be truly said that it is a time: for this might be the case, even if absolute theory were true, provided Time was unreal.

How then does the relative theory analyse the proposition?

It *may* say it = ($\exists$ e) : e was a seeing of S. Paul's by me . e was before *this*.

I.e. to have been before this = to have been at a time.

But it may add: & other things might have been *simultaneous* with e.

I.e. to have been at a time = to have been *before* this, & such that other things might have been simultaneous with it.

But how about the proposition: There was *a* time before there were any events?

This means: There was an event before *this* which no event was before, but it is logically possible that there should have been an event wh. preceded it & with wh. others were simultaneous.

Simultaneity

R. in *Monist* April 15,[1] takes simultaneity = overlapping to be ultimate—a relation wh. is *not* transitive, & is *not* what we mean by simultaneity, i.e. exact simultaneity. And we never *can* observe of 2 events that they are *exactly simultaneous*.

[1] [B. Russell, "On the Experience of Time", *Monist*, v. 25, 1915.]

Can it then be maintained that *exact simultaneity* is ultimate?
I think so, by maintaining that overlapping = having a *part*
exactly simultaneous with a part of. That is: though we never
perceive "*This* is e.s. with *that*" we do perceive "This has a part
wh. is e.s. with a part of *that*".

Overlapping *in space* = having a common part; but overlapping
in time does not: in time 2 events may overlap without having a
common part.

⟨We shd. naturally take A sim. B to be equivalent to A & B
occurred at the same time. But this *might* mean merely "There was
a time at wh. A & B were both occurring". This is why R.
supposes simultaneous with may mean merely "overlapping".
What it does mean is "*The* time of A's occurrence was same as
that of B's: i.e. there's one & only one time such that A occupied
whole of it & no more, & only one such that B occupied whole of
it & no more, & these were same.⟩

A is sim. with B = A & B occurred at the same time = not
merely there was a time at wh. A & B were both occurring, but
the period of A's occurrence was the *same* as that of B's = the
period such that A occupied the whole of it & no more was the
same as that such that B occupied the whole of it & no more.

A is sim. with B is *not equivalent* to "There is *some* period such
that A & B both occupied the whole of it & no more" though it
implies this: what it is *equivalent* to is: "There is *only one* period
such that A occupied the whole of it & no more, & only one such
that B did so, & the one occupied by A was the same as that
occupied by B". The former would *not* give a transitive relation,
unless the hypothesis that the same event may occupy the whole
& no more of 2 different periods is excluded by a special postulate.

6

BELIEF AND MULTIPLE RELATIONS

How to state R.'s theory of belief?

"Belief is a multiple relation" is liable to mean something merely obvious, not disputed by anyone.

For if you are asserting S believes that ARB, you are obviously asserting a relation to hold between S & A & R & B; & any relation that's asserted to hold between more than 2 terms is in a sense multiple.

Does R. want to say that the relation is not *logically equivalent* to any dual relation?

But it *is*: it's equivalent to the relation between S & B, expressed by saying that S is judging of B, that A has R to it. *Every* multiple relation is thus equivalent to a dual one: e.g. B is between A & C, is equivalent to the judgment with regard to A & C that they have B between them. S gives A to B: is equivalent to the assertion that "gives A to" holds between S & B; & to the assertion that the relation "gives to B" holds between S & A.

In all these cases, however, it is obvious, I think, that the equivalent dual relation is analysable in terms of the multiple one, not vice versa.

Can then we say he means: The multiple relation asserted is not analysable in terms of any dual relation to which it is equivalent?

Not *only* this; but (1) that it's not analysable in terms of any dual relation at all,

(2) that it's not *equivalent* either to any dual relation between S & a single object of wh. the other terms of the multiple relation are constituents.

(2) must, I think, be added, bec. a person who holds the propositional theory *might* be willing to admit that there was a multiple relation between S & A, R, B, *not* analysable in terms of the relation to the prop. ARB. It's very unlikely, I think, that any holder *should* hold this; & it's perhaps imposs. that the holding of a multiple relation between several terms should be logically equivalent to the holding of a dual between others, unless one of the two *is* analysable in terms of the other.

But R. does certainly mean to deny (2); & this denial is not sufficiently expressed by saying that what we mean by *belief* is the multiple one; because if the opposite of (2) were realised it is certain we should sometimes mean by belief the one & sometimes the other.

Thus if the absolute theories of time & space were true in the *equivalent* form, it is certain that by "A is before B" we shd. sometimes *mean* the multiple relation, in wh. absolute positions are involved, & sometimes the dual ones. Hence the absolute theory can be stated as asserting that "before" is *sometimes* to be analysed in this way; only it is wrong to state it as asserting that it is *always* to be so analysed.

As for R.'s def. of "multiple" (U. & P. p. 5)[1] "A relation is distinguished as dual, triple, etc. acc. to the number of terms it unites in the simplest complexes in wh. it occurs". Take the relation between A & C constituted by the fact that A is father of B & B father of C: i.e. the relation $\phi(x, y)$ where $\phi =$ "is father of B & B is father of". This relation is plainly *dual*, & hence we must not understand "unite" in such a sense that this relation can be said to unite B to A & C.

Moreover "in the simplest" implies that the very same relation which unites e.g. 2 terms in one complex, *may* unite *more* in another. And it may be doubted whether this is the case.

In the case of *belief* it is certain that many different numbers of terms may be united. But then you may, & should, I think, say that they are *different* relations, having a certain common quality. If I say S believes that ϕA, & S believes that ARB, I am not saying S has *some* relation of quality b to ϕA, & *some* relation of quality b to A, R & B: in wh. case I really should be asserting the *same* relation of different numbers of terms. What I am asserting is: S has some *triple* relation of quality b to ϕ & A; &; S has some *quadruple* relation of quality b to A, R & B. Or, rather, there is some type of b-relation appropriate to each different number of terms, & in each case I am necessarily asserting that some b-relation of the appropriate type holds. I *cannot* assert that some b-relation of another type holds.

[1] ["On the Relations of Universals and Particulars", *Proc. of the Aristotelian Society*, vol. XII, 1912. Reprinted in B. Russell, *Logic and Knowledge* (London, 1956).]

7

PROPOSITIONAL FUNCTIONS

R. defines a prop. function as follows (*Monist*, Ap. 1919, p. 192)[1]:
"any expression containing an undetermined constituent, or several undetermined constituents, and becoming a proposition as soon as the undetermined constituents are determined".

Expression is wrong; he means what is *meant* by such an expression.

Let ϕA, or ARB be atomic propositions.

We get a propositional function, if we substitute $\hat{x}$ for A; or if we substitute $\hat{\phi}$ for ϕ.[2] We *don't* get one if we take $\hat{\phi}\hat{x}$, since a propos. function *must* contain some determined constituent; what we here get is the form of a proposition.

That these 2 are strictly parallel can be shown by considering the props.

$$(\exists\,\phi)\,.\,\phi A$$
$$\&\,(\exists\,x)\,.\,\phi x$$

each of wh. R. would say is asserting of a propos. function that it is *sometimes true* (or "possible").

He does not, however, ever consider prop. functions of the form $\hat{\phi}$A.

Hence a temptation to say that the prop. functions he considers are *properties*.

But they are *not* properties for *relations* also are considered by him.

---

[1] ["The Philosophy of Logical Atomism." Reprinted in B. Russell, *Logic and Knowledge* (London, 1956).]

[2] ⟨No we *don't* get a prop. function if we substitute $\hat{\phi}$ for ϕ; but only if we substitute $\hat{\phi}$ for ϕ in the *equivalent* prop. "ϕ applies to A" or "ϕ characterises A". And though $\hat{\phi}\hat{x}$ is *not* a propos. function yet "$\hat{\phi}$ applies to $\hat{x}$" *is* one: it is the *relation* of predication.

R.'s ϕ!a, as distinguished from ϕa, means: ϕ has relation of predication to a. How define a propl. function?

Take any expression you like which expresses a prop. Take any single word in that expression wh. stands for something the prop. is *about*; understanding that ϕA *is* "about" A, but is *not* about ϕ; but that "ϕ applies to A" is *both* about ϕ & about A. Then what the prop. asserts *about* that something *is* a propl. function. Or, if a prop. is *about* more things than one, what the prop. asserts about them is a propl. function.⟩

95

Taking ARB, you again get $\hat{x}R\hat{y}$, & $A\hat{R}B$; but he never considers the latter.

But $\hat{x}R\hat{y}$ (or, in his language, $\phi(\hat{x}, \hat{y})$) really is a propositional function, of the sort he considers.

Hence the difficulty of defining *what* the sort he considers are; since they are *either* properties or relations.

He himself insists that $\phi\hat{z}$ or $\hat{x}R\hat{y}$, are *not* constituents of ϕA & ARB respectively; though they *are* constituents of $(\exists\ x)\ .\ \phi x$ or $(\exists\ x, y)\ .\ x\ R\ y$; or of $(x)\ .\ \phi x \supset \psi x$; or of $(x, y)\ .\ x\ R\ y \supset x\ S\ y$. Why?

x^2 is a *function* of x, really means: "square of" is a many-one relation: $=$ so soon as *value* of x is given, *value* of x^2 is determinate.

What is the analogy of this use of "function of" to "propl. function"?

$\phi\hat{x}$ is a propl. function: means: the relation wh. the prop. ϕa has to a is many-one (it is, in fact, one-one); or: the relation wh. any prop. which asserts ϕ of a thing to that thing is many-one.

$\phi\hat{x}$ is a function of x: means: "consists in asserting ϕ of" is a one-one relation.

8

THE PRESENT

It seems to be the plain truth that:—

Every event has, *when* it is present, a characteristic wh. it does not possess at any other time—a characteristic wh. is what we mean by saying that at that time & no other it is present.

But against this prop. there is to be urged

That no event possesses *any* characteristic *at* any time except the time at which it is.[1]

When we say, therefore: at *other* times it does *not* possess the characteristic of being present; all that we mean would seem to be: any judgment to the effect A *is* present, occurring at another time, would be false.

It would seem then that what the statement really means is: In the case of every event, a judgment to the effect "A *is* present", or "A *is*" is true only if the judgment is simultaneous with A.

It certainly can't be, as language suggests, that the same event *is at* all times, & possesses at one a characteristic wh. it doesn't possess at others. This would assimilate an event to a thing wh. persists & has at one time a quality wh. it hasn't got at others.

You get a definite contradiction: if you suppose an event *is* at any other time except that at which it is present: that at wh. it is present, *means* the time at wh. it *is*. How can an event have a characteristic at a time at wh. it isn't?

What we are really saying is that it is only if simultaneous with it that a certain kind of judgment would possess a certain property.

But we're not yet at the end of our difficulties.

We've said: if A be any event, a judgment to the effect "A *is* happening" will only be true, if it be simultaneous with A.

But now it is widely held & seems evident that whether a judgment is true or not depends only on its *content*, not on the time at wh. it occurs; & that hence if a judgment "A is happening" were true at one time, the same judgment, if made at any other, would be true.

[1] ⟨To suppose it to do so is assimilating it to a persistent thing, wh. is red at one time & not at another.⟩

Yet it seems evident that in this case it's not so. Are we to say that the very same judgment can be true at one time & false at another? or are we to say that when we say the judgment "A *is* happening" would *not* be true, what we really mean is that it would be true, but only could not be correctly expressed by "A *is* happening"?

Now it's certain "A *is* happening" isn't a correct expression for a true judgment, unless the use of the words is simultaneous with A.

If you *say* "A is happening", & your use of the words is *not* sim. with A; then, if you are expressing a true judgment, you are expressing it incorrectly (& nobody ever is guilty of this incorrectness); or, if you are expressing it correctly, your judgment is false.

That is, whether "is" can be correctly used to express a judgment, depends *not* solely on the content of the judgment, but on the question whether the use of the words is or is not simultaneous with something *about* wh. the judgment is.

⟨In the case of most words, if they're a correct expression of a true judgment at one time, they will be a correct expression of the same true judgment at all times. We take as part of the *meaning* of "is" what is only a condition for its correct use. "Red" means the same every time you use it; but "is" doesn't.⟩

The *content* of such a judgment is always to the effect that A is timelessly sim. with something given; & whether the words correctly express it or not, depends upon whether this something is or is not sim. with them.

Thus "is" if used correctly always expresses a *different* judgment for every different time at wh. it is used. (Like "I", "this", "here".)

We thus consider the class of judgments: "judgments wh. can be correctly expressed by the use of the present tense", & of 2 judgments with identical content, one will belong to this class, the other not. But we naturally *think* that they can't.

When you judge "A *is* happening" you are judging of some event wh. is, in fact, sim. with your judgment, that A is sim. with that; & whether your judgment is true or false depends on whether A *is* sim. with it. But you might make exactly the same judgment, when the judgment was *not* sim. with the event in question; & it would still be true, but *not* a judgment that A *is* happening.

R. says "present" *means* "presented".

But "A *is* happening" does not mean "A is (timelessly) presented": because such a judgment cannot at all times be correctly expressed by "A *is* happening". What R. suggests is that the condition for correct use of "*is* happening" is that the judgment shd. have a certain content. And this is not true.

But moreover even for the *other* case of present this is not right: because an event may have been present, even though neither presented nor simultaneous with anything presented.

9

PRESENT

Consider the 3 expressions: (1) "A *is* occurring", (2) "A *is* simultaneous with B", (3) "A *is* past"; where in each case A stands for an event.

These 3 expressions resemble one another in respect of the fact that

(1) can't be truly *said*, unless A is simultaneous with the use of the expression,

(2) can't be truly *said*, unless A's simultaneity with B is simultaneous with the use of the expression,

(3) can't be truly *said*, unless A's possession of pastness is simultaneous with the use of the expression.

Let us express this by saying that the "is" which occurs in each is a temporal "is" or an "is" with tense.

The fact expressed by each, if they *are* truly used, is nevertheless a fact which could theoretically be expressed by an expression such that that expression could be truly used even if the use of the expression was not simultaneous with the fact in question. No such expression is at our command in English. But suppose we agree to use the expression *"is timelessly"* in such a way that the expression "A is timelessly P" can be truly said, where A's possession of P is *not* simultaneous with the use of the expression.

We can then say that

(1) the fact which (1) expresses, is a fact of the form "A is timelessly simultaneous with C", where C is an event.

(2) that which (2) expresses is a fact of the form "A's simultaneity with B is timelessly sim. with C", where C is an event.

(3) that which (3) expresses is a fact of the form "One possession of pastness by A is timelessly simultaneous with C", where C is an event.

Now what I want to note is 2 things:

That, in one very important sense of "at a time" all 3 characteristics are *not* characteristics which are possessed by A *at* any time. In this sense we can say all 3 facts are timeless facts.

And since they are characteristics wh. A doesn't have at any

time, there is a corresponding sense in wh. they are characteristics which A does not seem to have.

The sense in wh. this is so, is the sense in wh. a persistent
thing may have a character at a time, & then cease to have it
though it continues to exist.

For instance my hand may at a certain time be *moving towards*
my other hand, & may then cease to move towards it. The sense
in wh. it has this character at a time, is that its movement is an
event, wh. is in the fundamental sense of simultaneity, simultaneous with another event. And to say that it ceases to have it,
is to say that this event ceases to exist = that it is followed by
another.

FUNCTIONS

What does "x is a function of y" mean?

Take Whitehead's 1st example, p. 145[1]

$$s = 20 \times t.$$

He says (1) "s is a function of t".

      (2) "20 $\times$ t is a function of t".

      (3) "s is the "value" of the function 20 $\times$ t".

(2) is the fundamental usage.

What does (2) mean?

It means (says Whitehead): "Whatever value be assigned to "t", the value of "20 $\times$ t" is uniquely determined."

But what does this mean?

Perhaps: "There is *some* = one & only one many-one relation such that anything whatever has that relation to that which is twenty times the thing in question."

But what is meant by "p $\supset$ q is a function of p & q"?

"There is one & only one many-one relation such that any 2 props. whatever have that relation to the prop. asserting of the first that it implies the second."

To assert: "p is true" is a function of "p" = There is one & only one many-one relation such that every prop. has that relation to the prop. that the prop. in question is true.

And to ask: *What* function of "p" is "p is true"? should be to ask: What many-one relation has every prop. to the prop. that it is true?

Ramsey's answer, however, is that: "p" is *the* function of "p" which "p is true" is.

Does this mean only: *The* many-one relation which every prop. has to the prop. that it is true is that of identity?

"x^2 is a function of x" = "There is one & only one many-one relation such that everything has that relation to the thing wh. is its square."

What function of x is x^2? = *what* relation is the one wh. everything has to its square?

[1] [A. N. Whitehead, *An Introduction to Mathematics* (London, 1911).]

The answer is "the converse of "square of" ".

This = "x^2 is *the* function of x, which x^2 is".

Take: " "x is a man" is a function of x":

This means "There is some many-one relation which everything has to the proposition that *that* thing is a man".

$\phi x \supset \psi x$ means "If you consider the pairs of props. which resemble one another in the way in which the pair "ϕA & ψA" resembles "ϕB & ψB", the relation $\supset$ holds between the first & the second of every such pair".

So " "x is a man" is a function of x" means:

"If you consider the pairs of entities, wh. resemble one another in the way in which the pair "A & "A is a man" " resembles "B & "B is a man" ", then there is *some* many-one relation which holds between the first & the second of *every* such pair."

Thus "x is a man" is an incomplete symbol: there is nothing which *is* the function "x is a man".

CAUSALITY AND INDUCTION

The mere assertion "(x) . ϕx $\supset$ ψx" is different from, & does not allow you to deduce, the assertion "If anything, which won't or didn't have ϕ, were to have or had had it, it would have or would have had ψ".

For from: "There *is* nothing wh. both has ϕ & has *not* got ψ", it obviously cannot be deduced, that, if a thing which never did have ϕ, had had it, it *would* still have been true that there *is* nothing which both has ϕ & has *not* got ψ.

What distinguishes *both* assertions of the form "ϕx entails ψx", *and causal* laws, is that they do allow you to deduce this: i.e. they allow you to deduce that, *if* a thing wh. didn't have a property, *had* had it, it would have had another.

Keynes confines himself to the problem of inductive reasons for the assertion that (x) . ϕx $\supset$ ψx has a finite probability.

This is different from the question of inductive reasons for "Fire burns you" (i.e. if you put your hand in a flame, you get a painful sensation of a certain sort); since that is always understood to include "If you *were* to do it, you would get the pain", & "If you had done it, you would have".

But still, if you only understand it to mean: At any time, past or future, at which a man has or will put his hand in a flame, he has or will have that sensation", the problem is difficult enough; for *you* haven't observed this; you have at most observed that every time *you* did it, you had the sensation, & you have probably done it very few times.

The properties in question here are that of "putting your hand into a flame", & that of being almost immediately followed by a certain kind of sensation *of yours*; i.e. every event which has the first (intrinsic) property, has the *external* one of being followed almost immediately by another kind of event related to it in a certain way.

In this case I think the induction depends upon your knowing that its having of the external property *causally depends* upon its having the intrinsic one; & I think you *can* know causal dependence directly, though certainly you don't always know it directly: you have to use induction to know it.

12

SPECIES OF A PROPERTY

I want to talk of species of the property "is conscious".
But there are 2 very different relations such that ϕ may be said
to be a species of ψ, if it stands in that relation to ψ.

(1) ϕ may *not* be definable in terms of ψ: e.g. "red" is not
definable in terms of "coloured", nor "is pleased" in terms of
"is feeling".

(2) ϕ may be definable in terms of ψ, *if* ψ be a relational property: e.g. "is father of a son" is a species of "is a father"; "is
seeing something blue" is a species of "is seeing", "is seeing a
tree" of "is seeing".

Again, among psychological relations (= relations such that
"has R to something" is a psychological property), some are
definable partly in terms of relations wh. are not psychological,
& some are *not*. And no psychological facts wh. assert of an
individual & a time a property defined in terms of a relation of the
former kind are capable of being known by introspection *alone*:
e.g. "I'm seeing a tree" can't be so known; since this means:
"I'm seeing a sense-datum wh. is *of* a tree".

It is certainly not proper to say that to perceive A is one *way*
of being conscious & to perceive B another *way* of being conscious;
although it is just possible to say that a person to whom A appears
to be green is *conscious* of A in a different *way* from one to whom
it appears to be blue, wh. is what defence there is for Johnson
(An. of Thinking).[1]

[1] [W. E. Johnson, "Analysis of Thinking", *Mind*, vol. XXVII, 1918.]

13

EXTERNAL WORLD

To say that anything is "external to my mind" means, I think, that it is something such that from its existence at any time it does not follow that I am conscious at that time.

Thus what is *not* external to my mind is things or events (if any) such that from their existence at any time it followed that I was conscious at that time.

With this definition "I" may be *external*, since I may exist when I am not conscious; & hence we must add to the definition: something wh. is *other* than me or any part of me, & also is such that . . .

"Not an experience of mine" is to be defined in this way.

"I am having an experience" = some predicate is true of me, which both (1) is such that any being who possesses it at a time must be conscious at that time, (2) is such that any being who possesses it at a time must be having a different experience at that time from what he would have had if he had not possessed [it]. The predicate "is looking at the binding of a book, which has red capitals inside" is a predicate, which does possess (1) & does not possess (2).

Call these predicates "psychological predicates". (They are, of course, not the *only* predicates dealt with in psych., but they have this connection with it: that no prop. is a psychological prop. unless it is about one of them.)

14

PROPER NAMES, CONNOTATION, DENOTATION, ETC.

The same word or phrase is sometimes *used as a proper name* & sometimes not used as a proper name.

The analysis of "is used as a proper name" does not involve an analysis of "is a proper name"; since, on the contrary, "is a proper name" means always *either* "is, in *this* usage, used as a proper name" or "is, in *all* ways, used as a proper name".

A word or phrase is being *used as a proper name, only* if in that usage it has neither connotation nor denotation. (This isn't *sufficient* to define "is used as a proper name", since, e.g., expressions which are being used to express a prop., have neither connotation nor denotation & yet are not being used as a proper name.)

But to say that a word, in a particular usage, "has connotation" may mean 2 different things, so that we get 2 correspondingly different meanings of "is being used as a proper name".

(1) To say that it has, in a particular usage, connotation may mean merely that there is some adjective to which, in that usage, it stands either in the relation in which "All red things" stands to the adjective red, or in that in which "The red thing I'm now seeing" stands to the adjective "is a red thing which I am now seeing", or in that in which "some red things" in "I am seeing some red things" stands to the adjective "is a red thing wh. I am now seeing".

We may call the adjective in question *its* connotation in that usage.

And to say that it has "denotation" in the corresponding sense, means that it has connotation, in this sense, & that the adjective in question does in fact apply to something.

Its denotation, therefore, if it has any, will be *all* the things to wh. the adjective wh. is its connotation applies.

Nothing can have denotation in this sense without having connotation.

A word is being used as a proper name, in Russell's sense, as a "name" in Wittgenstein's, only if it has no connotation in this sense.

But what are ordinarily & rightly said to be used as proper names, e.g. Bismarck, Mont Blanc, may, & *do* (if R. is right about "Bismarck") have connotation in this sense.

(2) The other sense of "having connotation", is one in wh. to say that a word is being used with connotation asserts *not only* (1), but also some such thing as that the connotation with wh. it is being used is one with which all individuals who are using it with the same denotation are using it.

This is Mill's & Keynes' sense: the sense in which only "*general* nouns substantive" have connotation.

And names can be "*proper*", in the ordinary sense, if they haven't connotation in this sense: Bismarck & Mont Blanc haven't.

Should we say rather (as suggested by J.[1]) they have connotation *only* if they contain an adjective-name, wh. is being used for the adjective, of wh. it is a name? "Le mont blanc" thus has connotation; but "le Mont Blanc" has not.

But usually a word is said to be used as a *proper name*, only if, *besides* having no connotation in this sense, it is *not* the name of an adjective.

J.[1] sees rightly enough that ordinary adjective-names have not connotation in this sense, & therefore calls them proper names: but it is part of the definition of a proper name in the ordinary sense, that it should *not* be the name of an adjective.

[1] [Johnson.]

15

VICIOUS INFINITE SERIES

Are those only which arise from a circular definition. E.g. "is good" = "is judged to be good".

16

CHARACTERISING

Attributes = predicates which actually belong to something = predicates which can be truly predicated of something.

Is the notion "predicable of something" a clear one?

Suppose A is bigger than B.

Then "A is bigger than" expresses an attribute of B; & "is bigger than B" expresses an attribute of A.

"A is bigger than" does *not*, according to me, express the *same* attribute of B as is expressed by "is smaller than A", although each entails the other: my reason for saying so being that *the* relation, wh., from the fact that A is bigger than B, it *follows* that B has to A, is different from *the* relation which, from the same fact, it follows that A has to B. Can any one deny that "less than" is a different relation from "greater than"?

17

THE PRESENT

Let us raise the question what is meant by saying of a given event, e.g. a sound which I am now hearing: "*This* is now present."

Blake (*Mind*, 136, p. 432)[1] gives, as the interpretation also given by R., that in each such case, I am referring to some particular *experience* which I am having: & am saying "This is present relatively to *this* experience". "Present relatively to" is only defined for the case where the experience in question is what R. calls "a total momentary experience": in this case it = (p. 431) simultaneous with some object wh. is an object of that experience.

[1] [R. M. Blake, "On Mr Broad's Theory of Time", *Mind*, vol. XXXIV, 1925.]

NOTEBOOK III

(Late 1930s to 1940)

1

KNOWLEDGE AND BELIEF

Johnson's Dict., Pref.: "Nothing can be proved but by supposing something intuitively known."

Johnson defines "believe": "to credit . . . from some other reason than our personal knowledge", which says that "S believes p" entails "S does *not* personally know p". But he defines "credit" [to mean] "to believe"; & if you substitute "believe" for "credit" in the first definition, it follows that "S personally knows p" is *not* incompatible with "S believes p". J., therefore, by implication recognises 2 different senses of "belief" the one compatible, the other incompatible with "proved knowledge".

Webster recognises the incompatible one: "to be persuaded of the truth of, upon evidence furnished by . . . circumstances other than personal knowledge"; but he also recognises the other by defining "persuade" [as] "cause to believe".

There certainly is *a* common use of belief in which "I believe" entails "I don't know for certain". Is there another in which "I know for certain" entails "I believe"? One reason why it seems so is because "I thought I knew" entails "I believed".

KANT ON "OUTER OBJECTS"

Kant, Pref. to 2nd ed. (p. 29, note). "Bleibt es immer ein Skandal der Philosophie und allgemeinen Menschenvernunft, das Dasein der Dinge ausser uns (von denen wir doch den ganzen Stoff zu Erkenntnissen selbst für unsern inneren Sinn her haben) bloss auf Glauben annehmen su müssen, und, wenn es Jemand einfällt es zu bezweifeln, ihenen keinen genugthuenden Beweiss entgegenstellen zu können."

Kant himself thinks he has given a strict (strengen) proof of this, which he calls "the objective reality of outer Intuition": & he thinks, also, the *only possible proof*. This proves "that we have direct consciousness of the existence of outer things".

The proof is: I exist in time: → my existence is "bestimmbar" in time; → my existence is related to something permanent (beharrlichs) outside of me.

P. 599 (1st edn.). "I have as little need to infer the reality (Wirklichkeit) of outer objects, as the reality of the object of my inner sense (my thoughts); for both are nothing but "Vorstellungen", the direct perception (consciousness) of which is at the same time a sufficient proof of their reality."

"Outer things & I myself exist on the direct testimony of my self-consciousness."

But "which given Intuitions, belong to outer sense & not to imagination, must be made out in each particular case according to THE RULES, which distinguish experience in general (including inner) from imagination" (p. 30).

P. 200. (Widerlegung, 2nd ed.). "Not every intuitive Vorstellung of outer things includes this existence: it may be the result of imagination (in dreams as well as in madness); but this can only happen through the reproduction of former perceptions, wh. are only possible through the reality of outer objects."

P. 199. "To imagine anything *as* external, we must already have an outer sense, & by its means distinguish *directly* the mere receptivity of an outer intuition from the spontaneity of imagination."

P. 199. "Inner experience is only possible *mediately* through outer" because "only through outer experience can we "bestim-men" in time our own existence". "The Vorstellung "Ich bin" contains *directly* the existence of a subject, but no *knowledge* of the subject, since this requires Intuition—namely inner, in view of which the subject must be "bestimmt", for which outer objects are necessary."

In order to distinguish false appearances (e.g. dreams), one uses the rule: "what is connected with *a perception* by empirical rules, is real". So p. 348 "Alles is wirklich, was mit einer Wahrnehmung nach Gesetzen des empirischen Fortgang in einem Context steht".

But how can one tell whether so & so *is* a perception?

In order to prove to anyone that there is a table, I need only to shew him this one. That there is one here now, when no-one but me is seeing it, is proved to him partly by the trustworthiness of my perceptive faculties, partly by the evidence that I am trustworthy in the sense of not lying, partly by the evidence of my being able to report *correctly* (use the right language for) what I see: but it can be confirmed by my fetching him & shewing him one when he comes. All this will prove to him that I am *seeing a table* now. Kant only proposes to be able to prove that we *sometimes* see external objects: never that, in a particular case, I am seeing one. The proof that in a particular case I am is *a scientific proof*. Could there be a philosophic one?

That I am seeing one needs no proof to me. If someone were to come & fail to see one, that *would* be a reason for me to doubt: might it be a reason for thinking I was dreaming?

Suppose Wittgenstein's case that it suddenly disappeared, & then appeared again. He seems to suggest that in such a case it wouldn't be true that there was, nor yet that there wasn't. The rules for the use of "There's a table" don't provide for this case.

Some things do look (& feel) *as if* they were at rest, & others as if they were moving. I.e. some sense-data *are* at rest, others are moving.

But it is said there is no sense in saying that a physical thing is at rest—only that this thing is at rest relatively to that; & no sense in saying that one is moving—only that this thing is moving relatively to that. It is also said, alternatively, that we have no means of telling whether a physical thing is at rest or moving absolutely: all we can observe is that it is at rest relatively to this or that, or moving relatively to this or that.

What is the reason for this? We can't define "x is moving" (where x is a physical thing) as "x would in normal circumstances look to be moving" as we can define "x is yellow" = "x would in normal circumstances look yellow"; because we use "is moving" in such a sense that we can say "the earth is moving", although in normal circumstances it does not look to be moving. Yet sometimes, perhaps very often?, we mean by "is moving", would to a normal observer in normal circumstances seem to be moving: e.g. on the cinema "her lips moved".

4

SENSE-DATA

Double images should be mentioned at once. Suppose one is to left of the other: the left-hand image is not *identical* with the right hand, yet the left hand is the *same surface* as the right. The left is to left of the right but not in physical space.

I *can* ask myself: Is that sense-datum a physical object? And I can say of those I now see: These *are* physical objects. But are they *identical* with physical surfaces? When I shut my eyes, the sense-datum I saw just now has ceased to exist (how prove this?), but the physical object has not.

A physical surface, when seen, is seen *in the same sense* in which an after-image is seen, with closed eyes. Is it?

It is certain that, when I point at an object I am seeing & say "That's a match-box" or "There's a match-box", I am *referring* to some object or set of objects which I am seeing (= "directly" seeing = in same sense as after-image with closed eyes).[1] But am I "referring" to it in the sense that it is of it that I am asserting that it is a match-box? Certainly not: I am, at most, asserting that it is part of the surface of a match-box. But am I even doing this? In what sense am I "referring" to an object (or objects) seen in sense 1? Suppose you've said "That's a match-box" (which would hardly be said unless (1) it were of an unusual shape, (2) you were explaining the meaning of "match-box" to a child or a foreigner), & the hearer asks: What is? What object are you referring to as "that"? All you can do is to point again more clearly, or perhaps touch, or take up. Or he may point or touch & say: Is this the thing you mean? If you say "Yes", that means you were referring to the thing he pointed at. But to you he will seem to have been pointing at a thing you are *seeing in sense* 1. You'll say "Yes" only if he does point to the one among the things you are seeing in sense 1 to which you were referring. But suppose, when you go nearer & point unmistakably, he says "But there's nothing there!" You still know quite well what you were referring to; & you may say "Why, don't you see *this* here?" If he still says: No, I see

[1] [Later on in this entry Moore also calls this sense of "seeing" "seeing in sense 1".]

nothing there, you won't know what to think. You may suspect you were having an hallucination; that the thing you still see in sense 1 *isn't* a surface of a physical object at all. You'll know that you were *referring* to this thing seen by you in sense 1; but you may doubt whether you were referring to a physical object at all.

Suppose what you said was: There's a match-box. And your hearer says: "Where?" You point again, perhaps more clearly, or go up & touch. You may say "there at the end of my finger!" Your hearer will then know what *place* you were referring to—but a *vague* place; he will know *whereabouts* you meant, but not *where* you meant, unless he sees the match-box.

5

HUME ON "CONTINUED EXISTENCE" OF BODIES

(*Treatise*, p. 187, IV. 2)

H. says he's going to ask "What are the *causes* which induce us to believe in the existence of body?"

Do we *believe* in the existence of body?

He means: believe in the existence of particular bodies: e.g. I of my body & my pen.

Do I *believe* in their existence? One reason for saying *No*, is that I *know* they exist. *When* do I know this? When I say, *in good faith* (i.e. not lying), things which *entail* that they exist: e.g. I have a scar on my right hand; this pen was given me by D. Perhaps, at other times too, but then certainly.

But he immediately *substitutes* for this, 2 different questions: viz. (1) "Why do we attribute a *continu'd* existence to objects when they are not present to the senses?" & (2) "Why do we suppose them to have an existence *distinct* from the mind & perception?".

Do we "attribute a continu'd existence to objects when we are not perceiving them?" To *some* objects, e.g. pains which we feel, we never do. To others we often do, i.e. whenever we say, *in good faith*, of an object which was or is perceived by us, something which entails that it existed at a time when we were not perceiving it. E.g. That scar on my hand has been there for more than 40 years. I have had this pen for about a year. For I haven't been perceiving the scar for 40 years, nor the pen for most of the time in the last year.

His question then must be: Why do we attribute *continu'd* existence in *those cases where we do*?

And as to this he says first: My *senses* can't give rise to my knowledge that my hand existed last night when I was asleep, bec. to say so would be to say I was perceiving it when I wasn't (p. 188). And also my *reason* can't (p. 193); but his reasons for saying this are obscure; and it's not at all clear my reason can't. However, he says: my *opinion* (it's not an opinion, but *knowledge*) must be entirely owing to *imagination*.

6

COGITO, ERGO SUM

Does "I've got a pain" or "I see the moon" entail "I exist"?

Certainly "Mr Chamberlain has got a pain" entails "Mr C. is still alive = is not dead yet". Does it? though Julius Caesar is dead, isn't it possible he still exists & has pains? but there's a great difference between "Mr C. is still alive", & "I'm still alive"— there's a sort of absurdity in saying the latter—if I say it, it *must* be true. Yet there *are* circumstances in which it's not absurd to say "I'm still alive", "I'm not dead yet"; e.g. if somebody had thought you were dead, or thought you were a ghost. (Athelstan.)

But does "Mr C. has got a pain" entail "Mr C. is a real person"? I think not. No. The *expression* "Mr C. has a pain" would *make sense* as part of a story about an imaginary Mr C.: the point is rather that in that case it would not make sense to ask: Has he really? As it is: the expression has a sense, wh. it could only have if Mr C. were being used as *a name of a real person*. But how about "Ariel has a pain now"? This has sense, though it's false, because we all know what "Ariel" means. "Ariel" here means "Shakespeare's Ariel" = "The *imaginary* being whom S. calls "Ariel" in the Tempest". But it's self-contradictory to say "That imaginary being has a pain now". When we say "Ariel" we are not saying that he is imaginary. We can suppose that S. was using "Ariel" as a name for a real being, though we know he was not: we can suppose that Ariel existed then & still exists. *What* are we supposing? "Did Jack the Giant-killer really exist?" a child may ask; & is asking a sensible question. And he's *not* asking *merely* whether a boy who did what Jack is said to do in the story ever existed: he's asking whether *you* were using "Jack the G." *as a name of a real person*? There might, by chance, have been a boy who did all those things; but if you weren't using "J. . . ." as a name for that boy, then Jack is *not* a real person. S. was not using "Ariel" as a proper name for any real being, though he did use "Richard II" as a proper name for a real person. He used "Ariel" much as Mrs Gamp used "Mrs Harris", except that he did not wish to make people think Ariel was a real person, whereas Mrs Gamp did wish to make people think Mrs Harris was.

Kant says, B 422 n., that *we can't say* "Whatever thinks exists". The reason he gives for this is absurd; but there *is* a reason, namely that it treats "existence" like a predicate, e.g. like "is alive". "Whatever thinks at any time is alive at that time" is not absurd; nor is "whatever thinks at any time *exists* at that time"; but then is "exists" being used as a predicate?

"I'm moving", "I'm eating", "I'm drinking", all entail "I exist"; don't they entail "I'm a real person"? When *I* use them, I'm using "I" to refer to a real person: but in a novel they may be used otherwise.

Kant also says (B 422 n.) that "I exist" is *identical with* "I'm thinking". "I existed at 12 last night" is certainly *not* identical with "I was thinking at 12 last night". So it might be the case that I was existing now, yet not thinking now; but could I *say* "I exist" without thinking? My body might *utter the words*, & yet I not be thinking; but if I say it & *mean* it, I must be thinking.

Tweedledum says "You're only one of the things in his dream. You know very well you're not real". "I *am* real!" said Alice, & began to cry. . . "If I wasn't real," Alice said . . . "I shouldn't be able to cry" (= I am crying, therefore I exist). "I hope you don't suppose those are real tears?" said T. "I know they're talking nonsense", Alice said to herself.

A person who saw me might think he was dreaming, & that I was one of the things in *his* dream; but it would be nonsense to suppose ⟨?⟩ that I was one of the things in somebody else's dream. But what T. *says* is *not* nonsense: we understand what he means.

T. also says: "If that there king were to wake, you'd go out bang, just like a candle." Alice answers "I shouldn't". This is a different matter. Even if she were real, & not merely "a sort of thing in his dream", it *might* be true that, if he were to wake, she would go out bang.

I'm *not* only one of the things in somebody else's dream. What am I saying when I say this? Is the supposition that I am, self-contradictory? Is the prop. one about how I use the word "I"? Or is it that the way I do use it is such that the prop. is self-contradictory?

One of the "things" in a dream of mine might *say* "I'm real; I'm not merely one of the things in someone else's dream". Yes: *in a sense*; but not in the sense in which *I* can say it. When I say "he might say it" what I mean is "*I* might *dream that* he said it". From "I dreamt that a person said so & so" there does not follow "Somebody *said* so & so".

"I'm not a thing in somebody's dream = "There is no person, x, & no dream-character, y, such that the fact that I'm now writing in a note-book is identical with a fact to the effect that x is now dreaming that y is writing".

What I mean by writing "I'm now writing in a note-book" *couldn't* be identical with any fact of the form "x is now dreaming that y is writing in a note-book".[1] Why not? I certainly didn't *mean* a fact of this form, when I wrote it. But mightn't it be that I had mistaken a fact of this form for one of another? When I have dreamt that a person of a certain description was writing, I may mistakenly think that a person of that description really was writing. If "I am writing" were of this form, then a fact of the form "x is dreaming that . . ." would be of the form "z is dreaming that x is dreaming that . . .".

T. says that he is merely one of the things in the red king's dream.

Can I understand the assertion that *I* am so?

A friend of mine can dream that *I* do so & so; but when he does so, *I* am not merely one of the things in his dream.

To say that I'm *merely* one of the things is to say that I'm one of the characters in his dream which can't be identified with any real person: therefore that [it] can't be identified with me, which is a contradiction??

But this is to assume that I *am* a real person, wh. is just what is in dispute.

What proves that I'm *not* merely a character in some one else's dream?

I am now seeing a note-book; & there's nobody, x, & no dream-character y, such that both (1) x is dreaming that y is seeing a note-book & (2) the fact that *I* am seeing one is identical with the fact that x is dreaming that y is.

The prop. that I am can't be identical with any prop. of the form "x is dreaming that y is". Why not? Bec. no prop. of the form "x is seeing a note-book" entails "Somebody is dreaming".

[1] ⟨It isn't merely that there isn't; but that there *couldn't* be. Why not? The assertion "There is a person x & a dream-character y such that . . ." is self-contradictory. Why?⟩

I say "I am writing in a note-book", & am using the word "I" in the correct English way—not e.g. as a proper name for Russell. The correct English way is such that the *words* have no complete meaning by themselves: in order that a person may be able to find out whether what is expressed *partly* by this means was true, he would have to find out whether the person who uttered them was writing in a note-book at the time.

"I" is not being used by me as a proper name, nor as equivalent to "the person who utters these words" bec. this latter phrase might be understood by someone who did not see the person in question, nor recognize who it was by his voice: it would be equivalent to "Somebody is both uttering these words & writing in a note-book". Yet, though "I" is not being used as a proper name, the proposition expressed by it & the fact that I am saying it, *is* the same as could be expressed by "Moore is writing". Children say "Georgie wants a sweet" instead of "I".

7

IS "BELIEVE" ALWAYS DISPOSITIONAL?

Take first the case where you believe what another person tells you, *while* he's telling it, things which you never heard before, so that there's no question of your having a standing dispositional belief.

If asked afterwards: And you believed his account of what happened? you might answer: Yes; *it never occurred to me to doubt it.* (And this *includes* "never occurred to me to disbelieve it".)

This *looks* as if, for belief in this sense, nothing *positive* need occur. But while you're reading a novel, no positive *disbelief* need occur (nor, of course, doubt): yet one *wouldn't* say here "it *never occurred to me to doubt it*", nor "I believed it". What is the difference?

At any time when you're reading a novel, you *know* it is fiction —a dispositional know = would, if asked, *say* (*believing* it, or *not lying*): Of course it's fiction.

This, of course, is *not* the case in listening to a man's story in those cases where you would say "I believed it", "it never occurred to me to doubt it". But is this the *only* difference?

In the case of listening to the story, you're saying also: It didn't occur to me to *suspect* it. It would be absurd to say this in the case of a novel, although of course you don't *suspect* it.

When a judge says "I don't believe the witness A", he means I *think* A was lying; but not necessarily I *feel sure* he was, but I'm *inclined to think* so = I *think* it's more likely than not that he was.

Degrees of belief are: I *think* it's more likely than not; I think it's *much* more likely than not; I have *no* doubt it's the case.

When a child says "I've got a pain" the parent *may* say "I don't believe you"; & it may be that, though he *doesn't* say this, he *would* say it, if he were asked whether he believed it or not.

8

THE *SAME* PAIN

W. says (does he? I'm only trying to reproduce his view) there is only one use of "the same pain", that, namely, in which "A & B have the same pain" makes sense & == "A & B have exactly similar pains"; & that therefore there's no use of "the same pain" such that "A & B have the same pain" is nonsensical. He contrasts this with "the same book", of which he says there *are* 2 different *uses*, one in which "A has in his hands at this moment the same book which you had in your hands yesterday at tea" will be true, provided, for instance, A has Tristram Shandy in his hands now, & you had T.S. in your hands at tea yesterday: another in which this sentence will only be true if A has in his hands now the same *copy* of some book which you had in yours yesterday. With the latter use of "the same book", "A in London has in his hands at this moment the same book which you have in your hands here in Camb." will be nonsensical, i.e. we can say "A *can't* have in his hands now the same book you have"; whereas with the former it won't.

It looks as if in this case of "the same book" it were a question *not* of a different use of "same", but of a different use of "book"—the difference between the use in "Tristram Shandy is a *book*" & the use in "Every *book* on that shelf is a copy of Tristram Shandy".

And that it is *not* a question of 2 uses of "same", but only of 2 uses of "book", seems to be borne out by the fact that the difference between "A in London & B in Camb. are both reading the same book" when it is nonsensical & when it's not, can be put without any reference to "same". Suppose I point at a copy of Tristram Shandy & say "A in L. & B in C. are both reading this book" this will be sense if by "this book" I mean "Tristram Shandy", nonsense if I mean "this copy of T.S.".

Similarly in the "pain" cases, it is not, I think, a question of 2 uses of *same*, but of 2 uses of "pain". And the justification for saying that there is a use such that "He has the same pain as I" is nonsense, is only if "pain" is sometimes used = "attack of pain": perhaps it isn't, but I think it sometimes is. E.g. this pain has lasted longer than the one I had yesterday morning, may

127

surely be used (?) & it = this *attack* has lasted longer. To say "You are having this attack of pain" is plainly nonsense; though it's not at all nonsense to say "You are having an attack of *this* pain"? Similarly "You are having the same attack of pain as I" is nonsense; but "You are having *an* attack of the *same* pain" is perfect sense.

There remains the point: W. says "A & B are reading (or holding) the *same* book" is *sometimes* true for *both* senses of "book". But is there any use for "the *same* attack of pain"? Yes: in "The attack B was referring to was the same as the one C was referring to: it was the one you had yesterday, *not* the one you had on Wednesday".

How about: "He has the same pain as I have, but in a less acute form"?

9

SELF-CONTRADICTION, AND "NO ANSWER TO"

Austin says: Suppose my cat suddenly began to preach the Gospel, there would be *no answer to* the question: Is that a cat or isn't it?

Would there also be no answer to the question: Is "This is a cat, but it preaches the Gospel" self-contradictory, or not?

It looks as if we must say, "There is an answer, namely that it's not self-contradictory". It looks as if we must say: The usage is *not* such that "This preaches the Gospel" entails "This is not a cat"; since, if it were, there would be an answer to "Is this a cat or not", namely "It isn't".

10

CERTAINTY AND SENSATIONS[1]

It seems to be often the case that we have a sensation of a certain sort without *knowing* that we have any of that sort.

In looking at a landscape it may happen that one of the objects in it looks red to me, without my noticing that object; & if I don't notice then I don't *know* that it looks red to me, although, if I had noticed it, I should have known this. But is it certain that, if I don't notice it, it *is* looking red to me?

In answer to the question: Is anything looking red to you? we may truly answer "I don't know", although in fact something is. But *if* we had been noticing the object, could we have truly said "I don't know"? If you are noticing an object which looks red, I think you can't be said not to know that it looks red; although, of course, very often you don't say to yourself that it looks red. You may be said to know that it looks red, even if you do not understand the word "red" or any synonym. But then "he knew that it looks red" seems to mean the same thing as "he noticed it & it looked red to him"; & in that case we should have to say of an animal who notices an object which looks red to it that it knows it looks red to it; and *this won't do*. You only *know* it looks red to you, if it is true of you that, if asked, you'd *be able to say* that it does. I.e. an object may be noticed by you & look red to you, without its being true to say that you know it looks red. But what would be a true answer, *if you were asked* "Does anything look red to you?", is a different matter.

If you are asked "Is anything looking red to you?", what you try to say is what is the case at the moment *when you have understood the question*. If at this moment you notice a thing which does look red, you will answer at once "Yes"; but, if the field is large & full of detail, & you don't at the moment notice anything looking red, you may answer preliminarily "I don't know: let's see", & then begin examining the field to see if you can find anything looking red: if you succeed you may answer: "Yes, there is", as if this were an answer to the original question; or, if you think you've examined the field completely, "No, there isn't"; or,

[1] [Above the title of this entry Moore wrote "U.S.A. Oct., 1940".]

if you don't feel sure that your exam. was quite complete "I think there isn't, but I'm not quite sure". But in all 3 cases your answer is really an answer as to the state of things *at the time when you make it, not* as to what *was* the state at the time when you were asked. And unless you remember (as often happens ⟨?⟩) that this state of things was also the state at the time when you were asked, there is no reason to suppose that it was. Suppose you are asked: Do you hear a clock ticking (= a sound like the ticking of a clock)? You may say "Yes" at once; but even though you know that the clock was ticking before you were asked, you have no reason to suppose you heard it then, unless you remember that you did. In this case you would only answer "I'm not quite sure" if the ticking was very faint; you might, then, by listening detect it; but there is no reason to suppose that you hear it, *till* you detect it—that you heard it when you said "I'm not quite sure".

If you doubted whether there was any difference in colour between two ribbons lying at a distance from one another, you would try to find out by putting them close together, but this wouldn't help to decide whether you saw any difference before: & even then mightn't you still be in doubt for a time, whether there was or not, i.e. whether you saw any?

Does it ever happen that you think you're *not* hearing, or seeing, or feeling *anything of a certain kind*, when in fact you are?

The question is ambiguous: in looking at a distant mountain-side you may think an object is a rock, when in fact it is a man; hence, in answer to the question "Do you see a man on that mountain?" you may say "No", when in fact you are. But in fact, in such a case, you would probably say: "Not, as far as I can see"; not "No". So it's not a good example. But "Do you see etc." in this case really means "Do you see anything that you recognise as a man?" so that "*No*" *would be correct*, even if something you saw & took for a rock was in fact a man. It would be true, *in a sense*, that you were seeing a man, but *not* in the sense meant.

⟨But so would "I can't be sure: I think it's just possible that dark object near the right end of the lake, is a man sitting down". This, of course, implies: If it is, then I *am* seeing a man.⟩

The fact is "x saw a man" ≠ A. "(∃ y) . x saw y . y was a man". Where latter is true we should hesitate to say x *didn't* see a man, just as we hesitate to say that the dog didn't go round the cow.

But it's only *unquestionably right* ⟨Questionable⟩ to say "x saw a man", where besides A there is also true $(\exists y) . x$ saw $y . y$ was a man $. x$ *recognised y to be a man* (or, at least, did *not* mistake y for something else).

"Surely that doesn't hurt you?" "It *certainly* does."

11

DIFFERENT SENSES OF "SEE"

There are cases in which in answer to, e.g. "Did you see H. at the theatre last night?", it would be quite proper to answer: "No: I only saw his reflection in a mirror: I never happened to get into a position from which I could see him himself." This shews that there is a usage of "see" such that "I saw a reflection of x" ↛ "I saw x". But I doubt if there is any in which "I saw a reflection of x" does entail "I saw x". Of course, (a) "I saw a reflection of my face in a mirror" → (b) "I saw my face in a mirror"; but (b) does not *entail* "I *saw* my own face" (*saw* used absolutely). ⟨Doesn't it? But certainly you might quite properly say: "I saw H. take some sugar out of the cupboard this morning", when you had *only* seen this in a mirror. So too: "I saw Jupiter", when you had *only* seen it through a reflecting telescope.⟩ We can say "A person can't see his own eyes", although, of course, it's perfectly easy to see your eyes in a mirror (this only shews original point). (a) "It's the simplest thing in the world to see your own eyes." "It's quite impossible to see your own eyes." (a) can only be true if "see x in a mirror" entails "see x", & it *does*.

Similarly to "Did you see H. yesterday?" it would be quite proper to answer: "No; I thought I did, but I found afterwards that it was only an hallucination". But in describing an hallucination it would be quite proper to say "I saw H. standing before the fireplace as plain as I see you; but it must have been an hallucination".

So too to "Did you see H. yesterday?" you can answer "No: but I did see him in [a] dream". Yet in describing a dream it would be quite proper to say "I *saw* H. sitting in a chair". But *is* this an *absolute* use of "saw"? Isn't it modified by your having said that it's a dream you're describing? In *one* sense it certainly is: i.e. it's not followed or preceded by "in a dream", or any other qualifying phrase *in that sentence*.

The *test* here used as a positive criterion of *difference of sense* is that a given sentence & its contradictory may both express a truth, which *can* only be if one of the words is used in a different sense. We have to be sure that none of the *other* words in the sentences are used in different senses.

12

NEITHER UNQUESTIONABLY CORRECT NOR UNQUESTIONABLY INCORRECT

A. "He was lying, when he told me there was oil on the estate."
B. "Oh, then there wasn't any oil on it?" A. "Oh, yes, there was."
B. "What! Then he can't have been lying when he told you
there was. What on earth did you mean by telling me he was
lying? You shouldn't have said that." A. "Oh, yes, I should. He
was lying, bec. he led me to suppose he knew there was, when
on the contrary he was quite convinced there wasn't." B. "Oh, I
see: you were using "lying" to mean merely that he said there
was, when he thought there wasn't. Well, *perhaps* it's not incorrect
to use it in that way. I withdraw my positive statement that you
oughtn't to have said he was lying; but I do think it's *doubtful*
whether you should. I do think it's doubtful whether it's correct to
say a man was lying, when what he said was true: I think it is
perhaps incorrect." A. "Well, I agree that it's *perhaps* not quite
correct; & you agree that it's *perhaps* not incorrect. We can sum
the matter up by saying: Under the circumstances it's not *unquestionably* correct to say he was lying, not yet *unquestionably*
incorrect." B. "I agree that's so: but here's something which
puzzles me. How on earth do we know that it's neither unquestionably correct nor unquest. incorrect?" A. "Well, I suppose
that's a matter of usage. It would be unqu. correct to say so,
only if *all* well-educated people who knew the language used "he
was lying when he said p" *merely* to mean "he thought or knew p
was false, when he said it", & *never* used it in such a way that
part of what they were asserting was "p was false". It would
be unquestionably incorrect, only if *all* w.e.p. who spoke English
well *never* used it in that way, but always so that part of what they
were asserting was that p was false." B. "Oh, I say, this won't
do at all! You are entirely forgetting the fact, which you know
perfectly well, that 2 (or more) different uses of a given word may
both (or all) of them be unquestionably correct: there are 2 unquestionably correct uses of "bank", & at least 3 of "bull". Why
shouldn't 2 *different* uses of "he was lying when he said p" be
both of them unquestionably correct?" A. "Let's say: It's unques-

tionably correct if all w.e.p. *frequently* use it in that way; unquestionably incorrect if *none* ever do. If all frequently used it in *both*, both would be unquestionably correct." B. "But how can we possibly know whether a person is using it *merely to mean* "he thought or knew p was false, when he said it", or whether part of what he's asserting is that p was false? How can you know yourself which way you were using it on a particular occasion? The fact is that whether it is unquestionably correct or not to use a word in a certain way depends just as much upon how w.e.p. *understand* it as on how they *use* it. But I don't understand what you mean by saying that they use or understand a word *merely* to mean so & so, or *not* merely, but to mean *something else* as well. How can we tell how much a person *means* or *understands* by a word?"

There are states of a man's head such that any w.e.p. who knew that A's head was in one of them would unhesitatingly say that A was bald; there are others such that any w.e.p. who knew that A's [head] was in one of them would unhesitatingly say that A was not bald. But there are others such that many w.e.p. at least would hesitate to say one or the other. E.g. they might say: Well, he's slightly bald; or "Well, he's hardly at all bald; but one can hardly say straight out "He's not bald" nor yet "He is bald" ". There's no well established convention with regard to such states of the head, to say "He's not bald", nor yet to say "he's bald": = it's not the case that all w.e.p., who knew the state of the head, would say either without hesitation.

Every w.e.p. who knew both (a) that A when he asserted that p knew it or believed it to be false & also (b) that p was false, would say that A had lied; and if, when a man knew (a) but knew that p was true, he would say unhesitatingly that A had not lied that would prove that part of what he understands by "A was lying when he said p" is "p is false".

13

SENSE-DATA AND "LOOKING"

A. "Whenever a physical surface is looking φ to me, I am seeing (in the sense in which I see after-images with shut eyes)[1] something which is φ."

This is not an empirical generalisation—something which has been found out empirically: it is something which (if true at all) follows from the meaning of "looking φ", just as that "whenever a creature is a brother, he is male" follows from the meaning of "brother".

But A doesn't in fact state nearly all that is meant. It is never meant merely that "A physical surface is looking φ to S" entails "(∃ x) . φx . S is seeing₁ x". The extra point can be expressed by saying: I must be seeing₁ something *corresponding* to the surface in question which *is* φ. And how is this to be expressed more clearly? We might say: I am seeing something which *is* φ, such that I identify the surface in question by reference to that something—either as identical with it or as that which is *the* thing having to it a certain relation. But what's meant by "identify the surface by reference to"? We might say: If challenged to point out any physical surface which is looking φ to me, I should point & say "This one is". And to say "I identify the surface by reference to x" = if I answered a challenge in this way, the prop. which I express by pointing & saying "This one is", would be a prop. about x, but perhaps only in the sense in which "The author of Waverley was Scotch" is *about* "Waverley".

This is one way of bringing out the point that the sense-datum problem can't be fully discussed without considering the kind of

---

[1] ⟨Sense 1 [i.e. seeing₁] = sense of "see" in which I see an after-image with eyes shut, or in which a man in d.t. sees something which *looks like* (looks as if it were) a snake. Yet he's not seeing anything which "*looks*" so & so, in the sense in wh. physical things *look* so & so.

When I see, without seeing double, a piece of pink blotting-paper, with nothing laid across it then I am seeing (in sense 1) something, such that if I were to say to myself "*That's* one side of a piece of pink blotting-paper", & were to ask myself which among all the objects I am seeing in sense 1 is the one, owing to my seeing of which, I know that *that* does look pink to me, it would be the one.⟩

prop. you express by saying "this" (or "that") & pointing. One chief point is missed if you stick to "I'm seeing a — — ".

Now take this piece of blotting-paper. I point & say "This surface looks (in the main) pink to me now". Acc. to what we have said, A maintains that this prop., if true, is *about* something which *is* pink in the main. But obviously this is not enough. A maintains that it is *about* it, because "this surface" refers in some way to a thing which *is* pink. But how? The mere words "This looks pink to me now" don't *by themselves express* any prop. at all, in the sense that they would convey any meaning other than "Something is looking pink to me now" unless something in the context or something accompanying their utterance indicated to *what "this" refers* = what surface you meant by "this surface." In the *context*, if I said: "I was looking at a piece of blotting-paper when I wrote this last night. This piece is looking pink to me now." (Referential use of "this". "Once upon a time there was a boy called Jack. This boy . . ." = Once upon a time there was a boy who was called Jack, & who etc. etc.). In this use *the words said before* are sufficient to make clear what "this" *refers to*. Not so in the demonstrative use. Here it is necessary that some gesture of some sort (possibly merely the direction of the eyes & a nod) should accompany the saying of the words, if they are to convey more than "Something is looking pink to me now"; just as this in its turn conveys no more than "Something is looking pink to someone now", or "to the person who uttered these words", unless the tone of the voice in which they are said or the sight of the speaker make plain whom "me" refers to. But now suppose I make a gesture of pointing. All that this *alone* will convey to a person who sees me pointing while he hears me say the words, will be that something *in that direction* is looking pink to me now. But this is obviously not all that I mean by pointing & saying "*This* is looking pink to me now". We might be tempted to say that what is meant is "The thing which is *nearest to me* in *that* direction". But, suppose my hearer sees nothing nearer to me in that direction than the floor: has he understood me? He might point at the floor & say "Is *this* what you meant is looking pink to you?" and your answer would be "No". He has understood that you are saying "There is a thing which is the nearest to me in that direction & which is looking pink to me" (i.e. *The* thing . . .) but he has not understood what you mean by

"This . . .", i.e. *this* ≠ *the* thing which is nearest in that direction. In order to understand you he must *see* the thing which is looking pink to you—the thing to which your "this" refers. You are in fact using this thing to convey to him what you wish to convey, just as much as you are using your gesture & your words, & as much as if you were taking it in your hand & flourishing it when you said "this". In fact you are using it, not indeed as a *name* for itself, but to *indicate* that it is what your "this" & pointing refer to.

⟨Sometimes the meeting point of the direction in which your eyes are looking with the direction in which your finger is pointing may serve to indicate *where* the object to which you are referring by "this" is situated, i.e. at what point along the line which is the direction in which your finger is pointing. This by itself would give us "Something *there* is looking pink to me" or "*The* thing that is *there*". And this is a prop. which your hearer could understand, even if he saw nothing in that place. But if he did see nothing there, he would not have understood what you were referring to by "this". He might know that you were referring to some object which seemed to you or which was there: but he would not know *what* object. I.e. "*that* piece of blotting-paper" does not, even when the place referred to by "there" is specified in this way, mean the same as "the piece of b. which is *there*". Very often however the point in the line indicated by my finger, to which I refer by "there", is indicated not by being the point at which my line of vision meets that line, but by being the point at which my hearer sees a piece of blotting-paper: i.e. "there" = "the place where *that* is", instead of its being the case that "that" = "the thing which is *there*".⟩

14

MOTION

Koffka says the pictures of people, animals, things which we see on the screen at a Cinema don't really move at all: no movement takes place within any picture on the screen: all that happens is that different static pictures move down as wholes.

If they did move, it would be in the same sort of sense in which a shadow moves, which is very similar to that in which a wave moves: no material thing is transferred from one place to the other; but one surface after another, is lighted with a degree of illumination less than that which lights surrounding surfaces, and this happens continuously—just as in the case of a wave, a certain form of arrangement of masses of water occurs successively in many different places, & that continuously.

But is this a different *sense* of "move"? Isn't it only that shadows & waves are quite a different type of object from material things, but that they *move* in the same sense? That they move perhaps only means that to any normal person they would look to be moving.

What is the difference in the case of the Cinema?

Suppose it were the case that it looked as if a black vertical line were moving from left to right. What really happens is that a vertical black linear image is thrown on the screen (is it?) for a very short space of time, during which it is moving down the screen; then another a little to its right; then another to right of this, & so on.

When we say *another* vertical image, we imply that it is *not* true that the same image has been there all the time, and therefore that, if we said "*this* image has moved" or "is moving", we should be saying something untrue. And so we should, if we *meant* by this that during the whole of the time in question *there had been an image of that shape on the part of the screen* in question (if this were *entailed*), in a sense which entails that during no interval of time, however short, was there no such image on that part of the screen, *by any test* or criterion. There is a test or criterion such that if we take *that* as entailing "it was at some time without such an image", then it was. But if we take as a test for its having been

blank that to any normal person looking at it, it would have looked
blank, then it *wasn't* blank at any time. "It was blank for a time
during this minute" & "it wasn't blank at any time during this
minute" don't necessarily contradict. Isn't one use of this phrase
just as correct as the other? People are certainly inclined to say
No: it's *more* correct to say "it was blank for a time", because this
tells us something which science has shewn to be the case.

Laz[erowitz] tells me that when a cinema is working, the
different pictures succeed one another without a break from
above to below; & therefore the screen is never blank even in
Koffka's sense. And *all* the images in each picture are constantly
moving from above to below; so therefore are Koffka's images.
What does happen is that no image ever *moves relatively to other
images* in the same picture. A series of pictures is thrown each of
which is static in the sense that, though all the images in it are
constantly moving downwards, no image is moving relatively to
any other image.

Koffka, when he says this succession of images really does pass
over the screen, is assuming that the same sort of thing is happening, *so quickly that nobody can see that it's happening*, as is happening if the machine is so slowed down that a succession of static
pictures would be seen by any normal eye. But *is* the same thing
really happening? Are there in fact successively on the screen a
number of different vertical lines, one above the other? There are
present at the surface of the screen movements of light-waves such
that, if they were continued longer, one static picture would be
seen with one vertical image in it moving downwards, &, if still
longer, at rest; and then after these movements other movements
such that, *if* they were continued longer, another static picture
would be seen containing a vertical image a little to the right of
the earlier one; & so on. That such movements of light-waves
exist is certain. But *they* are not images, and because, if they were
continued longer (or took place more slowly), there *would be*
images, it doesn't [in] the least follow that, lasting as short a
time as they do, there *are* any. We might say: There are images of
a certain kind on the screen only if a normal eye would see
images of that kind.—Of course, by saying these images are there,
Koffka might mean that, if an observer with a highly abnormal
eye & brain of a certain structure were present, he would see them;
and this may be true: it may be that there is logically possible a

structure of eye & brain, such that the light movements that are there would cause the observer possessed of them to see in a very short space of time the same sort of thing which we see when the machine is very much slowed down. But is it *logically possible* that such a thing should be seen in such a short space of time? I doubt it: we don't know what it would be like! though we think we do, bec. we say: "It would *only* differ in the rate at which successive pictures succeeded one another". But here it's a question *not* of, could they be seen in $\frac{1}{100}$ of a sec., say, but of what Einstein calls "psychological time": or is it? Any period in which they were seen *couldn't* seem to us as short as the period which the film-star takes to shut her eyes. But *could* a sufficiently long period of psychological time actually only occupy $\frac{1}{100}$ sec.? This *does* seem possible. But if it did the second-hand on a watch would seem to go so slow that we couldn't see it moving! And in that case would the period it took in going from one mark to the next be what we mean by "a second"? A second wouldn't then be a *short* space of time—i.e. the time taken by the hand to move from one mark to the next wouldn't. And this moving from one mark to the next is *not* our only criterion for a second. It must be such a movement on a *normal* watch. But what is a *normal* watch? A watch which moves at the pace watches now move.

SHADOWS, PATCHES OF LIGHT, ETC.

What name is there for the ? thrown upon the screen in a cinema?

They are not shadows, because they are not produced by the introduction of an opaque object between the source of light & the screen, but by the introduction of transparent (= translucent) objects between the 2—translucent in different degrees. (In an X-ray photo are the darkest parts *shadows* in the sense that they're due to the introduction of a body (e.g. mass of filling, or a shot) which is *opaque to* X-rays, between the source of the rays & the plate? & the rest due to intervention of objects "trans-X-ray" in various degrees?—In asking this question I am not only confusing plate or film with *print*; but also overlooking the fact that neither on the plate nor on the print are the "patches" we're talking of shadows, or patches of light or any such thing: they are real physical differences in the surface of the film or print, and in the case of the *film* not only of its surface but its substance right through? Whereas, when a picture is thrown on the screen, no change takes place in the surface of the screen: no doubt something new is taking place *at* its surface; but as soon as the picture ceases to be thrown, the surface of the screen is just as it was before. But when an unused film is exposed, the surface of the film becomes *permanently* different from what it was before: it is in a different state.)

Nor is it natural to call them "patches of light". When an electric torch is turned towards the wall in a dark room, a patch of light appears on the wall & may move. And if the glass is blue or a piece of transparent blue paper is pasted over it, a blue patch of light is thrown on the wall; and in a *colour* film many of the blue patches that appear on the screen seem to be blue patches of light in just this sense. But I think this is not so: I think to say there is a patch of light on a surface implies that the surrounding part of the surface is dark, & this is not in general the case with the ? in a film. Perhaps this is why you can't have a *black* patch of light; whereas you can have a black ? on the screen.

Let's call the ? "images".

16

TIME: WHAT IS A SECOND?

If a second is defined by reference to the rotation of the earth on its axis, i.e. as $\frac{1}{60}$ of $\frac{1}{60}$ of $\frac{1}{24}$ of the time between 2 identical positions of the Greenwich meridian relatively to the fixed stars, then, if the earth rotated 10 times more slowly than it does now, it would be possible to run 10 yds. in a second, instead of only a yard as now, and a second would be 10 times longer than it is now; but if cinema machines still moved as fast as they do now, it would still be quite impossible for any one to see a succession of static pictures instead of a moving one. Don't we mean by a second the length of time which is *now* $\frac{1}{60}$ of $\frac{1}{60}$ of $\frac{1}{24}$ of the time between etc.?

17

SEEING

(a) *What I see here* is the very same book which I saw in your hand yesterday; but (b) *what I see here* is different from what I saw in your hand yesterday.

(a) & (b) don't contradict: (b) follows from "This book *looks* different to me now from what it did when I saw it in your hand yesterday".

But now of an after-image: (a) I still see the same after-image as I did when I first closed my eyes, but (b) what I see when I see it now is different from what I saw when I saw it then: it was brighter then.

(a) & (b) = I saw THIS ⟨?⟩ after-image when I first closed my eyes, but it has changed since then—not merely "it *looked* different then". Yet instead of "it was brighter then" we might say "it looked brighter then".

N.B. (1) "I saw a blue after-image" ≠ (∃ c). I saw c . c was blue, although (2) "I saw a blue book" = (∃ b). I saw b . b was blue. The difference in (1) is that (1) entails "I saw a shade of blue" whereas (2) does not: "I saw a blue book, but it didn't look blue to me" is not contradictory, any more than "That white screen looks blue now". But when we say "The image I saw was blue" we *are* saying "it *looked* blue to me", though here the use of "look" is different from the other, just in that it *makes no sense* ⟨?⟩ to say "it looked blue, but it wasn't"; i.e. the prop. "So & so was *an image* & looked blue" contradicts "but it wasn't blue". If, however, we have a case of a sense-datum with regard to which we are in doubt whether it *is* an image ("subjective") or not, it *does* make sense to say "It looks blue, but perhaps it isn't", because it makes sense to say "it is objective", *if* this makes sense. And this *does* make sense, even if *is* only means here "is *of* a physical surface": or does it? ("You see that bright speck there? That's Jupiter" doesn't perhaps prove it, because perhaps "that bright speck" does not describe a sense-datum.)

18

SEEING

"The sky is blue" = The sky looks blue to normal people look-ing at it by daylight, if it's not covered by clouds. (If it is covered by clouds, though you can *look at* the sky, you can't *see* the sky. This shews 2 different uses of "the sky", because you can't look at what you can't see. We can say "the sky was *grey*".)

But "This book is blue" = This book looks (or *would* look) blue to normal people (= people of the sort, which is *now* normal) who look at it by *good* daylight at *normal distances*, i.e. not too far off or too near. In the case of the sky, you don't need to mention a distance, because you *can't* get too near or too far away from it.

"She moved her lips" (said at a cinema of a character on the screen) means "To any normal eye, with the illumination usual in cinemas, & at any of the distances usual in cinemas, her lips would have appeared to move" (*or* there would have appeared to be a movement of that *part of the figure which represented her lips?*).

LOOKING

Suppose a spot of red light is thrown on a white screen. That part of the screen will then "look red" to any normal person: & we can I think say it *is* red (e.g. "that part of the wall *is* darker than this: don't hang the picture there"), meaning it would look so to everyone under these circumstances, though it's also correct to say "It's *not* red", meaning that by ordinary daylight it wouldn't look so. Here are 2 meanings of "is red", in which a physical surface may *be* red. Can we possibly hold that the surface also *is* at that moment "red" in a third sense, viz. that in which an after-image is? In favour of saying so is this: that that part of the screen looks red to you, entails that you are seeing *something* which *is* red in this sense, & not only *something* but *something such that* it's *because* you're seeing it that *you know that* the spot is looking *red* to you. (Why not: "because you're seeing it, the spot *is* looking red"? Because it might have looked red without your seeing *that*, e.g. if you'd been seeing something of a slightly different shade, such that it was bec. you saw it, that you knew it was looking red.) And if you say to yourself "That part of the screen looks red" it seems as if this something which *is* red was what you are referring to by "that". Call this something A. If it is not A to which you are referring by "that", the only alternative seems to be that "that" is equivalent to "*the* thing which I know to look red because I see A" = "the thing to which A corresponds", or "the thing which is where A is". The temptation to think that A *is* what you refer to by "that" is very strong indeed: A is the only thing *seen* in sense 1 (= sense in which an after-image seen with closed eyes is seen) which *could* be identical with the part of the screen in question, & there is a great temptation to think that that part of the screen *is* seen in sense 1. But if A is identical with that part of the surface of the screen, then that part *is* red in this third sense, since A certainly is. But is it possible to hold that that part of the surface of the screen *is* red in this sense?

20

LOOKING

It is quite certain that when you say of a physical surface that it "looks blue", "blue" is being used in the same sense as when you say of an after-image (closed eye) that it *is* blue. Why? (It is a necess. condition of its looking blue to you, that you should see the colour blue, in the same sense as when you see an after-image which is blue.)

But this being so, the phrase "it looks blue, but it isn't blue" is deceptive, because it *looks as if* you were saying of the very same quality which the thing looks to have, that it hasn't got it; whereas if I am right that "*is* blue" in this usage = "would look blue to normal persons in good daylight at a proper distance", it's really only a play upon words: what you are saying is only that while it looks to have one *quality*, what it hasn't got is another *property called by the same name.* This seems strange; & this strangeness might be used as an argument that it isn't true, & that when we say a physical surface is blue what we mean is exactly the same as when we say that an after-image is. On my view, it throws a curious light on the use of "looks" of physical things: we only say "looks ϕ" when ϕ is a property which no physical thing *could* possibly have—which it's nonsense to attribute to any.

In order to explain to anyone what "blue" means, it's not sufficient (as Watson said) to shew him a physical thing which *is* blue; you must shew it under such circumstances that it *looks blue* to him.

As for "looks" of sense-data: we can rightly say of the man in d.t. that he sees things that "look like" snakes—(can we say "are like snakes"? or "are like the appearance of snakes"?)— though *not* physical things that do as, e.g., a stick may. We can also say that an after-image *looks* about a foot from the eye: they certainly do *look as if* they had a certain position in physical space, though here they *haven't* any.

NOTEBOOK IV

[c. 1941–1942]

1

LOOKS

From "x looks blue to me" there does *not* follow "x is blue".
But if we say of a blue after-image, seen with shut eyes, "it
looks blue to me", *that* is a use of "looks" such that from it
there does follow "it is blue".

You can't see a blue after-image without its looking blue to
you, but you *can* see a blue book without its looking blue to
you. When a book does look blue to you, does it follow that you
are seeing something which you couldn't see without its looking
blue to you? If so, this something can't be the book, nor any part
of its surface.

2

AFTER-IMAGES (SHUT EYE) AND
TAUTOLOGY

Any after-image you are seeing *must* exist while you are seeing it. This only says: (t, x, i) . x is seeing i at t →i exists at t.

But (a) "I'm seeing a blue patch" seems to be a purely empirical or contingent prop., although "this patch exists" is partly tautological ⟨?⟩, & (a) seems to follow from it, if the patch in question is blue.

Is "this patch exists now" partly tautological? It seems so, because anything which hadn't existed now couldn't have been "this patch". I.e. "this patch doesn't exist now" is self-contradictory. But it *doesn't* follow from this that "this patch exists now" *entails* any necessary prop., nor therefore any tautology.

But is it even true that "this patch doesn't exist now" is self-contradictory? It's certainly true that there might not have existed now any such thing as this patch: that place might have been red all over instead of green all over; & *if* that had been so, this green patch would not have existed now.

What is the reason for saying "This patch doesn't exist now" is self-contradictory?

Consider "This patch is brighter than that one". I take this (following Ramsey) to = "This colour (or continuum of colours) is here now, & that colour (or continuum) is there now, & this colour is brighter than that one". In "this patch doesn't exist" "this patch" seems to be being used in the same way. Hence it begins "This colour is here now", & to add "doesn't exist now", can only mean, it seems, "but this colour is *not* here now", so that the whole is a contradiction.

Instead of that continuum of blues which I see over there, there might have been a continuum of greens in just that place now. There is no contradiction in the supposition that there *is* a continuum of greens in that very place now. There is therefore no contradiction in the supposition that that particular continuum of blues *is* not in that place now. But if this had been the case, it would have been impossible for me to use "that patch" in the way in which I do now use it: it could not have referred to that to which it does now refer. If I had been seeing the same continuum of blues in another place of exactly the same shape & size, I should have been able to make the false proposition: This continuum of blues is in that place now—the place being that which, on this supposition, would then be occupied by a continuum of greens. But I should not have been able to make the prop. I do now make by saying "That patch is darker than this".

I think my point is the same as is made by saying "That table doesn't exist" is self-contradictory, whereas "There's no table there" is not. Of course, the first *could* be used to say the same as the second. But as we ordinarily use "that table", e.g. "That table is too small for 5", part of what we say is "There is a table there", so that if in "That table doesn't exist" we were using "That table" in the same way, we should be saying "There is a table there, but there's no table there". It's absurd to say "*That* table doesn't exist".

3

"THIS" AND PARTIAL TAUTOLOGY

"This is here" is certainly partly tautological, in some uses. See p. 8.[1]

⟨In what not? (a) In "this colour is here" as distinguished from "this coloured patch is here"? (b) In a sort of joke: In answer to "Where is Tim?" you may push Tim forward & say "This fellow's here".

(a) is the important case. If by "this colour" you meant "the colour which is here", then it would be partially tautological. And don't you? This isn't *all* you mean, in all cases, if "the colour which is here" has the meaning which Russell has explained: since your interlocutor might be able to see where you were pointing (a vague "here") without seeing the colour in that place; whereas e.g. "this colour here is brighter than I want" is *sometimes* used in such a way that it's not understood unless your interlocutor *sees* the colour in question. But though "this colour" doesn't always mean only "the colour which is here" in R.'s sense, doesn't it *always* mean "this colour here", & isn't "this colour here is here" always partially tautological? Of course, it isn't if, when you say the second "here", you point to a different place from the one you point to when you say the first. But how if you don't? isn't it tautological then?⟩

"There's something here", which follows from it, is in no degree tautological.

Compare "Somewhere in *this* area", where the area in question is marked out by a visible boundary, consisting in the line which separates the area in question from surroundings sharply different in colour from it; with "somewhere hereabouts", where the meaning of "hereabouts" is given by pointing to the middle of a black-board on which there are no sharply contrasted colours: e.g. "I'm going to draw a triangle somewhere hereabouts". Now "hereabouts" *could* be replaced by "in this area"; but in such a use "in this area" would be used in a different way from what it is when we are referring to the marked out area. In the latter the visible outline is a *property* of the area to which "this" *refers* in *referring* to the area.

[1] [I.e. entry no. 5 in this Notebook.]

In the case of "here" & "this" what they *refer to* are a place or a thing which, together with our saying of "here" & "this" & our pointing (in some sense), indicate *themselves*. By pointing at that & saying "this" when I point, I indicate ⟨?⟩ the thing at which I point, *if* it is seen. I use *it* in order to say something about *it*: just as I use the sound "long" to say something about itself when I say " "long" is a short word"; only we can't say that we use the thing pointed at as a name for itself, as we can say that we use "long" as a name for itself. If in answer to the question "Which one shall I take next?" you pick up one of the objects & hand it to him, this seems *almost* like using the object as a name for itself. The handing of it corresponds to the pronouncing of the word "long".

4

"PERCEPTS" AND "PLACES" (James)

James, *Essays in Rad. Emp.*, "World of Pure Experience", pp. 82–5.[1]

It's solely an empirical question whether "when you and I are said to know (he doesn't mean "know" he means "see") the "same" Memorial Hall, our minds do terminate at or in a numerically identical percept". He answers: "Obviously, as a plain matter of fact, they do *not*. Apart from colour-blindness & such possibilities, we see the Hall in *different perspectives*. You may be on one side of it & I on another." And then goes on (83) "Do our minds have no object in common after all?" And goes on (84) "Yes, they certainly have *Space* in common", gives as "a pragmatic principle" "we are obliged to predicate sameness when we can predicate no assignable point of difference" & asserts "there is no test discoverable, so far as I know, by which it can be shewn that the place occupied by your percept of the Memorial Hall differs from the place occupied by mine. The percepts themselves may be shewn to differ; but if each of us be asked to point out where his percept is, we point to an identical spot". (Point in *the same direction*, yes, but identical?)

And later " "There" for me means where I place my finger. If you do not feel my finger's contact to be "there" in my sense, when I place it on your body, where then do you feel it?"

Suppose J. & P. *were* on different sides of M.H., & were trying to point at their percepts. If a 3rd spectator could see both of them, he might find that their fingers were pointing at one another, & were therefore pointing at ever so many "identical spots", namely all those which lay between the points of the 2 fingers; but this would not shew that the spot in which J.'s percept was was identical with the spot in which P.'s was. If you point in a direction, you can't help pointing at *every* spot which lies in that direction, whether you can see it or not, but any percept of yours which lies in that direction will only lie in *one* of those spots, or, rather, will only encircle *one* of them. If J. & P. walked up to M.H. & touched it on opposite sides, J.'s visual percept

---

[1] [W. James, *Essays in Radical Empiricism* (London, 1912).]

156

would be imm. adjacent to the tip of his finger, P.'s to the tip of *his*, & it would be quite plain that the place where J.'s percept was, was *not* the same as that where P.'s was.

What "test could shew" that, if J. touches P.'s body with his finger, the place where P. feels the contact is *not* identical with the place where J. feels it?

If J. & P. were asked to touch the place where they feel *it*, J. would put his other finger in much the same place in which P. would put one of his. This goes to shew that the place *is* the same. But does it really shew this? Doesn't it only shew that the contact J. feels *seems* to J. to be in the physical place which they both touch, & similarly that the contact P. feels *seems* to P. to be in the physical place they both touch?

⟨This suggests that "here" or "there" = in the same place as this (i.e. the tip of my finger). This can't be exactly right, in the cases where you only point & don't touch; but it might be that to give meaning to "here" or "there", 2 things are required: that there's no sense in saying of *one* thing, "this is here" or "there": that "There's a chair here" = "There's a chair having (a certain relation) R to *this*".

"That colour is in that place" means then?⟩

What reason is there for thinking the places aren't really the same? Roughly (1) that the place where J. feels the contact is a place, not in physical space, but in J.'s sense-field; & the place where P. feels it a place in P.'s sense-field, & that these 2 sense-fields are not identical—have no place in common. (2) That what I feel when another person touches my body is very different from what I feel when I touch another person's, & that 2 such different kinds of feeling can't be in the same place at once.

J.'s touch-sensation (when each is touching the place on J.'s body where his sensation seems to him to be) *is* adjacent to his visual *sense-datum* of the tip of his own finger & also to *his* sense-datum of the tip of P.'s; P.'s touch-sensation *is* adjacent to *his* visual sense-data of those 2 things. I.e. J.'s is *where* 2 of J.'s sense-data are; P.'s is *where* 2 of *his* are. Are J.'s visual sense-data of the 2 finger-tips in the same place as P.'s visual sense-data of them? Only if the sense-data are identical with the surfaces—2 different sense-data both identical with the *same* surface.

"THIS" AND "HERE"; "THAT" AND "THERE"

Let us say "This thing" = "the thing that is here", & "that thing" = "the thing that is there".

Then "This thing is here" = "the thing that is here is here" = $(\exists x) . x$ is here . $y \neq x \supset_y y$ is not here . x is here, which is *redundant*, but *not* tautological in the sense of containing a part which is necessary. "What's here is here" *is* tautological = $(x) . x$ is here $\supset x$ is here.

What's that thing there? = (1) what's it called, (2) what does it do, what's it for? I asked this at The Manse, & the answer was "It's a "mixer", & is for beating up eggs etc.".

Now this question is one which would only be asked by a person who was *seeing* or had recently been seeing the thing in question (a blind man might ask "What's this thing here?" but not "What's that thing there?", the seeing man says "this thing here" when he's touching or nearly touching it), & he wouldn't understand the answer unless he was seeing it (the answer wouldn't be an answer to his question). Hence "there" for him does not merely mean, e.g. "the nearest thing in *that* direction", but "in the place where that thing is", where "that thing" *cannot* = "the thing that is there".

Can we say "that thing" = "the thing at which I am pointing" or "the thing to which this finger points" or "the nearest thing to which this finger points"? No, because the prop. is not understood unless the thing in question is *seen*.

"There's a match-box there" $\neq$ "That's a match-box": it answers "Is there a match-box anywhere about?". The other doesn't.

6

SCEPTICISM AND DOUBT

"I have no doubt that p, but I don't think it's quite certain",
is *not* self-contradictory ∴ x thinks that p is not quite certain ↛ x
doubts whether p is true.

7

TRUE BY DEFINITION

That "a brother is always male" or "any (every) brother is male" is true by definition; but that "any creature wh. is both male & a sibling, is male" is *not* "true by definition"—this is a matter of *logic*, not of words. This seems to shew that when we say things of form "p" is "true by def.", we are talking *partly* of the expression "p", not *merely* of the prop. expressed by "p".

We can say "That every brother is male *follows from the meaning (or definition)* of the word "brother"." But what follows from the fact that "brother" means "male sibling", is that the *sentence* "every brother is male" means "every male sibling is male", *not* that "every male sibling is male" is true. That "every male sibling is male" is true (understood *without* existential import) follows from the fact that "There is at least one sibling who is male & *not* male" is a contradiction, & that the negation of a contradiction is true: i.e. "It's not the case that there's a sibling which is male & not male" is true. But from what does it follow that this is true? We *can* say: from "Nothing is both male & not male". And, of this, that it follows from $\sim (p \,.\, \sim p)$, i.e. the Law of Contradiction. But is the Law of Contr. "true by def."? & what is meant by saying it is "true"?

8

DREAMS

How do I know that I'm not dreaming now?

I know that my body is in a certain position: e.g. that I'm sitting down, with my right leg crossed over my left knee, *not* lying in bed. Could I know this, if I were dreaming? Not, if my *whole* present experience were a dream; but I might perhaps be *half* dreaming.

But how do I know that I am sitting down? D.[1] disputes whether I do: he says he has often dreamed he was sitting down, when in fact he was lying in bed. I.e. he has discovered afterwards that at that previous time he was lying in bed. How did he discover this? & how does he know now that he has often discovered it? Or mayn't he be dreaming now that he has often discovered it?

He does imply that he may be dreaming now that he has often discovered it; for he implies that his whole present experience *may* be a dream, i.e. that he *doesn't know* that it isn't. If so, he doesn't know that he has ever dreamed: he *may* be only dreaming that he has dreamed. But could he dream that he has dreamed, without knowing what dreaming is? And could he know what dreaming is, without having ever known "That was a dream"? He might, perhaps, in the sense in which a man born blind may know what it is to see.

("I saw Russell in a dream last night" = "I dreamed I saw Russell". Miss Stearns wants to say: It wasn't really R. that I saw in my dream. And it's true that there is a sense of "see" such that nothing which I "see" in a dream in *that* sense *is* Russell, whereas of things which I "see" in that same sense in waking life, one of them *is* Russell, whenever I see Russell: one of them *is*, in the sense that, referring to it by "that", it would be true to say "*That* is part of the surface of R.'s body & clothes". I think it must be admitted that there are 2 senses of "saw in a dream", one in which it may be true that "I saw R. in a dream", another in which it's *logically imposs.* that I should ever see R. in a dream.)

How do I know that I am sitting down now, & not merely dreaming that I'm sitting down?

[1] [Descartes.]

PHYSICAL OBJECTS AND THE FUTURE

When I say "This is a chair", am I saying anything about the future? One reason for suspecting that I am is that sometimes, when we think "That's a chair", something happens *afterwards* which *makes it certain* that we were mistaken: e.g. something happens which makes it certain that what we took to be a chair was only a *reflection* of a chair. Accordingly when I say "This is a chair", I am (it seems) committing myself to "Nothing will happen in the future such as will make it certain that this is not a chair": and it isn't (it seems) *certain* that this is a chair unless it's *certain* that no such thing will happen. It seems, then, as if it is often certain that certain things won't happen in the future. There is so far no argument for the view that it is ever certain that so & so *will* happen.

In fact, however, it seems never to be the case that anything which happens subsequently does *by itself* make it certain that we were mistaken. It is always the *conjunction* of what happens subsequently with what happened *at the time when* we were mistaken & previously to that time. When we say "That's a chair" we are, therefore, only committing ourselves to: Nothing will happen subsequently such as *in conjunction* with what is happening now & has happened previously would make it certain that we are mistaken. But is anything even conceivable such as, in conjunction with what is happening now & has happened previously, would make it certain that I'm not now sitting in a chair? or even (then) doubtful whether I was?

Can I think of any particular thing which would? I can think, as a logically possible thing, that there should next minute be to me all the appearance of there being a reflection of a chair in that place; that I should see & touch a mirror in front of it; & see in an appropriate place a chair of which the reflection was a reflection. But, if all this happened, (as it might), I should say: This mirror *certainly* wasn't here just now; nor was a chair like this here: something unaccountable which I can't explain has happened: but there certainly was a chair there, where now there is only a reflection, a moment ago. And this would be the only reasonable thing to say, if I remembered, as I do now, the whole state of things when I said "That is certainly a chair". Of course, I *might* become unreasonable & say "I must have been mistaken" or "Perhaps I was mistaken"; or I might lose my memory, & it might then be reasonable for me to say "There certainly wasn't a chair there", though this would not be true.

People might say to me: There was a mirror there all the time, & this chair here. This would be very unaccountable, but, with such a memory as I have now, it would not be reasonable for me to believe them. Suppose they were to say that to me now: that there really is a chair in a place where I see none, & a mirror where I see no sign of one. It would not be reasonable for me to believe them, & it would be *certain* that they were wrong.

This case differs, in ways which I cannot detail, from cases in which I *thought* there was an object in a given place, & found it was only a reflection. I don't now merely *think* there is a chair there: I know there is.

I don't know now that there won't be, a minute hence, a reflection of a chair there & not a chair; but I do know that, if there is, it won't make certain that there is not a chair there now, nor even uncertain that there is a chair there now.

Of no kind of thing do I know that it won't happen or that it *will*: all that I know about the future is that nothing will happen which, if I retain my memory, will make it reasonable for me to doubt that there was a chair there now, & nothing which will make it certain that there wasn't. I don't know that I shan't lose my memory: and, if I did, certain things which might happen would make it reasonable for me to doubt whether there was a chair there now or even to feel certain that there wasn't. Nothing could *make it certain* that there wasn't: but, of course, I might *feel* certain that there wasn't.

Part of above is wrong. Take this. I am at present sitting in an arm-chair in my room at Princeton, & writing this by electric light: I know all this for certain. But I do not know for certain that I shall not, in another half-minute, be, to all appearance, lying naked on a beach of white sand by a deep-blue lagoon, under a bright sun. If that were to happen, and I remembered sitting here half a minute ago, it would be *reasonable* for me to *doubt* if I had been sitting here—to doubt if I really was remembering; and still more if people lying near me on the beach told me I had been there for the last half hour. If my remembrance of having been here was as clear then as it is now, I *shouldn't know what to think*. It would be reasonable for me to doubt, e.g. whether what I remembered wasn't only a dream; i.e. I shouldn't *then* know for certain that I had been here. But this is nothing against my knowing for certain *now* that I am sitting in a chair etc.

Would it be reasonable for me to suspect that I might be dreaming *then*? Not if, to *all* appearance, I was lying naked etc.—certainly not if the appearance lasted a considerable time. But how, if after 2 mins., I appeared to be in my chair again? & then after another 2 on the beach again? Certainly I shouldn't know what to think. But I *do* know what to think *now*.

But now suppose that five minutes hence I not only am, to all appearance, lying naked on a beach of white sand, but also *feel as if I remembered* having been there for half an hour past, & have *no* recollection of having been here. There seems to be no contradiction in supposing this might happen. Is it also true that I don't know it won't? It seems to be true that something *might* thus happen such that I should then have *just as good reason* for supposing I had been lying naked there for the last half hour, as I have now for supposing I have been here for the last half hour. Yet, *ex hypothesi*, I shouldn't *know* that I had, because it wouldn't be true that I had. Hence from the fact that I have as good reasons as I have for saying that I have been here for the last half hour, it doesn't follow that I *know* I have.

Does it follow that I *don't* know I have?

I think it does; & hence we must deny that it is *logically possible* I should have as good reason for saying I had been lying naked, as I have now for saying I have been here. We must say that, when a thing didn't happen, I *can't* have as good reason for saying it did as I have when I *remember* it: that in the latter case my reason *doesn't* merely consist in my feeling as if I remembered it—in *any* present feeling. Yet it seems as if that it *did* happen can't be any part of the reason I have *now* for saying that it did.

I remember perfectly that I have been sitting for some time with this book before me. I *have* been thus sitting. But I can't distinguish anything that it seems natural to call "feeling as if I remembered it". My ground for saying "I have" doesn't seem to consist in my having such a feeling. My ground for saying I have a pain (when I have one) *does* consist in my having the particular pain I have. But my ground for saying I had one just now, does *not* consist in my having had just now the particular pain I had.

10

DEFINITION OF "SENSE-DATUM"

Suppose a round area (enclosed by a black line) of the surface of a white screen is *looking red* to me now, because red light is being thrown on it. Malcolm says:

I am having a red sense-datum *of* that round part of the surface $=_{def.}$ That round part is looking red to me now.

So it does: but does this serve to explain the use of the term "sense-datum"?

Far from it: for (1) It throws no light on the question whether, when I have shut my eyes & the white round patch is no longer looking red to me, it still makes sense to say that the red sense-datum which I *had* still exists but is no longer *had* by me: the given equation is quite consistent with its making sense, & being true. From the fact that the patch has ceased to look red to me, the equation shews that it follows that I have ceased to *have* a red sense-datum which is *of* it. But it doesn't shew that it follows that the red sense-datum has ceased to exist. (2) It throws no light on the question whether "I am having a red sense-datum, but nothing is looking red to me now", is or is not contradictory. The equation is quite consistent with its *not* being contradictory. We need only suppose that there *may* be sense-data had by me, which are not *of* anything: & there are. (3) It throws no light on the question whether the sense-datum I have "*is* red" in the same sense in which an after-image seen with closed eyes may "be red".

11

"AUTONYMOUS" USE OF WORDS

I sometimes use the sound "B" as a *name* for itself.

But I can't use the sound "B" without pronouncing *a* "B", and then I am using *the* "B" which I pronounce, *as a name*, not for itself, but for the sound "B".

We must distinguish 2 different uses of "use as a name": (1) a use in which what is "used as a name" is e.g. the sound "B" (a type); (2) a use in which what is used as a name is e.g. a particular "B" which I pronounce (a token).

(1) is by far the commoner use of "use as a name". The second (2) occurs e.g. if, in talking of what I said when I said "In this box I've got a bee which has a "B" on its back", I were to say "The first "B" I pronounced in saying that was being used as a name for a kind of insect, the second as a name for the letter "B" ". But the same could be expressed by "The first time I pronounced "B" in saying that, I was using "bee" as a name for an insect, the second time I was using it as a name for the letter "B" ", where the use of "use as a name" is (1).

Do we ever use a token as a name for *itself*? R. was so using it in his lecture when he said (p. 37)[1] "I made a noise closely similar to the noise I am about to make: "A"." And we should so use it if we said (a) "Try to *imitate* this sound ——". On the other hand if we say (b) "Try to *make* this sound ——" (which is simply another way of making exactly the same request) we are using the sound (token), *not* as a name for itself, but as a name for the type. What proves that we are using the sound in a different way in these 2 cases? That, using "this sound ——" *in the same way as* in (a), we could truly say "this sound —— has never been made before nor ever will be made again", or *cannot* have been made before & *cannot* be made again. Whereas using "this sound ——" as in (b) we can truly say: This sound —— has very likely often been made before, & very likely will often be made again.

A. If I were to point at *the* "A" I have just written at the

---

[1] [B. Russell, *An Inquiry into Meaning and Truth* (New York and London, 1940).]

167

beginning of this line, & say (a) "This *is* (the letter) "A" " (which is perfectly good English for something that is true), this would *mean the same as* if I were to point at it & say (b) "This is *an* A". And perhaps "this" in both cases refers to the token: if so, "is", in (a), does not mean "is identical with", if "the letter "A" " is being used as in (c) "The letter "A" has been written 5 times in the last 4 lines"; since that token has been written only once. (c) is another way of saying (d) "5 "A's" have been written in the last 4 lines"; but we could not substitute "5 "A's" " in (d) for "the letter "A" " in (c), nor vice versa.

[Note added later, with an arrow referring to the words "this would mean the same as" in the preceding paragraph.]

Would it? Not always. (a) might naturally be used in teaching someone how to pronounce the *type* symbol "A": meaning "This *sort* of symbol is pronounced "A" ". In this case "this" does *not* refer to the token. (b) on the other hand might mean "Here is one A", e.g. if you're trying to count the number of A's on a page, or trying to prove that there's at least one on this page. Thus in (a) you would be using "A" as a name for a type-sound; but in (b), though you would be *using* a token-sound, & therefore also a type-sound, you would not be saying anything *about* a type-sound—i.e. "this" wouldn't "refer to" a type-sound.

12

NECESSITY

Primrose yellow *is* lighter than Oxford blue. This is a necessary prop.: it is *not possible* it should not be. But what has it to do with "must"? If a ribbon is primrose yellow & a second is Oxford blue, the first must be lighter than the second: for all x, y, from the prop. that x is primrose yellow & y Oxford blue, it follows that x is lighter than y.

Also, if x is a shade of primrose yellow, & y a shade of Oxford blue, x *must* be lighter than y.

How about: *This* shade *is* darker than *that*? Is this equivalent to: "For all x, from x is of this shade, there follows x is of a shade that's darker than that?"

This experience is worth having for its own sake → Any experience exactly like this would be = From x is an experience of this sort there *follows* x is worth having for its own sake = If an experience is of this sort, it *must* be worth having for its own sake.

This sort of experience *is* worth having for its own sake.

The *is* in these cases[1] doesn't mean "is now" or "is always", but is like the "is" in 2 + 2 *is* 4.

From "This sort of experience is liked by everyone always", there does *not* follow "From the fact that an experience is of this sort *it follows* that it is liked by the person who has it". But it *may* follow that it is a pleasure.

[1] [I.e. in "Primrose yellow is lighter than Oxford blue" and "This sort of experience is worth having for its own sake".]

13

THE LIAR

From the 2 premisses: (1) S uttered the sentence at t "I am saying something false at this moment", & (2) the only sentence S uttered at t was "I am saying something false at this moment", it is supposed *to follow that S said at t something* which was neither true nor false. It is certain that the conjunction *of* (1) *&* (2) *may be true.* Does it follow that S said something which was neither true nor false? Let's use C as a name for what S said at t, ⟨the sentence S uttered?⟩ i.e. for "I am saying something false at this moment". From the hypothesis that C was true, it will follow that S said something false at t, since this is what C asserts & "C is true" = C; & from the 2 premisses (a) S said something false at t & (b) the only thing S said at t was C, there follows "C was false". How about the hypothesis that C was false? From this premiss, i.e. "C was false", together with (1), i.e. "S said C at t", there follows "S said something false at t", & from this there follows at once that C was true, since, in saying C, S was merely saying that he was saying something false at t. Hence it does really follow from (1) & (2) that S said at t something which was neither true nor false; since from (1) it follows that S said C at t, and from the hypothesis that C was true together with (2) there follows the contradictory of C was true, while from the hypothesis that C was false together with (1) there follows that C was true.

Where is the puzzle in this? All that is shewn is that if (1) & (2) are both true, as they certainly may be, then C, i.e. what S said, can't be either true or false. I suppose the puzzle is (a) that it *looks* as if the sentence "I am saying something false at this moment" is *in all cases* meaningful, & (b) that it looks as if, if meaningful, it must be either true or false, whereas the argument shews that, if (1) & (2) are true, then it is neither true nor false, & therefore if (b) is true, must be meaningless. The puzzle is, therefore, to explain *why* it is meaningless; or alternatively, how it can be neither true nor false without being meaningless.

R., on the other hand, tries to shew that it does *not* follow from (1) & (2) that C is neither true nor false: his argument being apparently that from "C was *false*" & "S said C at t" there does not follow "S said something *false* at t", since in "C was *false*" "false" can't have the same meaning as in "S said something *false* at t": if C = (∃ p) . S said p . ∼ p, then C can't be a possible value for p, so that from "S said C & ∼ C" there won't follow (∃ p) . S said p . ∼ p . "(∃ p) . S said p . ∼ p" only has meaning for some restricted *type* of p, & cannot itself belong to the type for which it has meaning.

⟨It looks as if R. *must* be wrong, because if we say of a man "He said something false in the course of that speech", then, if he did say something that had *any* order of falsehood, our statement will be true.

Suppose a man says: "I said something false just now": we ask "What was it?": he answers "I said that I was saying something false". We should be puzzled. Suppose he did say "I'm saying something false now". He now says that this which he said then was false. How can he or we tell whether it was false or not?⟩

I.e. his argument is that from (1) & "C was false" there does *not* follow "C was true". But he would apparently allow that from "C was true" & (b), there *does* follow "C was false": so that his conclusion would be that it follows from (1) & (2) that C must be false, & can't be true; since it follows from (2) that S wasn't saying anything of the type such that what C asserts is that he was saying something of that type.

R.'s view seems not to apply to the form of the puzzle in which it is supposed that a man says, not "I am saying something false" but "*This* that I'm saying now is false".

Let C be what he says, i.e. "This that I'm saying now is false". This by itself is equivalent to "It's true that this that I'm saying now is false" or "C is true". But since what he's saying is C, he is, in uttering the sentence C, saying that C is false. It seems to follow that C can be neither true nor false. Why? It seems right to say: He hasn't told us *what* he's declaring to be false. Yet if he'd said "This sentence I'm now uttering will end with the word "false" ", he *would* have told us what he was declaring would end with "false"; & we can see whether what he said was true or false. Hence it seems we must admit he *would* have told us what prop. he was declaring to be false, *if* his words had expressed a prop. at all. But his words are such that there's no possible way of telling whether what they express (if anything) is true or false. If he'd said "That it's snowing now is false", we should have known how to settle it, viz. by finding out whether it was snowing.

(a) "This statement is false" = " "This statement is false" is true". But in (a) you can substitute for "This statement" " "This statement is false" ", so that (a) also = " "This statement is false" is false".

14

IMMEDIATE KNOWLEDGE

Blake asks: Why do I say that I do not know "immediately" such things as "That is a dog", when I see a dog?

It's admitted that I don't infer them.

I have grounds or reasons for them.

But then haven't I grounds or reasons for "I've got a pain" when I've got one or for "I felt a stab of pain just now" when I remember that I had, both of which I should say *are* "known immediately"?

(a) In the case of "I've got a pain" it doesn't seem right to say "I have *evidence* that I've got a pain". It's true that if I've got a pain, it must be a pain of some particular sort; & from the fact that I have a pain of this particular sort, it *follows* that I have a pain. But if you're asked: What evidence have you that you've got a pain? you must answer: None. You can also say "None is needed: I know it without needing any evidence". *You* may have evidence that I've got a pain: that I say I have is some evidence, & you are said to "have" this evidence if you *know* that I say so (hearing me say the words is not enough—you must understand them)[1]; other sorts of behaviour on my part may *be* evidence that I have one, & you are said to "have" this evidence if you *observe* this behaviour. If you observe this behaviour, and in consequence say or think that I'm in pain, perhaps you may be said to have *inferred* that I'm in pain; although we should commonly say "I *saw* that he was in pain". (This is like "I *saw* that the thing was made of some *hard* material" or "I saw that it was a *soft* thing".) *I* may have the same sort of evidence that I'm in pain, but I know it *independently* of any such evidence. It's not because of my knowing or observing something *else* that I know I'm in pain, but because I'm in pain or rather because I have just

---

[1] ⟨Is hearing me say them, & understanding them, having any evidence? A parrot might be taught to say "I've got a pain", & though we understood the words we shouldn't say we had *any* evidence that it had a pain. We must not only hear the words & understand them, but also *have evidence* that the speaker (a) isn't misusing the words, (b) is understanding them, (c) isn't lying, or acting, or reading the words out of a book, or saying them merely as an example of what might be said, e.g. as I've written the words above.⟩

that pain. To have that pain is to *have* an absolutely *conclusive reason* for *asserting* that I'm in pain? (This won't do; for I may have "reasons" for *not* asserting that I am, when I am. Nor can we say: reason for thinking—for I don't "think" it.) If I am in pain, & say that I am, I know that what I say is true, *because* I have a particular sort of pain. But if Stace is speaking to Malcolm, & I say that he is, I know that what I say is true, *not* because he *is* speaking in a particular way to Malcolm, but because I *see* that he is or see him doing it. *That* he is wouldn't be sufficient to enable me to *know* that what I say is true, though it would be sufficient to *make* it true. (Seeing him doing it is having evidence that he is doing it?) But having a particular pain *is* sufficient not only to make it true that I'm in pain, but also to enable me to know, *if* I say so, that what I say is true. AB. "That A has a B on its right." My seeing that B to the right of that A is sufficient to enable me to know that what I just said is true; but its being there is not sufficient. Having a particular sort of pain is, of course, *not* sufficient to enable me to know that my words "I am in pain" are *a correct way* of expressing something true: it's only sufficient to enable me to know that what I meant by them is true.

⟨That Stace is speaking to Malcolm is something which might be the case without my knowing it, & such that I don't know it without *having evidence* that it is so—"having evidence" consisting here in, e.g., simultaneously seeing & hearing things, such that from the fact that I hear & see them it doesn't *follow* that he is, perhaps *also* perceiving a certain relation between what I see & hear—sounds that I hear must seem to me to *come from* Stace's mouth. But that I have a pain is something which *couldn't be the case without my knowing it* ⟨?⟩, & is such that I do know it without having evidence for it: *for* ⟨?⟩ having that particular pain is something from which it *follows* that I have a pain. Perhaps, rather, I have no evidence that I am feeling just *that* pain?

"Have you any evidence that he kicked her?" "Yes, I saw him do it"; or "No; but I saw him do it"? From "I saw him do it" there *follows* "he did kick her". But "I saw him kick her" ≠ "I saw *that* he kicked her"? Seeing him doing it *was* having evidence that he was kicking her? But you don't have *that* evidence *now*: having evidence *now* consists in knowing (by memory) that you saw him doing it.

When Crusoe saw the footprint on the sand he had evidence that a man had been there, & he knew that a man had. A dog or an idiot might have had that evidence, & *not* concluded that a man had been there. Crusoe's knowledge that a man had been there was a genuine case of inference. So with the dinosaur marks in the Conn. River Valley: there is *no doubt whatever* that they were made by the foot of an animal: this is *known*: but it is certainly a case of inference—inference by *analogy*. So too when I see the marks of birds' feet in the snow, or dogs' in the sand, or horses' hoofs in the mud.

But now compare Crusoe's inferential & indirect knowledge that a man had been on the island, with his knowledge, at the moment when he sees the footprint, that there is a footprint on the sand there. That it is a *footprint* means that it was made by a man, & *this* is inference. But what we have to consider is his knowledge that it *is sand* which is formed into *that pattern*: this is what I was saying to Blake was *not* immediate. That it's a pattern *in sand*, not an hallucination of a pattern in sand, not an *image* of a pattern in sand or a dreamt pattern in sand. This Crusoe certainly *knew*: but didn't he know it directly? What he knew was that that was *the surface* of a good thickness of fairly solid material (*not*, as in the case of the dog, that it had another side to it); that it was the surface of something much thicker than paper. Now he didn't see below the surface & therefore he didn't know *directly* that there was a good thickness of solid stuff below the surface. Was this as much an inference as that a man had been there? Perhaps. But that it was a *physical surface*, the surface of *something* solid, seems to be different. Suppose he had found he could put his hand through it, without in any way affecting it, & without feeling any pressure against his hand? What he knew, in knowing it was a surface of something solid, was that if he had been putting his hand there at the moment, he would have been meeting with resistance, *not* that if he were to put it there the moment after, he would.⟩

(b) If I say "That's a dog", one thing I'm saying is

(α) That's got another side. A shut-eye after-image hasn't got any other side; nor has a reflection.

(β) Its other side isn't as near to this side as the other side of a piece of paper is: it's of substantial thickness.

G   *Commonplace Book*

(γ) It therefore has a considerable inside—not as little as a piece of paper has—& isn't empty.

These are all things I've learnt by past experience, if I'm merely seeing the dog from one angle. Does it follow from this that I don't know them immediately?

I don't think of them, when I say "That's a dog"; but if I found any one of them wasn't the case, I should take this as proving that it wasn't a dog. I.e. when I say "That's a dog" it looks as if I were making a prediction: I shan't find that this has no other side; I shan't find that it's as thin as a piece of paper; I shan't find that it's empty. Can I possibly know that I shan't find these things? I don't know that I shan't get experiences, which, if I hadn't seen as much as I have seen about this surface, would make me sure that it wasn't a dog. But, having seen what I have, the result would be only that I shouldn't know what to think—e.g. whether a dog had suddenly changed into a thing as thin as a piece of paper, or such a thing been substituted for it. I.e. such experiences wouldn't *prove* that it wasn't a dog. But they would give me some reason to think that it wasn't.

It's not immediate, because I only know it because I have learnt by past experience that things that look like this always have a substantial thickness & an inside. If I only saw, felt & remembered what I do at this moment, I shouldn't know that it was a dog: this knowledge is due to my having learnt by experience how things generally behave. E.g. I don't now remember having seen the other side of these chairs (though I know I have seen them from various angles), but even if I did, I shouldn't know that these other sides still existed, but for knowledge by experience that things like that do go on existing after I cease to see them. *See p.* 16.[1] My grounds are *generalisations* which I've learnt by past experience; and I don't *remember* generalisations. Having learnt these things *is* having reasons for *saying* that this chair has another side & is of substantial thickness.

I look at a match-box & then feel one of its corners with my hand. How do I know that what I am feeling is the thing which I saw just now? How do I know that what I saw just now still exists? I look at the match-box & shut my eyes, & then look again; how do I know that what I see the second time is the same thing as what I saw before; & does it follow from the fact that it is, that it

[1] [I.e. entry no. 9 in this Notebook.]

existed all the time my eyes were shut? I turn the match-box round in my hand; how do I know that the different-looking surfaces I see are all surfaces of the same thing? How do I know that they are surfaces at all?

One can say: because, when things we see & feel are *related as* these are, i.e. our *seeings & feelings* of them are related, we *say* they're the *same* thing. What *kind* of relation? No-one can formulate it exactly. We know that it's right to say—"this is the same", in all sorts of different circumstances.

"I see that match-box." Do you see *the whole* of it? "Of course not; I *only* see the sides that are turned towards me: there are sides of it that I don't see." Consider the relation you have to this side, which you express by saying that you see it: have you got *that* relation to the match-box? "Certainly not: the relation I have to the match-box, & which I express by saying that I see *it*, is not the same as that which I have to this side, & which I express by saying that I see *it*, but is the relative product of the relation I have to several sides or parts of sides expressed by saying I see them, & the relation these have to the match-box expressed by saying they are sides of it. The criterion for saying that you see a match-box, is that you should see a considerable part of the surface of one; but the criterion for saying that you see a surface is not that you should see a considerable part of *the surface of* a surface—which is nonsense. Similarly the criterion for saying that X married money is that he should have married *a woman who owned a great deal of money*; but the criterion for saying that he married Mary Smith is *not* that he should have married a *woman who owned a great deal of* Mary Smith. The relation between him & *money* which we express by saying that he married money, is not the same as that between him & Mary Smith, which we express by saying that he married Mary Smith. But we need not say that "married" is used in a different sense in "He married money" & "He married a woman who owned a great deal of money". We can say, if we like, that both "married" & "money" are used in the same sense in both sentences. What we must say is that, even if they are, the relation to money which both sentences assert him to have come into, is not the same as the relation which the second asserts him to have come into to a woman. Similarly in the case of "I see this side of that match-box" & "I see that match-box", we may say, if we like, that "see" is used in the same sense in both cases, but the relation which the first asserts me to have to the side is not the same as that which the second asserts me to have to the match-box. Accordingly, *if* we use "see" as a name for the first relation, we shall be using it in a different sense from that in which we use it, *if* we use it as a name for the second."

15

SAYING THAT *P*

To say or write the words "I've got a pain" is not the same thing as *asserting* that you have a pain or even as *saying* that you have.

(1) You may both assert & say that you have one without using those words at all. You can do it *by* using words in another language, which mean the same (not *only* by saying such words). Whether you can be said to do so by groaning etc. is a doubtful question. If you groan on purpose to make people think so, you are using the groaning as a symbol, & may be either lying or telling the truth. But groaning, not done on purpose, is not even *used as* a symbol; though it is a sign that you are.

(2) When you do say or write the words, you certainly need not be *asserting* that you have a pain.

(a) When I wrote them above, I was neither asserting nor saying that I had a pain.

(b) In reading a book aloud if you read "I've got a pain", you are certainly not asserting that you've got a pain, & it could only be said in joke, by one who knew the circumstances, that you said you had.

(c) If a parrot is taught to say "I've got a pain", it has certainly not asserted that it had, though it might perhaps be said to have said that it had.

(d) Can an actor who says the words in acting a part, be said to have asserted or said that he had?

(e) A person, through some extraordinary accident, or in another language, uses "I've got a pain" to mean "I hear a hissing sound."

In all these cases something is lacking, or something present, or both, such that the presence of that something, or the absence of that other something, or both, is a *necessary* condition for having *asserted* that you had a pain, when you said the words, in our most ordinary use of "*assert*".

What is lacking?

(α) In (c) the parrot *attaches no meaning* to the words. One necessary condition for asserting is that you should *attach some meaning*. But what this consists in needs enquiry.

(β) In *all* 5 cases there is lacking the *intention* to make people believe or to let them know that you are in pain. But in the first four there is lacking the intention to make them believe or let them know (call this "convey") that what *you* mean by "I'm in pain" is the case, as well as the intention to convey that you're in pain; in (e) the intention to convey that what *you* mean by "I'm in pain" is the case may be present. Owing to this difference ⟨?⟩, there is a use of "assert" in which it's right to say in case (e), that you were asserting that you're in pain; there certainly is such a use: you *were* asserting it, only that you were in pain was not what you meant: you certainly *said* so.

I doubt if anything is *present* in any of these cases, the absence of which is necessary for "asserting" in the commonest sense.

We say then that there's *a use* of assert such that you only assert you are in pain when (1) you say or write "I am in pain" or equivalent words, (2) you attach the right meaning to these words, (3) you intend to convey that you are in pain.

There are 3 cases where you do this: (1) when you *have* got a pain, (2) when you haven't, subdivided into (a) are lying, (b) are joking (only intending to make people think so for a short time, & intending to undeceive them later).

What's meant by saying that in these cases you are "attaching the right meaning" to the words or "using them in their proper sense"? You are also doing so, in cases (a), (b) & (d); and the difference between them & these is only that there you don't intend to *convey* the idea that you are. ("Communicate", as distinct from "convey", seems to me to suggest only "let them know", not "make them think". If you're lying or joking, are you communicating that you're in pain? I think you can be said to be *conveying* the idea.)

When you are asserting, by means of saying the words, you certainly are, in a sense, using the words in a different *way* from that in which you use them in (a), (b) & (d), but, it might be said, *not* in a different *sense*. It's not *incorrect* to say you're using them in a different *way*; but is there any fixed sense of "way", such that it *follows* that in that sense you are? Cf. what Wittg. says about using a hammer in a different way.

But now what's meant by "attaching the right meaning" to "I've got a pain", when you say those words? We can say it means: *using* the words "I've got a pain" *to mean* that I've got a pain. This is something which is *not* the case in (a), (b), (c), (d) & (e): so that we should have to say I'm not attaching the right meaning to "I've got a pain" in (a), (b), & (d); & yet in a sense, I may be. And if I say these to *myself*, I've no intention to *convey* the idea that I have.

In the cases of lying & joking, to say that you use them to mean *that*, as distinct from e.g. using them to mean that you are hearing a hissing sound, is to say that you know what it would be like, if you had got a pain, & that you intend to convey that something *like that* (= of that sort) is the case. And you know what it would be like to have a pain, if you *can imagine* having a pain? You couldn't know what it would be like, if you'd never had one. Or does knowing what it would be like, merely consist in a capacity to *apply the words* correctly, i.e. to *say* you have, *only* when you have—that you haven't, *only* when you haven't? If you *can* do this, you *understand* the words; & you can do this, only if you *can tell* when you have & when you haven't. You can't lie, unless you *could* tell the truth. This capacity is knowing what *the words* mean.—No: it's not! A child might be so trained as to say "two", if he liked, *only* when "one" was said, & to say "not two", if he liked, *only* when it wasn't: but it wouldn't follow that he attached any meaning to "two": but he couldn't do this unless he *could tell* when "one" had been said & when it hadn't.—"Apply the words correctly" can be applied, perhaps, also to Wittg.'s case of understanding an order: you bring a brick only when "brick" is said.

You can understand a language, without necessarily being able to use it.

You "attach the right meaning" both when you understand, & when you use it correctly.

There's no such thing as "feeling sure" that you've got a pain, when you haven't; perhaps, therefore, also there's no such thing as "feeling sure" that you've got one, when you have. There is such a thing as "feeling sure" there's a table there; & *hence* this may happen both when there is & when there isn't.

There is such a thing as *knowing* that you're speaking the truth, when you say "I've got a pain"; because there's also such a thing as *knowing* that you're not, i.e. are lying or joking. But you may know you're speaking the truth in saying it, when you haven't in fact got one; namely if you use & understand "I've got a pain" in an unusual sense—a sense such that you may have a pain in the sense you mean, without having one in the ordinary sense; e.g. you might use & understand "I've got a pain" to mean "I'm hearing a hissing sound".

If you know that you're speaking the truth, when you say "I've got a pain", & also *are* using these words in the ordinary sense (you needn't know that the sense you're using them in is the ordinary one), do you *know* that you've got a pain? It seems to follow that you do; since the possibility (which exists in the case of "There's a table there") that you're speaking the truth because you *think* you have a pain, though you haven't, is excluded. (Speaking the truth, need not necessarily mean "saying something true": it *may* mean merely not lying or joking—not saying something which you know or believe to be false.)

"Are you sure?", said to a child who says she's got a pain, means "Aren't you lying?" *not* "Aren't you perhaps making a mistake?" *Can* a person lie, without knowing that he's lying?

There is a possibility of mistake & therefore also of a correct opinion about such things as "There's a table there", "There's no table there (it's a reflection)"; & I was inclined to think this means merely "Sometimes people do make mistakes about such things". But "There's no possibility of mistake about "I've got a pain", "I haven't" " doesn't seem to mean merely "People never do". What does it mean? *Not*, merely, surely "We have given no meaning to "I think I have a pain" "? "I thought I had a pain, but I hadn't" is *absurd*. Why? I want to say something like: If we are using both "I thought that" & "I had a pain" in their ordinary senses, then it is self-contradictory: like "He was a female brother".

Is it *logically impossible* that you should think you have a pain, when you haven't, or that you haven't, when you have? Yes, I think so. But what does this mean? & why is it? If it is, it's also logically imposs. that you should *think* you have, when you have, or that you haven't, when you haven't. Is it also *logically imposs.* that you should *know* you have, when you have, or that you haven't, when you haven't? or is it, on the other hand, *logically necessary* that you should *know* you have, when you have, & that you haven't, when you haven't?

If you have, you *can tell* that you have; & if you haven't, you *can tell* that you haven't.

But is this true of an animal, or any creature that hasn't a language?

16

SEE

Miss M. says, like Prichard: "Nobody has ever seen the moon, nor a chair etc."

They might say this on 2 quite different grounds, wh. I doubt if they distinguish:

(1) That what we *mean* when we say "I see the moon" is often true enough, but that this is not a correct or accurate way of expressing what we mean.

To this the answer is (a) It's not bad grammar like "There ain't no jam on the table".

(b) If it's not bad grammar & also everybody English, including the best educated, uses it & understands it in the sense I do (i.e. you're not misusing it as you would misuse "Broad" if you said by a slip "I saw Broad" when you meant "I saw Moore"), then it *is* accurate.

(2) That what we *mean* by "I see the moon" is always partly false.

The ground may be (a) that there is no such thing as the moon, (b) that we think, falsely, that we are having to the moon the same relation which we have to a closed-eye after-image = that our sense-datum of the moon is identical with the moon = Naïve Realism.

17

POSSIBLE

I distinguish 3 senses: (1) logically possible, (2) causally possible, (3) the sense in which "It's possible that p" = "It's not certain that not-p"

(1) People *in philosophy* say: The *props.* that I'm not sitting down now, that I'm not male, that I'm dead, that I died before the murder of Julius Caesar, that I shall die before 12 to-night, are "logically possible". But it's not English to say, with this meaning: It's possible that I'm not sitting down now etc.—*this* only means "It's not certain that I am" or "I don't know that I am". What we say is: I might have been standing up now, I might have been born & died before the murder of J. C., it might be true that I shall die before 12.

To say these props. are "logically possible" is to say *not* that it's logically possible they *are* true, but that it's logically poss. they *should have been* true, or log. poss. that it *should* be true that I shall die tonight: *should have been* only when we *know* it's not true?

On the other hand the props. "I'm both sitting down now & lying at full length on the floor", "I'm not male, & yet am a brother", "My tie is scarlet & yet isn't red", "I wasn't alive before 55 B.C. & yet I died before that" are *not* logically possible or *are* "logically imposs.". And here we *may* say: It's not possible that I am, *not* possible that my tie is, not possible that I was: though also "It's not possible that I should be or should have been", not possible that I might be.

But we should hardly say It's *imposs.* that my tie *is* scarlet & yet not red. But also my tie *couldn't* have been scarlet, without being red.

(3) I *may* go out this evening = I don't know that I shan't nor yet that I shall = It's possible I shall, but also possible I shan't. What proves that this doesn't mean merely: That I shall go out this evening is not a self-contrad. prop.? The proof is that where a prop. is *not* self-contradictory, I often know it's false: e.g. that I'm not sitting down now. If any one says: It's just possible that you're not; it's right to answer: No, there's no

chance that I'm not; I know I am. But: It's *possible* that I should not have been sitting now—I might not, is compatible with I know I am.

Contrast: "I *could* go out this evening, but I shan't," where "could" implies causal possibility, as opposed e.g. to the condition of a person in prison. We express this by: "It is possible for me to go out" not by "It's possible *that* . . .". "I could have come but I didn't" = It's not possible *that* I came, but it *was* possible *for* me to come.   I didn't come ↛ I couldn't come.

(2) But now about "causal poss.": does it differ both from (1) & from (3)?

That cat *can* climb trees; my dog *can't*. It's not logically imposs. that my dog should have been climbing a tree now, or should have in the past. But it is *imposs.* that he should be climbing one now: could this merely mean "I know that he isn't"?

No; because I may know that my cat isn't, & therefore it may be imposs. that she *is*, while yet it's not imposs. she should have been.

It's not logically imposs. that I should have been able to drive a car; but that I *can't* drive one is true though it's not logically imposs. that I should be driving one now.

If I can't, it follows that I'm not; but from fact that I'm not, it doesn't follow that I can't.

"My cat may be climbing a tree" → "My cat *can* climb trees"; but "My cat *can*" does *not* entail "My cat may be"; because I may know that she isn't.

"My cat *may* climb that tree" is (3); "My cat *could* climb that tree" is (2) (causal).

You can't have turned the light off = It can't be that you turned the light off = It must be the case that you failed to turn it off → I know you didn't, but I know you didn't ↛ It must be the case that you didn't = it can't be true that you did, bec. the latter implies: I know other things from which it *follows* (*not* logically; e.g. fact that the light is on, & nobody else has been there since you left) that you didn't, whereas "I know you didn't" does not entail this: it may be that I noticed you didn't, & know this because I remember.

"He *may* have been in London on Tuesday." "No, he can't have been, because he was in Vladivostock on Wed., & it's *imposs.* to get from London to V. in 24 hours." This isn't logical imposs., but it is *causal*: & we should certainly say "it *follows* he wasn't in London on Tu.", though it's not logical "following". This sort of reasoning is constantly used in Detective stories. Is it "causal"? "He can't have swallowed all that arsenic, bec., if he had, he would be dead."

"He got from London to Vlad. in 24 hrs." "That's *imposs.*: he can't have; nobody can."

My cat can climb trees = It's *possible* for her *to* climb trees = She has the power of climbing ≠ it's logically possible she should (since this is also true of dogs), nor yet "I don't know that she never does". This can't be put in form "It's possible that".

In 1850 it was not *possible* to travel at 200 miles an hour, now it *is* possible. There were not then any machines which made it *possible*, now there are.

Consequently, if any one had said in 1850: "A was in London at 12 & at Newcastle an hour later" it would have been right to say "That's imposs.: he can't have been: it's impossible that he should have been". But if any one said that now, it might be right to say: "Well, it's possible that he should have been; but it's not *possible* that he *was*, because in fact he was in Cambridge at 12." If any one objects: But isn't it *possible* he wasn't in Camb. at 12? The answer may be: "No; because I saw him there." If it is still objected: Isn't it *possible* you didn't see him there? the answer may be: "No: I remember quite clearly; and there was at the time no *possibility* of mistake." There is now no *possibility* of mistake as to my being sitting down: it's not *possible* that I'm standing up = I know I'm not. It's *possible* I *should be* (or should have been) standing up, both (1) in the sense that it's logically possible & (2) in the sense that it's *causally* possible (I am *capable* of standing up—I'm not paralysed): but it's not *possible* that I *am*, in the sense that I don't know for certain that I'm not.

How do I know I'm not? Is it because it's causally imposs. I should be having my present experience & be standing up? How could I have learnt that it is? Surely only if I *knew* on other occasions, when I had this kind of experience, that I was not standing up. And it's imposs. I should ever have *known* this, if before *knowing* it I had to know on other occasions that I was not standing up.

18

POSSIBLE

(1) *Logical.* It's possible that I should have been seeing exactly what I am seeing, & yet should have had no eyes.

I *might* have been seeing what I am & had no eyes.

It's possible that every dog that has ever lived should have climbed a tree.

(2) *Causal.* It's possible that I should have been blind now.

I *might* have been blind now.

It's possible that I should have travelled 200 miles since an hour ago.

(3) *Epistemic.* It's possible that Hitler is now (12 p.m. Oct. 26) dead.

Hitler *may* be dead.

It's possible T. is at 86.

That (1) and (2) both differ from (3) is shewn by the fact that "I know he's not" contradicts (3), & doesn't contradict (1) or (2).

(1) "He had on a tie which was scarlet & yet not red." But *that's impossible*! i.e. it's imposs. that a tie *should be* scarlet & not red.

"That woman is Smith's brother." But *that's* imposs. i.e. it's imposs. that any woman should be anybody's brother. It's not *imposs.* that she should once have been his brother. "That woman *was once* Smith's brother" is something wh. it's not imposs. should be true.

(2) "The switch may have turned on by itself without any one's touching it." No: that's imposs. *Causally* imposs. it is; but not *logically*, since one can quite clearly conceive a switch doing it. Switches *can't* turn on by themselves! Why not? & what does this mean? Simply that they never do? Animals *do* move of themselves; a cat *can* jump, a chair can't.

"Perhaps Fido has been climbing a tree." "How did Fido get up into that tree?" "Perhaps he climbed there himself." No, that's imposs.: dogs can't climb trees. If they could, they some-times would; but they never do. There's some difference between their paws & those of a cat, which makes it imposs. for them to

climb: scientists may be able to tell you what the difference is—
why they can't climb. They don't climb, *because* they can't; &
hence that they can't doesn't simply mean that they never do.

(3) "Perhaps we're not in a room now." No; that's imposs.;
there's not the smallest chance that we're not. Why not? & what
does *this* mean? Simply that people who have the sort of visual
experiences we have, always are in rooms? "We *must* be in a
room now" doesn't seem to mean the same as "It's impossible
that we're not". "You *must* have omitted to turn the light off"
means: "There's conclusive evidence that you didn't." The
evidence is: It wouldn't have been on now, if you had turned it
off; for (a) nobody else has been in the room & (b) switches can't
turn on by themselves. But "you certainly didn't" doesn't = "You
must have omitted": we shouldn't say the latter if we *saw* you come
out without turning it off: we then shouldn't have *inferred* that
you didn't.

"Why did the light go on then?" "Because somebody turned
the switch." This means: It wouldn't have gone on, unless somebody had turned the switch. But how about: It wouldn't have
happened that somebody turned the switch without the light
going on? "If you turn the switch, that will make the light go on."

At any time at which I *can* move my arm, something is *possible*
which is not possible at a time when I can't. *What* is possible?
That I *should* move my arm. But this doesn't mean that the prop.
"I should move my arm" which can only mean "I ought to" is
possibly true. What it does seem to mean is that the prop. "I
shall move my arm" is possibly true: so long as a person *can*
move his arm, you can't be sure that he won't. But "I can move
my arm, but I shan't" is not a contradiction, whereas "It's
possible that I shall, but I shan't" *is* a sort of contr. Hence "I *can*
move" $\nrightarrow$ "It's possible I shall": only "it's possible I should",
"it's possible for me to". "He can move his arm, but he won't" is
good sense, whereas "It's possible he will, but he won't" is *not*.

NOTEBOOK V

[c. 1942–1943]

RUSSELL'S DEFINITION OF "ONE"

"There is *only one* apple on this plate" $= (\exists\, x)$. x is an apple on this plate . nothing *other than* x is an apple on this plate.

Now $(\exists\, x)$. x is an apple on this plate $=$ There are one or more apples, or There is at least one, or There are not no apples, $\neq$ There are *some*, but this notion can be understood without understanding the difference between "only one" & "more than one" (many) $\therefore$ there is no vicious circle in above def.

But "only one" $\neq$ "one". What is the meaning of "one" in: If there are 2, there must be 1?

A "unit class" is a class with *only* one member. Does "there must be 1" $=$ "There must be an apple on this plate, which belongs to some unit class $=$ which is the only member of *some* class"?

No: rather "There must be 1 apple" $=$ There must be an object of which it can truly be said "This is *only one* apple"?

THE ACHILLES

Is every length infinitely divisible?

It seems as if, whatever length you take, it can be divided into 2 equal parts.

If so then in any length there *are included as parts an infinite number* of smaller lengths.

But on the other hand, if l_1 be any length, then, whatever smaller length, l_2, you take, some finite number of lengths l_2 will be greater than l_1.

Hence there is *no* length such that an infinite number of those lengths are included in any finite length; but there is an infinite series of *different* lengths, such that one of each *is* contained in any length you like to take, but will not make it up.

If t_1 & t_2 be 2 (finite) periods of time, of which t_1 is longer than t_2, then, no matter how small t_2 may be, there cannot be an infinite number of periods, of length t_2, contained in t_1.

Yet, if t_1 is infinitely divisible, an infinite number of periods of *different* lengths must be contained in it, but will not make it up.

If every one of an infinite series of successive periods has to pass away before Achilles catches the tortoise, he will never catch it.

If one second has passed since noon, it does not follow that every one of an infinite number of successive periods, each shorter than the one before, has passed since noon; since this latter could not have happened. But then aren't we denying that time is infinitely divisible?

3

KNOWLEDGE

I said at Ann Arbor "There is a window in the roof"; and said also later that if I didn't know this, when I said it, I never know anything of the kind.

Paul ? told me afterwards that this was a mistake: that what looked like a window merely covered an opaque portion of the dome.

When I said "There's a window" I certainly *thought* there was; but did I feel sure there was? or did I think it was certain there was? When I said that other thing *later*, I can be said to have thought *then* that it was certain there was. But when I said "There's a window" I don't think I did feel sure—if anyone had said at once "that's not a window", I should have been surprised, as I was when Paul told me, but I shouldn't have refused to admit I was mistaken: I shouldn't have asserted "I feel sure there is". But does this prove I didn't feel sure? No: how about Cook Wilson's slap on the back? Here the man would have said "I *felt* sure it was my friend"; but I doubt if I should have said here, I felt sure it was a window: only, I *thought* it was.

4

SENSE-DATA AND PHYSICAL OBJECTS

Suppose we say, as I want to say, that the directly seen object (the one which contains as parts or qualities all the others about which I should be speaking) about which I should be making some assertion if I said "This is one side of a page", *is* one side of a page, & *is* therefore this side of this page.

We have to admit (1) that I shouldn't be seeing this directly seen object, but for the occurrence of processes in the nerves of my head; i.e. that the fact that I do see it is causally dependent upon such processes, & (2) that the existence of this side of this page does *not* depend on the processes in the nerves of my head on which my seeing of it depends: that it *would* have existed at this moment, even if those processes had not occurred.

But it seems also (3) that this directly seen object would not have existed, if I had not been seeing it (Berkeley): (is it "could not"? that it's logically imposs. it should?) & that therefore its existence depends causally on the nervous processes on which the fact that I see it depends (how is this to be shewn?)

Taking these 3 together, we get

There have occurred in my head nervous processes of which it is true both (1) that this directly seen object would *not* have existed but for them & (2) that this side of this page *would* have existed even if they hadn't existed.

But if this directly seen object *is* this side of this page, isn't this a contradiction?

We seem to be committed to

There have been nervous processes upon which this directly seen object both (1) *does* causally depend & (2) does *not* causally depend.

I have tried to avoid this contradiction, by saying that though this directly seen object *is* one side of this page, yet to say that this side would have existed now, even if my eyes had been shut, does not mean that this directly seen object would have *existed*, in *one* sense of "exist", a sense namely in which "exists" entails "is perceived", but only that it would have in *another* sense, namely— (What? that, if I'd had my eyes open & had otherwise been as I am, I *should* have seen it?)

This seems like what Berkeley says about his study-table; but it doesn't seem at all satisfactory.

To say of a closed-eye after-image, that I have ceased to see it; of a pain, that I have ceased to feel it; of a subjective sound that I have ceased to hear it, seems to be the same thing as to say that it has ceased to exist.

But to say of this directly seen object that, if I close my eyes, I shall cease to see it, doesn't seem to be the same thing as to say that, if I close my eyes, it will cease to exist.

5

"RECOMMENDING" A USE OF WORDS

Take the case of the dog & the goat, or the man & the squirrel. Suppose A insists that the dog did go round the goat, & B that it did not. Are A & B merely "recommending" different uses of "go round"; & *not* differing in opinion? They're not differing in opinion as to what happened: aren't they differing in opinion as to the correct use of "go round"?

The facts are: (1) the dog was successively N, E, S & W of the goat, & also at every intermediate point of the compass from it; but (2) the dog was never at the back of the goat, nor at either of its sides, so that it is not the case, as it would have been if the goat had remained at rest, that, if the points on the goat's surface which were successively nearest to the dog, had been joined by a black line, this black line would have run right round the goat.

Now as a rule, when we go round an object, the object is not itself rotating, so that *both* (1) & the other condition, which (2) says was *not* fulfilled, *are* fulfilled—call it (3).

Now usage has established that if D had to G, *both* relation (1) *&* relation (3), then it is correct to say D "went round" G: and this means that if, in such a case, anyone were to say "D didn't go round B", he would be either *misusing* (using incorrectly) "went round", or denying what actually occurred—making a mistake or lying.

But usage has *not* established that if D had (1) to G, but did *not* have (3), it will be *incorrect* to say "D did *not* go round G", nor yet that it will be *incorrect* to say "D *did*".

It would certainly be *incorrect* to say "D did", if neither (1) nor (3) were fulfilled; & certainly *incorrect* to say "D didn't", if both (1) & (3) were: but this is all that has been established by usage.

Now what are A & B doing, if A insists "D did", & B insists "D didn't"?

A is definitely making a mistake, if by "D did" he means "It would be definitely incorrect to say "D didn't" ", or, *as* definitely incorrect as to say "D didn't", when (1) & (3) are both fulfilled.

Isn't it possible A does mean one or both of these? He certainly has not *realised* that he means these: but very probably, if he were brought to admit that they were both untrue, he would cease to insist that D did; which would shew that he *did* mean one or other of them. It is only if he wouldn't cease, that there would be ground for saying that he is recommending—saying "You *ought* in such a case to say "D did" ". And even then, there is another alternative: he might mean: "It would be misleading to say "D didn't" without an explanatory qualification"—which is true, & is a prop. about usage.

Similarly B is definitely making a mistake if by "D didn't" he means it is as definitely incorrect to say "D did" as it would be if neither (1) & (3) were fulfilled.

Isn't it possible B does mean this? He won't have realised that he does: but he might cease to insist "D didn't" if he realised that this *was* a mistake; which would be a reason for saying that it was what he meant. But he might still insist that it would be misleading to say "D did" without explanatory qualification—which is true, & a prop. about usage; and he might be brought to see that "D didn't" is not a proper way of saying this. Only if he still insisted "D didn't", would there be ground for saying that he is making a recommendation—saying "You ought to say, "D didn't", though in refusing to do so you won't be going against usage as you would if you refused to say "D didn't" when neither (1) nor (3) were fulfilled": is saying "The usage ought to be altered", so that it would be as wrong to say "D did" here, as it would be where neither (1) nor (3) are fulfilled.

6

WHAT IS FIXED BY USAGE?[1]

(1) Anybody who knew that conditions (1) & (3) were both fulfilled by D & G, & was using "not" correctly, & yet asserted in earnest (not joking) that D did *not* go round G, would be either lying or, if he spoke sincerely, would be misusing "go round"—using it *incorrectly*.

(2) Anybody who knew that *neither* (1) *nor* (3) was fulfilled, & yet asserted in earnest that D did go round G, would be either lying, or, if he spoke sincerely, using "go round" *incorrectly*.

Usage fixes therefore that 2 uses of "go round" are *incorrect*; but, of course, it fixes also that lots of others are also incorrect.

(3) Anybody who *used* the words "D went round G", *to assert* that conditions (1) & (3) were both fulfilled, would be using "go round" *correctly*.

(4) Anybody who *used* the words "D did not go round G" *to assert* that neither (1) nor (3) was fulfilled, would be using "go round" *correctly*.

Usage fixes that these 2 are *correct*, but it does *not* fix that they alone are.

There may be usages which usage does not fix as either correct or incorrect.

Now a person like A, who knows that (1) is fulfilled & that (3) is not, & who yet insists that D did go round G, may mean that *usage has fixed* it that a person who knows this, & the use of "not", & yet asserts in earnest that D did not go round G, is either lying or using "go round" *incorrectly as strongly* as it has fixed (1).

If A does think this he is making a mistake. He need not know that this is what he means; but, if, on its being pointed out to him that this is a mistake, he ceases to insist that D did go round, we may say it was what he meant without knowing it.

Condition (1) is: There was a plane such that D moved through a curve in that plane, such that every radius of a circle in that plane of which G was the centre cut that curve in some point or other.

---

[1] [Cf. the preceding entry.]

Condition (3) is: D so moved that at one point he was opposite (nearest to) G's head, at another opposite G's tail, & at others opposite to all points on G's body intermediate in some plane between G's head & tail.

Now, if (1) & (3) were both satisfied, it would be *definitely wrong* to say D did *not* go round G.

What does this mean? That, if, in such a case, a man said "D did go round G", he would not mislead anyone, bec. this phrase would not lead anyone to expect *more* than that (1) & (3) both happened?

(But do we need to say: Anyone who *knew English*? or, who understood "went round"?)

But in the case where (1) is true, & (3) not, it is *not* definitely wrong to say "D didn't", nor yet to say "D did".

But in both cases it may mislead, *unless* you add a qualification.

You ought to say "D didn't, *but* he did fulfil (1)"

& "D did, *but* he never got opposite G's tail".

Where (1) & (3) are both true, *no* qualification is needed to avoid misleading in saying "D did"; & where *neither* is true, none is needed to avoid misleading in saying "D didn't".

A says, in case where (1) is fulfilled & (3) is *not*: D did go round G, meaning It is correct to say D did, & *therefore* not correct to say D didn't.

B says: D didn't, meaning It is correct to say D didn't, & *therefore* not correct to say D did.

Which, or whether either, is right, depends upon what would be conveyed to a person, who didn't know what sort of case they were considering, i.e. one in which (1) was, & (3) wasn't [fulfilled].

Now "D did" *might* convey to such a person that both (1) & (3) were, & therefore mislead.

And "D didn't" *might* convey that neither (1) nor (3) was, & therefore mislead.

If, on the other hand, (a) the case were one in which both (1) & (3) held, "D did" would mislead nobody; & if (b) it were one in which neither (1) nor (3) held, "D didn't" would mislead nobody.

Let us express the difference between A's "D did", & the

"D did" in case (a), by saying that in the latter "D didn't" would be *definitely* incorrect, in the former *not*.

And the difference between B's "D didn't" & the "D didn't" in case (b), by saying that in the latter "D did" would be *definitely* incorrect, in the former *not*.

If A means to say that "D didn't" would be *definitely* incorrect he is making a mistake.

And if B means to say that "D did" would be *definitely* incorrect, he is making a mistake.

And unless they do mean this, they are not contradicting one another; though they might be *recommending* different things— i.e. that it should in such cases *be made* definitely incorrect to say (A) that "D didn't", (B) that "D did".

Aren't they contradicting one another? If they are, they're *not* making recommendations.

If A says there's *no* difference in point of correctness between his "D did" & that in (a), he's definitely making a mistake; & similarly B is making one, if he says there's no difference between his "D didn't" & that in (b).

(X) "D didn't, although he fulfilled (1)" is *not* a contradiction; & (Y) "D did, although he didn't fulfil (3)" is *not* a contradiction. A, on my view, is saying that X *is* a contradiction, & B is saying that Y is a contradiction: & both are wrong: but then can they be contradicting one another? Yes, they can: because A is *also* saying that Y is *not* contradiction; & B *also* that X is not.

The "recommend" people have to shew that A & B are *not* contradicting one another on a point of usage like this.

It's not *definitely* incorrect to say "D did", & also not *definitely* incorrect to say "D didn't". These 2 are logically equivalent to it's not *definitely* correct to say "D did", & not *definitely* correct to say "D didn't".

If A is saying that "D did" is *definitely* correct & "D didn't" *definitely* incorrect, he is wrong; & so is B, if he says "D didn't" is *definitely* correct, & "D did" *definitely* incorrect.

But if A & B are *both* wrong, can they be contradicting one another?

Yes, because A is *also* saying a true thing, viz. " "D did" is *not* definitely incorrect", which B denies; & B a true thing, viz. " "D didn't" is not definitely incorrect", which A denies.

"D did" is *definitely correct* $\rightleftarrows$ "D didn't" is definitely incorrect, & hence → the weaker prop. "D did" is *not* definitely incorrect.

Similarly "D did" is *def. incorrect* entails the weaker prop. "D did" is not def. correct.

So that A is saying the truth in implying "D did" is *not* def. inc., & a falsehood in saying "D didn't" is def. incorrect; B is saying truly "D didn't" is *not* def. inc., & falsely "D did" is def. inc.

Usage has not fixed that "D did" *entails* that (3) holds, & also not fixed that "D did" does *not* entail that (3) holds. Either usage is *allowable*, i.e. correct, but not *definitely* correct.

A & B, no doubt, have not distinguished between "correct" & "*def.* correct"; & "incorrect" & "def. incorrect".

" "D didn't" is incorrect" is true, if it means merely " "D did" is not def. inc."; & is then quite compatible with " "D didn't" is not def. inc.", which is also true.

7

EXTERNAL OBJECTS

Is the statement "There are external objects" "empirical"?

"A soap bubble existed at noon yesterday" *entails* "An external object existed at noon yesterday".

Why?

Because A. " "A soap-bubble existed at noon" does *not* entail "Somebody was having an experience at noon" ".

A is, of course, *not* empirical.

B. $(\exists \phi) . (\exists x) \phi x t_1 \nrightarrow$ Somebody was having an experience at t_1. [B] is not empirical.

"There are external objects" = There are now & have been in the past objects of some kind, ϕ, such that $(\exists x) \phi x t_1$ does not entail x was being perceived at t_1.

We might say: x is an external object = x has a property such that to say that a thing has that property is to say that it *can* exist unperceived (= from the prop. that there is a thing with that property it does *not* follow that anything is being perceived).

Suppose a philosopher says (a) "There's a hand" is self-contradictory, ∴ (b) There are no hands.

(a) is non-empirical, (b) is empirical; though, *if* (a) were true, (b) would be a tautology, since, if p is a contradiction, $\sim p$ is a tautology.

From " "There's a hand" is contingent" there follows " "There's a hand" is *not* self-contradictory".

From "There are hands" there follows " "There are hands" is not self-contradictory".

From "There are hands" there FOLLOWS "It makes sense to say "There are hands" " but *not vice versa*.

⟨No: nothing follows about the *words* "There are hands".⟩

But "That there are hands" can be established by empirical evidence: anything which can be established by empirical evidence, can't be self-contradictory.

8

PERCEPTION

1. I saw a man, but I didn't recognise that it was a man, didn't think that it was, didn't see that it was: *thought* I was having an hallucination, doubted whether I wasn't, thought it was a rock.

Those bisons saw the Indians in wolf-skins, but didn't *recognise* them *as* men.

Animals may recognise an object which they see *as* a man; and can be said to *know* that it is a man, or to see that it is? Can they be said to *think* that a scare-crow is a man, to mistake it for a man, to doubt whether it is a man or not?

2. A dog can *see that* you have a piece of meat in your hand; & can be said to *know* that you have.

9

"ABSTRACT" UNIVERSALS (*RE* BLANSHARD)

There are attributes & relations, such that nothing *can* (logically possible) possess the attribute in question, & no things can be related by the relation in question, unless the thing or things in question also possess some more specific (determinate) attribute or relation, which is such that this more specific attribute or relation is *not* a *conjunction* of the first with other attributes or relations.

To have shape, to be coloured, to be triangular, to be red are attributes such that it is a contradiction to suppose a thing to have shape, & yet not to have any particular shape, to be coloured, but not to be of any particular colour, to be red & not to be of some particular shade (or shades) of red, to be triangular & not to be either scalene or isosceles or. . . . I.e. to be triangular but not to have any shape is a contradiction, but not because "triangular" is a conjunction of which "having shape" is one conjunct: "triangular" does not *include* "having shape" in the sense in which "hard & round" *includes* both "hard" & "round".

Similarly, "to be at some distance from", "to be related to" (in the sense in which "I am related to my cousin", means "I am a relation of my cousin's"), "to have begun before".

We may, if we please, say that such attributes (or relations), are not "abstract", meaning that they cannot belong to a thing, unless the thing has some other attribute, which entails them, without being a conjunction in which they are a conjunct.

10

UNIVERSALS

How can we explain what is meant by saying "So & so is a universal"?

A beginning of explanation can be made by saying that we sometimes *assert the same thing* about two different things: e.g. "Socrates was a Gk.", "Plato was a Gk.", "This (pointing) is white & so is that" (pointing to something different), "Red is a colour & so is blue", "To be triangular is to have a shape, & to be square is also to have a shape."

But, of course, to assert "Socrates was a Gk." is *not* to assert the same thing as to assert "Plato was a Gk."; yet we can say that in asserting the first we are asserting *the same thing about* S. as we are asserting about P. when we assert the latter. That which we *assert about* both in this sense is "a universal"; and anything which *can* be asserted, in this sense, *about* each of two different things is a universal.

But suppose a Gk. one day had pointed to a man & said "That's Socrates" & then on another had pointed to a man & said "That's Socrates": would what he asserted about the man pointed to on each occasion be a universal? It would, by our definition; since even if it was the same man he pointed to on each occasion, he *could have* asserted (mistakenly) the same thing about a different man. Yet it does not follow from this that Socrates is or was a universal. Why not? It does seem to follow that "being Socrates" *is*. It has sometimes been asserted (quite rightly) that the "is" of predication must be distinguished from the "is" of identity; and it seems as if one can say here that "That *is* Socrates" = "That *is identical with* Socrates", & that "being identical with Socrates" *is* a universal, though Socrates isn't. But what is meant by "is identical with Socrates"? S. was not identical with himself: it is nonsense to say that he was. And, of course, "That is Socrates" does not mean "That man is called "Socrates" ": *but perhaps it does mean* "That is the man who is most *often meant* by the word "Socrates" " ("most often" either in my circle, or in general).

I think it's doubtful, whether "universal" is so used that in such a case what a man would be asserting about what he pointed

at would be a "universal"; &, if so, we ought to modify our
definition in such a way as to say that [a universal is] anything
which can be *asserted about* each of 2 different things, *except* the
sort of thing you *assert about* an object at which you point when
you use a proper name & say "is x" where the only value x can
take is a proper name.

But now how about relations? A relation is always a "universal",
but no relation is "what can be asserted about" any single thing.

(a) Let's say: When you *can* assert the same thing about one
couple or *trio* or . . . of things as about another couple, what is
asserted about a couple or trio etc. is a universal & a relation.

E.g. what you *assert about* George V & George VI when you
say "G. V was the father of G. VI" is the same as what you assert
about Edw. VII & George V when you say "Edw. VII was the
father of G. V".

What you assert about red, orange & yellow when you say
"red is more like orange than it is like yellow" is *the same* as
what you assert about blue, green, & yellow when you say "blue
is more like green than it is like yellow".

But now you can *assert about* George V & George VI "G. V
& G. VI were both male", & you are asserting *the same about*
Edw. VII & G. V if you say "E. VII & G. V were both male".

Is what you *assert* about these couples in this case a "relation"?

I think "relation" is sometimes used in a wide sense in which
it is; but

(b) in a narrower sense, some people would say: You only
have a relation, when what is *asserted about* a couple (or trio
etc.) is such that the assertion is not logically equivalent to a
conjunction of two conjuncts in each of which the same thing
is asserted about one member of the couple as in the other is
asserted about the other.

Thus in this narrow sense: "G. V & G. VI were both male"
won't assert a relation between G. V & G. VI; but G. V & G. VI
were *of the same sex*, though entailed by the last, *will*: "A & B are
both one foot square" won't, but "A & B are the same size" will.

Relations in the narrow sense may be (1) symmetrical, e.g.
"x is the same size as y", from which there follows "y is the
same size as x", (2) non-symmetrical, e.g. "x loves y", which is
consistent both with "y loves x" & with "y does not love x", &
(3) asymmetrical, e.g. "x is larger than y" which *entails* "y is

not larger than x" ($\sim$ (y is larger than x)); the battle of Waterloo happened before the battle of the Marne; I wrote the words on the last page *before* I wrote these words; blue is darker than yellow.

But now: I, this sheet of paper, the sun can't be *asserted about* anything, or any couple or trio etc. of things, in the sense in which either an attribute or a relation can. These things, therefore, are *not* universals.

Also, suppose, with my eyes shut, I see an after-image containing two blue spots, of exactly the same shape, size & shade of blue, these blue spots are not universals.

Also, suppose I say "now": that utterance of "now" is an event, & is *not* a universal, though it may, internally, be exactly like another utterance of "now".

I distinguish the two spots by their being in different places; and this is different from distinguishing them by their relations to other things, although they can't be in different places without having different relations to other things (?). So, if I say, "now, now" I distinguish the two "nows" by their being at different times—one *before* the other—& this is different from distinguishing them by their relations to other things.

When I say "now" I am using the utterance (the token) to say something about itself; just as when I say "That ash-tray is mine" I am using the ash-tray to say something about itself.

Ramsey urges against this that "Socrates is wise" = "Wisdom characterises Socrates", and that you may just as well say, therefore, that Socrates is something that can be asserted of wisdom, as that wisdom is something that can be asserted of Socrates. If you say "Socrates is wise" & "Socrates is a Gk.", you are asserting *the same thing* about "wisdom" & "being a Greek". Wisdom once urged that what you are asserting of "wisdom" & "being a Gk." is *not* "Socrates", but "characterises Socrates". But why should you not say equally that what you are asserting of Socrates is *not wisdom* but "is characterised by wisdom"? Does "red" = "is red"?

⟨Ramsey's argument to shew that there are no complex universals, can, I think, be completely met by saying that though complex universals are never *ultimate* constituents of props., they *are* constituents. A prop. can only have one set of *ultimate* constituents, but it can have many different sets of *constituents*.⟩

11

"PERSPECTIVES"

In the Lowell Lectures,[1] one way in which R. uses "a perspective" is = "a direct visual field".

He suggests that *the* place in which a physical object is, is *the* perspective which is related in a certain way to all perspectives in which there is an "aspect" of the object in question, e.g. a penny.

But from his description of the kind of relation which this perspective must have to the perspectives in which there is an "aspect" of the penny, it turns out that there is no single perspective which has this relation to them all, but a whole group of perspectives each of which has this relation to *one* group (series) among the perspectives which contain aspects & *not* to others.

To be consistent, then, we must say that there is *no* perspective which is *the* place in which the penny is; but that there are a number of different perspectives, each of which is a member of the *group* that is that place.

The perspective I have now, i.e. my present direct visual field, is a *member* of the group which is *the* place in which my head is now; but it cannot be said that it is *the* place in which my head is now, nor yet that it is *in* that place in the sense in which my head is in that place: it might be said to be *included* in that place, in the sense that it is a member of the class that is that place.

It cannot even be said to be *the* two-dimensional region in physical space (the "point of view") from which I see what I do see, since every two-dimensional region in physical space is a *group* of perspectives, namely all the perspectives, each of which stands in a certain relation to any series of perspectives (from one direction) each of which contains an aspect of any physical surface which occupies that region.

More important still: any "aspect" which is in my present perspective in the sense in which an aspect of part of the surface of my piano is *in* it, can't possibly be "inside my head" in the sense in which my brain, or any part of it, or any surface of any part of it, is "inside my head". It is only "in$_1$" a perspective which is a member of a group of perspectives, which is the place

[1] [B. Russell, *Our Knowledge of the External World* (London, 1914).]

where my head is; whereas any part of my brain is only "in₂" that group of perspectives in the sense that all perspectives in which there is an "aspect" of that part have a certain relation to some member of that group. An "aspect" could only be "in" a physical place, or "inside" one, in the sense in which a physical thing or surface can be, if there were "aspects" of that aspect—if it were a "logical construction" out of other aspects, which of course it can be; for to say that a physical thing or surface is "in" or "inside" a certain physical region, is to say that *aspects* of it are related in a certain way to that region.

The place where my brain is is inside the place where my head is. What does this mean in terms of perspectives? We must imagine that my skull were transparent, so that my brain could be seen inside. If that were so, an observer approaching my head would reach a perspective which was one of the group constituting the place where my head is, *before* he reached any member of the group constituting the place where my brain is. Can we say that the perspectives constituting the place where my brain is are part of (included in) the perspectives constituting the place where my head is?

Suppose we could approach the full moon. We should reach a perspective constituting part of the place where the moon is as soon as we reached one in which we could no longer see the whole circular outline of the moon. After that we should have perspectives in which there were "aspects" of *parts* of the moon, but no "aspects" *of the moon.*

Suppose you could continue *through* the moon. You would never come to a perspective containing an aspect of the moon, and yet you would get beyond perspectives which formed part of the place where it is. How distinguish those which do from those which don't? Those which don't are those such that, *if you turned round in that place,* you would get a perspective which contained an aspect of a part of the moon. And, "if you *turned round*" can be replaced by "if you got a set of perspectives related to one another in the way in which when you turn round in a place, you get them": the theory being that *part* of what you mean by saying you've turned round is that you get perspectives related in that way: that you *get* such is one reason for saying you are turning round. Kinaesthetic sensations of a certain sort are another, but usually the two go together.

12

PHENOMENALISM

What do I mean by saying that this is a sheet of paper, when I'm not touching it?

Part of what I *mean* (but only in the sense that this is *entailed* by my prop.?) is that *if* my hand had now been *there, and* I had been, as I am, capable of tactile sensations, I should have had that sort of tactile sensation.

But what does "if my hand had been *there*" mean? It means if, starting from a little while ago, i.e. from a sense-field I had a little while ago, I had had, instead of those I did have, a series of the sort I should have had if I'd moved my hand into contact with this piece. But what does this mean?

When I am feeling (touching) a surface adjacent to a surface I am seeing, there is usually an *immediately perceived* relation between the touch-sensation & the visual sensation, & that these sensations are related in that way is *part* of my reason for saying that the one is of a surface adjacent to the surface *of* which the other is.

There is also (?) an immediately perceived relation between a visual sensation & a subsequent tactual one, which makes me say (is part of my reason for saying) that the tactual one is of the *same* surface of which the visual one *was*. (*Or* the other way about.)

"Put your finger on that spot." How do I know that I have done this? (1) The spot has disappeared = I no longer have a visual sensation of a certain kind in the part of my visual field in which I had it just now. (2) I have a visual sensation of my finger *in front of* that part. (3) I have a tactual sensation, *behind* the visual sensation of my finger, & adjacent to visual sensations which *were* adjacent to the visual sensations of the spot.

When I say the tactual sensation is *directly perceived* to be "adjacent" to one visual sensation & "behind" another, I mean by "adjacent to" a directly perceived relation which is not I think the *same* as that meant by "adjacent to" in the case of 2 visual sensations, & by "behind" a relation which perhaps (how about *transparent* visual sensations?) [is] not identical with any directly perceived relation between 2 visual; though of course one visual can be directly perceived to be *further off* than another.

Perhaps therefore there is no directly perceived *spatial* relation between a visual & a *subsequent* tactual (or vice versa). Of course there is a directly perceived *temporal*. But the directly perceived spatial are only "*behind*" & "*adjacent to*" *simultaneous* visual, and that the tactual is of the same surface of which the previous visual *was* is said because of the *conjunction* of these facts with the fact that the adjacent visual is of the same surface of which a previous visual *was*.

13

NUMBER

(1) Why is mathematics useful in physics?

From the fact that you have put first 3, & then 2, balls into an empty bag, & that no more have been put in, nor any taken out, it does not follow that there are 5 there *now*, though it *does* that 5 were put in. If the result of thus *physically* "adding" 2 to 3 was always that there are 6 there or 0 or 1 etc., it would not follow that 3 + 2 = 5 is untrue. The arithmetical prop. 3 + 2 = 5 is quite independent *logically* of any prop. about the results of *physically* adding, which is a *physical* prop. From the arithmetical prop. *no* prop. about the results of *physically* adding follows; nor from any prop. of that sort does the arithmetical prop. follow.

How, nevertheless, arithmetic is useful is as follows. Suppose you know that your bank balance on the 10th was $100; and that you have drawn cheques since for 27, 9, 8, 17, 11, 14, 3, 31, 5. You *want* to know whether you've over-drawn. From your knowledge of these 2 facts by *themselves* you can't tell at once (perhaps a lightning calculator could). You have to calculate—here in one of the simplest forms—by addition. I now have calculated: 125 is the result. And I should then know, as I didn't before, that I *have* over-drawn. Of course it isn't the *mere* arithmetical fact that the sum of those numbers is 125, that enables me to know this. I must also know the physical facts that the numbers I wrote on the cheques, & the number entered in the bank-books as my balance, won't have changed automatically. But the arithmetical fact *together* with the physical do enable me to know something I shouldn't have known *without* the arithmetical fact. Of course some people would say that to know you've drawn cheques for 27, 9, 8, 17, 11, 14, 3, 31, 5 is *the same thing* as to know that you've drawn cheques for 125; whereas Kant, holding that the prop. 27 + 9 + 8 + 17 + 11 + 14 + 3 + 31 + 5 = 125 is "synthetic" would say it's *not* the same thing. But, whichever of these you say, it's certain that to know you've drawn cheques for 125 does enable you to draw an inference which the mere knowledge of the accounts of the separate cheques does *not*. The arithmetical prop. is *useful*.

(2) Is a number a "second-order" property—a property of a property?

When you say: *These* dots are 5; these dots are 3; ⟨But you don't ever⟩ it seems not to be. And "This group of dots is a *quintet*", seems to mean the same as "This group is a group of 5".

One wants to make a distinction between A. "This group is a trio" & B. "*This* is brown".

A = This group is a group of 3 & no more.

R. seems to suggest that e.g. This group is a trio = The property of being identical with either this or that or that, belongs to 3 things & no more. This seems at first sight to be very artificial. But we *can* say: either this dime, or that one, or that one must be the one I got at that shop, i.e. the property of being identical either with this or with that or with that *does* belong to that dime I got.

⟨"I'll give you a trio of dimes" = "I'll give you 3 dimes" = "I'll give you 3 dimes & no more".

So that in one usage "three" seems = "a trio *of*".

But does "being 3" = "being a trio"? Perhaps in one usage. You can count down 3 dimes & say "*That's* 3", but hardly "*Those* are 3"; while you can say "Those are a trio" *or* "That's a trio".

But "a trio of dimes" = "a group of 3 dimes & no more", and *this* is a use of "three", where "three" ≠ "a trio of". You can't say: "This pile is a pile *of a trio* of dimes", while you can say "This pile is a pile of 3 dimes". You *can* say "This pile consists of a trio of dimes" or "This pile consists of 3 dimes". "There *are* 3 dimes here" = "There *is* a trio of dimes here" = "There is a group of 3 dimes here".

But where "3 dimes" = "a group of 3 dimes", has "3" the same meaning in the first expression as in the second?

"I'll give you 3 dimes" = The property of being a dime given you by me shall belong to 3 things & 3 only. Here for "3 things & 3 only" you can substitute "a trio of things & *not* any group larger than a trio".⟩

"This group is a group of 5" = these *collectively* are 5; "These are brown" (This group is a group of brown things) = "*Each* of these is brown".

Does "This group is a group of 5" = "this, that, that, that & that *are* five"? No: *make a group* of 5.

Does "This group is a group of 5" — "there are 5 dots there"
or "the dots that are there are 5 in number"? No!

"There are 5 dots there" = "The property of "being a dot
there" belongs to *five* things" = ($\exists$ x, y, z, w, α) x is a dot there,
y is, z is, w is, α is. If 5 = *only* five, we have to add: "& nothing
else is". But, if it doesn't, this account seems inconsistent with
saying that ($\exists$ x) ϕx = it's not the case that nothing is a ϕ.

"There are some white dots there" = ($\exists$ x, y, z . . . .) x is a
white dot there, y is, z is . . . .

"That group of dots is five in number" = "the class consisting of this dot, that, that, that & that has 5 members".

"This collection is a trio" = The number of members of this
collection is 3, and this seems equivalent to saying something
about the property "being a member of this collection".

"This collection is a trio" = This collection is a collection of
3 things.

This collection of dots is a collection of 5 dots (= 5 & no
more). What are we saying of a collection when we say it is a
collection of 5 dots?

"This, that & that, taken together *make up* a group of 3 things."

"That group there is a group of 3 things."

"This, that & that are all brown" = "This is brown, that is
brown & that is brown" a conjunction of 3 independent props.

But "This, that & that make up a trio" is *not* a conjunction of 3
independent props.

"That group has 3 members."

Which group? Answer: "The group which consists of this,
that & that".

But we can't say "This, that & that have 3 members"; i.e. "this,
that & that" does *not* mean the same as "that group".

But we can say "This, that & that *are* (or "make up") a group
of 3 *objects*".

If we say "That's a group of 3", there must be some answer
to the question "3 *whats*?" Whereas if I say "That's brown",
"brown" doesn't need a supplement. We *can* ask "a brown *what*?"
But "That's brown" is a complete prop. by itself; whereas "That's
a group of 3" isn't.

"There are 5 dots in that region" *entails* "There are 3 dots
there". But "That group of dots is a group of 5 dots" *contradicts*
"That group is a group of 3".

"That's *one* thing" is not like "That's a brown thing": it does *not* mean that's a thing which has the property of being "one" (which is nonsense!)

"I'll give you *one* thing" ≠ "I'll give you a thing which has the property of being "one" ", whereas "I'll give you *a* brown thing" = "I'll give you a thing which has the property of being brown". We can't say "I'll give you *a* "one" thing".

It does look as if a group of 3 dots is *identical* with those 3 dots, i.e. with this, that & that: yet we can say "That group has 3 members" & *can't* say "This, that & that have 3 members."

A group of 3 hasn't got the property of "being 3": it only has the property of "having 3 members". There is no such property as that of "being 3": "3" is *not* a property; not even a property of a property: "having 3 members & no more" *is* a property—a property of a group.

(a) "There are 3 dots here" is profoundly different from (b) "There are white dots here". (b) = "There are *some* white dots here" = "There are here some dots which are white" = "some dots *each* of which is white". But (a) ≠ "There are some dots here each of which is 3". (a) = "There's a group of dots here which is a *group of white dots*": but "group *of* 3 dots" & "group *of* white dots" are profoundly different: "group of white dots" = group of dots, each of which is white; "group of 3 dots" ≠ "group of dots each of which is 3".

"Having 3 members" is not like "having *brown* members" in the respect that a separate meaning can't be given to "3" as it can to "brown".

"There are 3 dots here" = "There is here a group of dots having 3 members & no more".

To say of a group that it has 3 members & no more, is to say of some *property* which belongs to each member of the group that it *applies* to 3 things & no more.

"Applying to 3 things & no more" is the ultimate conception. Is it?

We understand what's meant by saying of a group or collection of things that "it has 3 members & no more."

We also know what's meant by saying of a "property" or "characteristic" that it applies to 3 things & no more.

What's meant by "This, that & that *form a group*"? Only

that there's some property which belongs to each & to nothing
else?

"*The* group of which this, that & that are the only members" =
The group of which each member has the property of being
either this or that or that. This is a property which *can't*
belong to anything but this & that & that. But there may well
be other properties which do *in fact* only belong to this & that
& that.

What is "the number 3"? Can we say it is "the property of
having 3 members & no more" or "the property of applying or
belonging to 3 things & no more"? It is certainly a property
which belongs to all trios & to nothing else: but *this* property
is that of "having 3 members & no more". But is there only *one*
such property? Not necessarily: the number 3 is *the* property
which we ascribe to a trio when we say it is a trio—i.e. the property of being a trio.

Why should R. say that the number 3 is the class of trios? or
that it is the class of classes similar to *this* class—where *this*
class is any trio? This latter is equivalent to saying that the
property of *being a trio* is that of being similar to *this* class—where
this is a trio. But then there are as many different properties each
of which is that of being a trio, as there are trios.

We *don't* understand what's meant by saying of a *group* that
it "has only one member"; since by a group we mean something
which has more than one.

But we *do* understand what's meant by saying of a property
that "it applies to only one thing".

Can we say that the number 1 *is* the property of applying only
to one thing?

We can say "This is *one* dot & only one". Are we saying: This
has the property of being a dot? This is *a* dot → This is only *one*
dot. Does this = The property of being *both* this & a dot, belongs
to only one thing?

This is brown ⇄ This is a brown thing ⇄ This is one &
only one brown thing ⇄ This is one & only one instance of a
brown thing.

But we can't say: This is one instance of a thing that's *one*—of
a "one" thing.

But: "*This* is *one* brown thing, & not more than one". "There's
only one brown thing *here*".

There *can't* be more than one instance of a brown thing which is identical with *this* thing.

This thing must possess some property which no other brown thing possesses.

This thing must possess some property which nothing else possesses.

It *must* be the only thing to which some property applies = There must be some property which applies to it & to nothing else.

This is a specimen of a white dot, & that is a specimen of a white dot; ∴ this & that, *taken together*, are two specimens of white dots. The group formed of this & that, has 2 & only 2 white dots for members. This, that & that, *taken together*, are a *specimen* (= one & only one specimen) of a trio = of a group, which has 3 & only 3 members. But what does "taken together" mean?

Montague relies on likeness between "That's a specimen of a brown thing" and "That group is a specimen of a group (of 3) having 3 members" or "Those 3 dots are a specimen of a group of 3".

"Those dots there" are 3 *in number*, is *not* like "Those dots there are brown *in colour*": the latter means "*Each* is brown in colour", the former does *not* mean "*each* is 3 in number", but only, those dots, taken together or taken collectively, are 3 in number.

Suppose that at a given time 3 dimes & only 3 existed. We can so use "group" or "collection" that to say this *entails* that there existed at that time *a group* or *collection* of dimes, which had 3 members & no more—a group or collection, of which *the* number was "3" (this being a use of "group" or "collection" in which to say that 3 things form a group or collection is *not* to say that they are "grouped" or "collected" together); and it is *equivalent* to saying that there existed at that time *only one* group of dimes that had 3 members & no more. Would that group of dimes be *identical* with those 3 dimes? Certainly it would. We could say: "This, that & that are the only dimes in existence" *or* "This, that & that are the only *group* of dimes in existence". (But we couldn't say this unless we saw (or perceived) them all at once; in which case they would *have* to be "grouped" or "collected" in some way.)

When we do see 3 dimes grouped together, we don't *say*

"Those 3 dimes have 3 members" or "contain 3 dimes & no more": we *may* say "This group of dimes *contains* 3 dimes & no more" or "has 3 members": but yet what we call "this group of dimes" is *identical* with those 3 dimes.

Actually many more than 3 dimes do exist; and from this it *follows* that "3 dimes do exist". How is "3" being used here? To say this is not to say that *only 3* exist; but it is to say that *a* group exists which has *only 3* members: if more than 3 dimes exist, there must be more than one group of dimes, which has *only 3* members.

The fundamental use of numbers is in answer to the question: How many so & so's are there? Hence, if we answer "3", we so use it that this entails "not more than 3": "3" = "3, & no more". But it looks as if the "3" in the definiens must be *more* fundamental than the "3" defined, and simpler. So it is: There are 3 dimes in existence = $(\exists \, x, y, z) \, . \, x \neq y \, . \, x \neq z \, . \, y \neq z \, . \, x$ is a dime . y is a dime . z is a dime: & "& not more than 3" adds $(x, y, z, w) \, . \, w$ is a dime $\supset$ either $w = x$, or $w = y$, or $w = z$.

But if $(\exists \, x) \, . \, x$ is a dime = There is *either* only one dime or several = It's not the case that there are none, we have no means of expressing the meaning of "There's one" which follows from there are several. $(\exists \, x) : x$ is a dime $. \, (y) \, . \, y \neq x \, . \, \supset \, . \, y$ is not a dime = There's *only* one; but $(\exists \, x) \, . \, x$ is a dime, *entails*, but is not equivalent to, "There's one"; or is it equivalent to "There's one" in *this* sense, which doesn't say "and no more"?

If I were to say "My piano has 2 pedals", everybody would understand this to mean "It hasn't got 3"; so that $2 = 2$ & no more.

14

VELOCITY OF LIGHT ARGUMENT

That when I see a physical surface light from that surface has reached my eyes before I began to see it, proves that every surface I see existed (for however short a time) before I began to see it.

If, therefore, no visual datum which is given to me ever exists before I began to see it, it follows that no visual datum which is given to me at the time I am seeing a surface is ever identical with that surface.

But if a surface has "phases", this does not prove that a visual datum seen at that time may not be identical with one of the *phases* of the surface.

But if the phase of the surface which I see began before I began to see the visual datum it does follow that the visual datum is not identical with *that* phase.

If however the datum has phases as well as the surface, it does not follow that one phase of the datum may not be identical with one phase of the surface.

What L.[1] wants to prove is that neither the datum itself nor any phase of it is identical with any phase of the surface seen. Has he *any* argument for this?

Ạ Ḅ Ç If I move my pen from A to C, passing through B, the fact that the movement from A to C began before the movement from B to C proves that the former is not identical with the latter; but nevertheless the movement from B to C is a *temporal part* of the movement from A to C. So my argument did not shew that the datum may not be identical with *a* phase of the surface seen, though it did shew it can't be identical with the surface.

[1] [Lazerowitz?]

15

"PHASES" OF CONTINUANTS

The *fact* that this sheet existed from noon till 12.2 is, of course, a different fact from the fact that it existed from noon till 12.1, & from 12.1 till 12.2, although both these *follow* from the fact that it existed from noon till 12.2. And it is also a different fact from the fact that it existed from 12.2 till 12.3.

Now what is meant by a "phase" of this sheet is (1) a supposed entity, having temporal parts (& in that respect like an "event") which is such that from the fact that this sheet existed from 12 till 12.2, it *follows* that there was an entity of the sort which existed from 12 till 12.2, and existed *only* during that period— was restricted to it; & which is therefore not identical with this sheet, because (a) this sheet has no temporal parts & (b) this sheet did not exist *only* from 12 to 12.2; and (2) is such that whenever I say "this sheet", I mean by this "*the* sheet of which *this* phase is a phase", *this* phase being a phase which I see when I say "this sheet".

Similarly every datum which is seen for longer than the shortest possible time, is supposed to have phases, which are not identical with it.

Now if my arm was moving during the whole of a given second it does seem to follow that there occurred during any part of that second a movement not identical with the whole movement nor with any movement which occurred during any other part—i.e. that for each part of that second there existed a movement *restricted to that part*, in the sense that neither it nor any part of it was occurring at any period which either preceded or followed that part.

Let A be a continuant which began to exist at t_1, & ceased to exist at t_2. Call the period from t_1 to t_2 N. It is obvious that, if you consider any period n_1 which is a proper part of N, from the prop. that A existed during the whole of N, it follows that A existed during the whole of n_1. And it is obvious also that if n_1 & n_2 are 2 different proper parts of N the prop. that A existed during the whole of n_1 is a different prop. from the prop. that it existed during the whole of n_2, & that both props. follow from the prop. that A existed during the whole of N. Now the "phase" hypothesis is that if you consider *any* set of proper parts of N which together "make up" N, e.g. 3 (n_1, n_2, n_3), then ($\exists$ x, y, z) such that x existed during the whole of n_1 & did not exist during any proper part of N *external to* n_1. . . .

Suppose a particular movement began at noon today & ended at 12.1. Let us say that, in that case, it "occupied" the period between 12 & 12.1.

There are 2 other relations, besides "occupation", that a movement may have to a period of time: viz: (a) "was going on during the whole of P": shall we call this "covered"? Then any movement which *occupied* the period between 12 & 12.1 must have *covered both* that period itself & every proper part of it, e.g. that between 12 & half a minute past 12.

And (b) "fell wholly within P" = "was restricted to P" = "did not cover any interval which was outside P". p_1 is outside p_2 = p_1 is neither identical with p_2 nor a proper part of p_2, nor has for a proper part p_2 or any proper part of p_2 (= doesn't overlap p_2).

Then M "occupied" P = M *both* covered P *and* was restricted to P.

Now "M occupied P" *entails* "Every different proper part of P (if any) was occupied by a different *part* of M".

And if p_1, p_2, p_3 are 3 proper parts of P which together "make up" P, and m_1 is the part of M which occupied p_1, m_2 the part which occupied p_2, m_3 the part which occupied p_3, then the conjunction of the 3 props. "m_1 occupied p_1", "m_2 occupied p_2", "m_3 occupied p_3" is *logically* equivalent to "M occupied P". But we must not say that M is *identical with* the sum of m_1, m_2 & m_3? unless it is part of the def. of m_1, etc., that m_1 occupied p_1, etc. But I *think* it is, just as it is part of the definition of M that it occupied P. If P is the period from noon till 12.1 today, then of course it is no part of the definition of M that it began at noon & ceased at 12.1: that it did so could only be discovered by the use of a clock, i.e. empirically: i.e. we should find out *empirically* that when M began it was just noon, i.e. empirically that the beginning of M was simultaneous with that of another event, & likewise the end.

We understand "I *am* smoking while I write", "I *sang* that

note at exactly the same time at which the piano sounded it",
"I *shall* sing that note at exactly the same time as the piano
sounds it". But can we understand "*is* simultaneous with" in
any non-temporal sense, i.e. unless it means "*either* is now *or* was
or will be"? If not, then "now" can't be defined in terms of
simultaneity.

16

"KNOW THE MEANING OF"

Is it "by introspection" that I know the meaning of words I use = know what *I* mean by them?

(a) In *one* use "know the meaning of" = "understand". And it seems I can *understand* words *I* use in the same sense in which I understand those used by others. And it is *not* "by introspection" that I do this. *Using them with a meaning* is sufficient for understanding in this sense.

(b) It can happen that I give an order, & when a person does something say "Yes; *that's* what I meant". Here I am saying of something which I *see* that it was *meant* by words that I used. How do I know this? Certainly partly by *memory* (direct or introspective) I remember that I wished that done; and it might be said I know "by introspection" that *that* was what I wished. But surely *not* the thing that I see? I know that that's what I wanted, before I saw it done; & to know this was *not* to know that my words had a certain relation to what I saw.

(c) I understand "The battle of Waterloo was fought in June, 1815". But how could I answer the question: What do you mean by those words?

(d) It is "by introspection" that I know that I am (or was) lying; and therefore also that I am not or was not. And if I was lying, we *can* say that I did not *mean* what I said—but this only in the sense that I didn't *believe* what I said: it is "by introspection" that I know whether I did or didn't believe what I said, & in *that* sense *mean* what I said.

But this is not the sense of "mean" that is in question.

(e) If, by a slip, I say the wrong word, e.g. "Broad" instead of "Moore", I can say afterwards "That wasn't what I *meant*: I meant "Moore" ". How do I discover this? It seems to be a case of using words in an unusual sense & therefore *understanding* them in an unusual sense. But it is not by introspection that I know that a certain use of words is unusual.

I might make a mistake of this sort in lying, & therefore actually assert something which I *did* believe, though I *meant* to assert something which I didn't. I should then *not* be saying what I *meant* to say: I *meant* to lie.

In such cases—where by a slip I use the wrong word—what I know is e.g. that I invited Moore—though I *said* I invited Broad. I know that though I *said* "I invited Broad" I *meant* "I invited Moore". I know by *direct or introspective memory* that I *meant* "I invited Moore". And if you ask: *What* did you mean by saying "I invited Broad", the only answer is "I meant "I invited Moore" ". At the time when I make this answer I *understand* the words "I invited Moore". But *understanding* these words does not mean knowing a certain relation to hold between them & something else which is "what I meant by them", & to which the words I formerly used "I invited Broad" had the same relation. What I mean by them is not "given" to me in the same sense in which the words are.

17

TWO MEANINGS OF "RED"

You can say that in "This book is *red*", "I'm having a red after-image", *red* is used in the *same* sense, and that in saying of a book that it "*is* red" & of an after-image that it "*is* red", "is" is being used in a different sense, but "red" in the same: that "is" in the first case = "would look to a normal eye by a good light", and in the second something indefinable. "*Is* red", "*was* red", "*will be* red" certainly have different meanings in the 2 cases, but *one need not say* ⟨?⟩ that "red" has.

But need not one? Is it not in terms of "being red" as applied to an after-image that you have to define "being red" as applied to a book? Does "being", in the first case, express a *relation*? for, if it does, *what* is the term expressed by "red"? It is tempting to say that an image which *is* blue, has the same *relation* to the colour "blue", as one which is "red" has to the colour "red". But what *are* the colours "red" & "blue"? We understand what it is for an image to "*be* red", & to "*be* blue"; but can we distinguish "red" & "blue" from "being red" & "being blue"?

An absolutely specific shade of red is a "universal" in the sense (Braithwaite's) that it can be in 2 places at once: but is it a "universal" in the sense that it can be "predicated" of something? What can be predicated of something is that that thing "*is* of that specific shade".

In answer to the question: What does "red" mean? you can produce a red book & say: *This* (colour) is red. But this won't by itself be sufficient, because if the shade of red shewn happens to be scarlet, the hearer might think that only shades of scarlet were shades of red.

18

GOOD AND BAD

Blanshard tried to prove as follows that: (1) "It's a bad thing that that whale should have suffered such pain" can't be identical in meaning with: (2) "Anybody who thought of that fact *impartially* would disapprove of its being a fact".

He said: Let us ask, with regard to what is meant by (1), & what is meant by (2): Is it true that anybody who thought impartially of these whole facts would disapprove of their being facts? And answered that this *is* true of (1), but not of (2): ∴ (1) & (2) cannot be identical.

Did he also say: Let us ask, with regard to what is meant by (1), & what is meant by (2): Is it true that it's a bad thing that (1) should be a fact? Is it true that it's a bad thing that (2) should?

He thought it's plausible to say: "It's a *good* thing that (2) should be a fact"; but not plausible to say "It's a good thing that (1) should be: ∴ (2) & (1) can't be the same.

I said that it's nonsensical to ask either: "Is it a good thing that it's a bad thing that that pain should have been suffered?" or "Is it a bad thing that it's a bad thing that that pain should have been suffered?" (If one is nonsensical, the other certainly is too.) But I don't feel at all sure of this.

Let's consider: "It's a bad thing that it's a bad thing that that pain should have existed." What reasons are there for thinking (as I think B. did) that this is *true*?

It's worth noting that: (a) "It's a bad thing that that pain *should* have existed" entails (b) "That pain did exist". Hence "It's a good thing that (a)" *seems* to entail "It's a good thing that (b)"; and, in that case, "It's a good thing that (a)" would be self-contradictory, since there would follow from it *both* "It's a bad thing that (b)" & "It's a good thing that (b)". But does: "It's a good thing that (a)" in fact entail "It's a good thing that (b)"? Not if: "It's a good thing that (a)" means "That pain existed *and* it's a good thing that the existence of any pain like that always would be a bad thing". The second of these two conjuncts is like saying "It's a good thing that things which would be bad, would be bad"; and this is absurd, because it supposes that it might not have been true of a thing which would be bad, that it would be bad. It is as absurd as to say "It's a good thing that $2 + 2 = 4$"; which would only have meaning, if it were possible that $2 + 2$ should *not* have been equal to 4. It can only be a good or a bad thing that so & so *is* the case, if so & so is something which *might* not have been the case. It is absurd to say of the fact that the multiplication table is true, that it is either a good or a bad thing that it is.

Why did B. think that it's at least plausible to say: It's a good thing that (2) is true? i.e. it's a good thing that anybody who viewed the occurrence of that pain impartially *would* disapprove of it?

Because he confused this with: It *would* be a good thing that a person who viewed it impartially *should* disapprove of it.

19

TRUE

How are people using "true" when they say that "sentences" are "true" (as R. does in *Meaning & Truth*)?[1]

So far as I can see, they are certainly so using it that from "The sentence (b) "The sun is larger than the earth" is true" there will *follow* "The sun is larger than the earth"; i.e. (b) can't be "true", unless the sun is larger than the earth. But how must "true" be being used, if this condition is to be fulfilled?

It will be fulfilled if (a) "(b) is true" *means* "(b) means that the sun is larger than the earth, and the sun is larger than the earth"; and I don't see how it can be fulfilled unless (a) means this.

If this is so, then though (a) does entail that the sun is larger than the earth, the latter does *not* entail (a). For in order that (a) may be the case, it is necess. that the words which occur in the sentence "The sun is larger than the earth" should have *been used with certain meanings*, & that the form in which they are combined should have *been used in a certain way*; and it is obvious that from the fact that the sun is larger than the earth it certainly does not *follow* that those words or that form of combination have ever been used at all. To say that (b) *means* that the sun is larger than the earth, is certainly to say (in part) that the separate words *have been used*, & that the form of combination *has been used*. Hence "the sun is larger than the earth" is certainly not logically equivalent to (a): it is entailed by (a), but does not entail it.

It follows that (a) is not identical with (c) "*It is true* that the sun is larger"; since this *is* logically equivalent to "the sun is larger". Yet I fancy that why people talk of sentences being "true", is because they imagine that when we say (c), we are saying that (b) is true. They suppose that we are saying something about the *sentence* (b): but we certainly are not; we are *using* that sentence, but not saying anything *about* it. If I assert that the sun is larger than the earth, I am certainly not asserting that the sentence (b) is true. I could assert it in French or Latin. If I do assert it by the use of the sentence (b), I do indeed *imply* though I don't assert, that I am using (b) to assert that the sun is larger than the earth:

[1] [B. Russell, *An Inquiry into Meaning and Truth* (London, 1940).]

I *imply* this, because that's how most people would use it, and hence people who heard me would expect that that was what I meant. But I don't *say* that I'm so using it: all that I *say* is that the sun is larger than the earth—a prop. from which no assertion about the sentence (b) follows: I do utter the *words* "the sun is larger than the earth", and by uttering them in a special way I assert that the sun is larger than the earth; but I don't assert *these words*—(to say that I did would be nonsense: you can't assert a set of words)—nor do I assert anything about them—not, therefore, that they are "true", nor that they mean that the sun is larger than the earth.

But this prop. (d): "the words "the sun is larger than the earth" *mean* that the sun is larger than the earth" seems a queer one. People may be inclined to think it is a tautology: to say "of course, they do"; "they *must* mean that". But that they do mean that is nevertheless a contingent & empirical fact: they *might* never have been used at all, or *might* have been used only with a different meaning. If I were to say in French (e): "Les mots "the sun is larger than the earth" veulent dire que le soleil est plus grand que la terre", everybody would recognise that this was far from a tautology, & was an empirical & contingent prop.; & yet if I said (e) I should be merely saying in French exactly what (d) says in English. (d), therefore, can't be a tautology any more than (e) is. Perhaps, why (d) *seems* to be, is because nobody could *understand* the words I used in saying (d), unless he *already* understood the words (sentence) (b): that is to say, unless he already knew what I was telling him; for to understand the words (b) *is* to know that they mean that the sun is larger than the earth. It is, therefore, always *useless* to assert (d) *in those words*, because anybody who understands those words will already know the contingent fact which I assert by means of them. I *might*, it is true, be using them in such a sense that what I asserted by their means was false: if, for instance, I were using "the sun" as a proper name for the moon; and, in that case, a man who understood (b) would not understand what *I* meant by them. But, in that case, I should not be using them to assert (d): to use them to assert (d) is useless bec. anybody who understands them will already know that (d) is true; and to use them to assert anything else than (d) is useless, because they will not convey to anyone else the false prop. which I should then mean by them.

That use of "true" in which "It's true that the sun is larger than the earth" is log. eq. to "The sun is larger than the earth" *seems* to be such that "true" has *no* meaning, or, if any, a different meaning in the case of every prop. which is expressed by the use of it. But from: "He said that the sun is larger & it is larger" there follows "He said something which is true". This, as Ramsey implies, is equivalent to $(\exists\,p)$. he said that p . p. We can say that "He said something true" is a short way of saying this; and that is why the word "true" is useful. So, if somebody says, "The sun is larger than the earth", & we say "True" or "That's true" or "Yes, it is", these are shorter ways of saying "The sun is larger than the earth".

But there is a strong feeling that somehow *the* meaning (really only *a* meaning but perhaps the *original* one) of "true" is such that, if there had been no beliefs, nothing would have been true. We don't often speak of "true beliefs"; what we do say is "He believed that the sun, etc., & he was *right*". But we do sometimes say "He had a true idea of the state of affairs", which does mean "He believed that the state of affairs was such & such, & he was right". This use of "true" used as an adjective of "idea", is one such that nothing can be "true" except an "idea". And "that idea of his was true" = corresponded to the facts = was an idea *that* the sun was larger, etc., *&* the sun was larger, etc. For *this* use of "true" the problem is, as Ramsey says, to *settle what's meant by* "He had the idea that the sun was larger than the earth" or "He believed that. . . ". We know quite well of course what *is* meant by it: i.e. we understand the expression.

And we could express what people mean by saying that sentences are "true", e.g. the sentence "the sun is larger than the earth", by saying that people would in general use this expression to express belief or knowledge that the sun is larger & that such a belief or knowledge would be a true idea. Of a man who believes or knows that the sun is larger we could say "He has a true idea as to which of the two is larger" or "of their relative sizes"; or "The idea that the sun was larger turned out to be a true one". And (d) "The sentence (b) means that the sun is larger" may be said to mean "Most people who used that sentence would be expressing an idea, on their part, that the sun is larger". Hence, in order to explain what (d) means, & therefore what (a) means, we have to discover (what we know) what is meant by "He believed that the sun was larger".

There *is*, therefore, *a* sense of "true" other than that which occurs in "It is true that", & other also than that illegitimate sense in which people use it when they say that sentences are *true*. What can we say about this? His idea that the sun is larger is true = He has the idea that the sun is larger, & the sun is larger. Here *what* does "true" mean? for: His idea that the moon is smaller is true = He has the idea that the moon is smaller, & the moon is smaller. It looks as if "true" meant something different in the case of every different idea. We can say that to call an idea "true" means that there is a fact *corresponding* to it; but this only means that, if the idea you are talking of is somebody's idea *that* the sun is larger, then in asserting that *this* idea is true, all that you are asserting besides its existence is that the sun is larger: you are asserting "he believes that the sun is larger & the sun is larger", and you would be able to assert this even if the sun were *not* larger: so that it can't be of *this* fact that you are asserting that the idea has a certain relation to it. It looks as if in asserting "He believes p" you are asserting that one relation holds between certain objects, and in asserting p are asserting that another relation holds between the same objects. But in the case of different props., the relations which in asserting p you are asserting to hold between the objects involved are often quite different!

When we say "He *found* that p", e.g. "he found that Smith had already got there", we are certainly asserting *both* (a) p & (b) *he* was in a certain mental state, i.e. something more than p. But it does not seem that we are merely asserting a *conjunction* of p & that he was in a certain mental state, as when we assert p *and* he believed that p. It seems as if the kind of state we are asserting him to have been in, is such that from the fact that he was in that state it *follows* that p. But how is this possible?

ARE ALL VISUAL SENSE-DATA EXTENDED?

Is every coloured speck extended? Only if it has parts. But what is meant by saying of a uniformly or continuously coloured sense-datum that it *has* parts? This: that there *might* be another sense-datum of the same size (no larger) such that one part of it was of one colour & another of another sharply contrasted colour, so that there was a sharply defined boundary between them. If a speck is so small that we *do not know what it would be like* to see a speck equally small, half of which was of one colour & the other of a sharply contrasted colour, then that speck has no parts & is not extended. I was tempted to say: When this is true of a speck, then no visual sense-datum *could* be smaller than it; but could we not have 2 specks, of both of which this is true, such that nevertheless one was visibly larger than the other?

What bearing has this on infinite divisibility, & whether an extended patch can be *made up of* unextended specks? Start with a patch half of which (a) is of one colour & the other half (b) of a sharply contrasted colour. Now consider (a): could you have another sense-datum (c) of exactly the same size & shape as (a) half of which was of one colour, & the other of a sharply contrasted one? If so, then (a) is "divisible" into 2 parts of the same size & shape as the 2 parts of (c). Then take one of the parts of (c), say (d), & ask the same question about it. It seems to me evident that, after a finite number of steps, you would arrive at a coloured speck such that you could not have a speck equally small half of which was of one colour & another of a sharply contrasted one. Take the smallest speck which *is* so divided: will it not then be *made up* of 2 indivisible & unextended specks? But what will the boundary between them be like? It can't be a straight line. In the case of any speck which *is* divided by a straight line, the 2 halves must have shape & therefore size. It looks as if you must be able to find a speck which is divided by a straight line, such that one of its parts can't be divided by a straight line.

DOUBLE IMAGES

A kind of experience sometimes occurs, which is often expressed by saying that x is *seeing* some physical object *double*; and it has been customary to use the expression "x is having a *double image* of the physical object y" as a synonym for "x is *seeing* y *double*", in the sense in question. In the expression "x has a double image of y", "has a double image of" seems to be used to mean "has two images of"—*not* to mean "has a *single* image of—only *one* image of—but an image which is in some sense "double"" (in what sense a single image could be said to be "double", I do not know). And when a man has this experience, he has no difficulty in distinguishing the *two directly seen* objects, which in this terminology are called two "images" of the same physical object. There is no doubt whatever that the one "image" is not identical with the other. They *are* in different places (*not* in physical space, for neither is in physical space at all; though each *looks as if* it were in a different place in physical space), i.e. the one is *not* in the place in which the other is. A *quality* (e.g. an absolutely specific shade of colour) can (in a sense) be in 2 different places at the same time; but an "image" is not a quality: and an image which is in one place *cannot* be identical with an image which is at the same time in another, even if it is *exactly like* it in colour, shape & size. Why "cannot"? Because from the fact that an object was in two different places at the same time it would *follow* that it was not the kind of object we are calling an "image".

It is a contradiction to say that the right-hand image is identical with the left-hand image. By "the right-hand image" we might mean *the* one of these two images which appears to be more to the right than the other—we need not assume that it *is* more to the right.

There is a place in which the right-hand image appears to be, and a different place in which the left-hand: and the first of these places is more to the right than the second. Now the same thing (if a universal) *might* appear to be in both places: if it did we should say: the thing which appears to be in the right-hand place also appears to be in the left-hand. But the thing which appeared to be in the right-hand place could not then be called "*the* right-hand thing", because it would *not* be more to the right than the thing which appeared to be in the left-hand place.

The right-hand image does *not* appear to be in the place in which the left-hand image appears to be; & also appears *not* to be in the place in which the left-hand appears to be.

Mace suggests that though the place where the right-hand image looks to be is really different from that in which the left-hand looks to be, nothing looks to be in either place but that part of the surface of the physical object you are seeing, which you are seeing.

This is certainly not true universally because

(1) Where the object you are seeing is convex towards you like a ball, or a cylinder like a pencil, the part of its surface which you are seeing does *not* look to be either in the right-hand place or in the left-hand. You can make 2 marks on a ball such that, if you shut the right eye, you will see the left-hand mark, but *not* the right-hand, and, if you shut your left eye, you will see the right-hand mark but *not* the left-hand. And similarly, if you see it double the left-hand image will contain something *corresponding to* the left-hand mark, but nothing corresponding to the right-hand mark; & the right-hand image will contain something *corresponding to the* right-hand mark, but nothing corresponding to the left-hand mark. In other words the surface corresponding to the left-hand image is *not* the same as that corresponding to the right-hand, though the 2 surfaces have a common part which is a much larger part of each than the part of each which is not a part of each. The part of the surface of the ball you *see* in double vision contains both marks, & is identical with the part you see in single *binocular* vision, which also contains both marks. If you were to mark out on the surface of the ball the part of its surface which you see in single *binocular* vision & in double vision, it would contain both the part you would see with the left eye alone, & the part you would see with the right eye alone, both of which are circular, but would not be itself circular, but of this sort of shape ∞.

(2) Even where this is not the case, e.g. where the surface seen is a flat one, e.g. one rib of a flat ruler, in which case, so far as I can see, the surface corresponding to the left-hand image *is* the same as that corresponding to the right, there is difference

of quality in the 2 images, e.g. one looks less substantial than the other. (Perhaps that this is so in my case, is due to the fact that my left eye's more short-sighted than my right.) This quality is *directly seen*, so that the surface isn't the only thing directly seen. Mace would say that the surface *looks to have* one quality *in* the one place & the other quality (or pattern) in the other place.

In such a case what would be meant, on his view, by saying that I have two images of the surface, would be that I directly see (1) the surface, (2) 2 "places", (3) 2 different "patterns" or "essences", & that the surface looks to be of one pattern *in* one of the places, & of the other in the other. It not only looks to be of this pattern & to be in this place; but looks to be of this pattern *in* this place. Can we say that the left-hand image *is* the fact that the surface looks to be of that pattern in the left-hand place? In that case it's not identical with the surface.

In what sense can I *see* a "place"? I do see places in *physical* space. E.g. in looking at the looking-glass opposite I see a reflection of the right-hand top corner of the wooden frame of the doorway behind me. This reflection *looks to be* some way behind the glass in physical space; and its outline marks out *the* place in physical space in which it *looks to be*. The reflection *is* not in that place in physical space, but only *looks to be* there, although the *same* reflection could be seen by another person. It looks as if the reflection, in the sense in which it can be said to be a physical reality—to be seen by several, is something happening at the surface of the glass. But it doesn't seem as if *this* is what is said to *look* behind the glass. What looks to be behind the glass is a sense-datum, which looks to be in a physical place, but *is* not in any physical place. Is it also in a place in another space—*my* visual space? And do I *see* this place? The place in physical space in which it looks to be *might look to be* smaller & of a different shape & has no absolute size: the place in my visual space *couldn't* look different & has an absolute magnitude.

22

PLACES

Suppose, with closed eyes, I see 2 small, round, blue spots, of exactly the same colour, size & shape, such as might be parts of an after-image I am seeing, or perhaps each of them a different after-image.

It seems as if the one would differ from the other solely in respect of the fact that each is in a place or position in which the other is not. And it seems as if the fact that the one exists is simply identical with the fact that that colour (or colour-pattern) is in that place now, & the fact that the other exists with the fact that that same colour (or colour-pattern) is in this other place.

Let one be to the left of the other.

It seems to be true that that left-hand one might (conceivably) have been at another place, might have been of another colour & of a different shape & size. This is conceivable because I might have seen *it* at another place (e.g. more to the left) before. I should have done so, if I had seen it continuously from that time to this, & seen it moving from that place to this. If this had happened, it would have been true to say of *it* at the earlier time: this *might* move to that place (not the one where it is) & keep its colour & size & shape, or change to different ones. In other words, we can say, with truth: This spot *might* have been there half a minute ago; and, *if* it had been, it *might* have moved by now to this other place & been of a different size, shape & colour. *If* something which is logically possible had been the case, then something else would have been logically possible. But can't we also say: If *both* these possibilities had been realised, *this* spot wouldn't have *existed*? If the first had been realised, but *not* the second, it would, of course, have been right to say: this spot *might* have been there instead of here & of these different colours, sizes & shapes. But if neither has been realised, though it's right to say the first might have been, it's not right to say the second might have. Since *I* did exist long enough ago to have got from the place where I then was to London, it's right to say *I* might have been in London now. But if I'd only just come into existence, it would not be right to say that I *might* have been in London?

It is a contradiction to suppose *both* possibilities to have been realised. For if this spot had moved from there, it couldn't also have moved from there to a different place. There's no contradiction between: "This did move from there to here, & this *might* have moved from there to a different place." This is *there*, & not here (where it is) *is* a self-contradictory proposition. I am there is a self-contradictory prop. ⟨?⟩; although it's true that I *might* have been there. There would have been no contradiction in saying of me in the past, you *will* be *there*.

"I'm here" as understood by someone to whom I shout it, is *not* a tautology: he hears from what direction the voice comes—learns that I am in that direction. But "I'm *not* here" would seem to be a contradiction?

If I point to a chair, on which I'm not sitting, & say "I'm sitting on that chair", I think this is self-contradictory, although it's true that I might have been sitting on that chair.

If I point to a chair, on which I am sitting, & say "I'm sitting on this chair" that doesn't seem to be a tautology. But isn't it, in spite of the fact that I might not have been sitting on it? When a man sees that I am, he is learning a contingent fact. If he had said, when he didn't see me, "Moore isn't sitting", he's certainly not saying something self-contradictory. But if when he sees me & the chair on which I'm sitting he says "Moore isn't sitting on that chair", isn't he contradicting himself? He wouldn't be if he said: "I'm only dreaming that Moore is sitting on that chair: that isn't a chair, & that isn't Moore". But then he's misusing "that chair", which says "that is a chair". But he might suppose, without contradiction, that he was having an hallucination of me: "that isn't really Moore" (just as Macbeth might have said "That isn't really a dagger").

23

[NO TITLE]

Can two different places in physical space be "given" to me (directly seen), in the sense in which 2 such places are given when I see a thing double, or in which one such place is given when I see that reflection,[1] without its being the case that there is an object which looks to me to be in the one place & *not* in the other, & also an object which looks to be in the second & *not* in the first?

I think not: & what we call the right-hand image & the left-hand *are* such objects. The left-hand no more looks to be in the right-hand place, than a left-hand after-image looks to be in the right-hand place.

But what's meant by saying that a "*place*" is "given"?

It is sometimes suggested that to be in a certain place *is* to have certain kinds of relations to *the* surrounding objects ⟨some of them?⟩. You specify a place by coordinates. And it is true that if something *other* than that reflection had *looked* to have the same spatial relations to all the other physical objects in my present field of vision, as the reflection looks to have, it would have *looked* to be in the same place in which the reflection looks to be.

∴ *looking* to have the same spatial relations to these objects is a *sufficient* condition for *looking* to be in that place.

But is it a necessary condition? Couldn't something else have *looked* to be in that place, even if *different* objects had been in my field of vision?

It would have looked to be in that place, if it had looked to be at that distance in that direction from *me*; and it might have done this even though quite different objects had seemed to surround it.

We can observe that a physical object is in the same place *relatively* to another, over a period of time; but is there any sense in asking whether it is in the same place *absolutely*?

[1] [Cf. p. 235.]

24

"TAUTOLOGY"

Is now sometimes used = prop. of which the negation is self-contradictory. How Wittg. was using it I don't know, but what he calls tautologies all are props. of this kind, though perhaps they are only a sub-class. I will use "necessary prop." for this.

But I don't think in popular use it is so confined: I think "Some brothers are male" or "This brother is male", "That cat is an animal" might be called tautologies: but negation of first is not self-contradictory, since if "There are no brothers", which is not self-contradictory, were true, it would be true (what is entailed by a prop. which is not a contradiction can't be a contradiction). As for "That cat is an animal", this entails "That object is a cat", and "That object is a cat but is not an animal" *is* a contradiction. But "that cat is an animal" is not the negation of this: it does not merely say that the conjunction "That object is a cat . That object is not an animal" is false, since it asserts that one of the conjuncts (that object is a cat) is true, and there is no contradiction in supposing this to be false. "That cat is an animal" asserts "That object is both a cat & also an animal" or "That object is a cat . That object is an animal", of which the negation is *not* a contradiction, but which is *redundant* or *tautologous*. I think we should say "That person is both a brother and male" is *tautologous* as well as *redundant*. "Tautologous", by etymology, means "saying the same thing twice (or more) over", and this *does* do this. How did "tautologous" come to be *confined* to *necessary* props.? & *do* they say the same thing twice over? *Why* should $\sim (p . \sim p)$ be said to be "tautologous"? Does it say the same thing twice over?

Now "This is not here" *is* a contradiction, but "This is here" is *not* its negation, if they both entail "This exists" and this is significant (= "There is such a thing as this spot"), as it seems to be because there *might* have been no such thing. "This colour is here" is again not the negation of "This colour is *not* here", but *not* because there might have been no such thing as this colour, but because there might have been no such place as this place. But is "This colour is not here" *not* self-contradictory?

If I point at a thing & say "This is here" or "That is there", or if I say these things to myself without pointing, these things *are* *tautologous*.[1] "Here" = "in this place", "there" = "in that place"; & "here" = *roughly* "in the place in which this is", "there" "in the place in which that is". Obviously "This is in the place in which this is" is a *tautology*,[2] if "this" is in a place at all; and any *particular* which is *in a space*, must be at one place & *only* one in that space. But it is not true of a *colour* that it need be in *only* one place.

But it's only *roughly* that "This is here" = "This is in the place in which this is". For

(1) We often use "here" to mean "*near* the place where this is", or something more specific, e.g. "I want you to sit here" = "*on* this chair", *not* "in the place in which this chair is": or "Write your name *here*" = "*on* some part of this blank space on this paper", where "*this* blank space" has not a perfectly definite outline. "Here" = "in *some* place on this chair", "in *some* place within this blank".

(2) "This is here" does *not* mean "$(\exists x) . x$ is a place where this is . nothing but x is a place where this is . this is in x." In other words if we say "This is here" = "This is in the place where this is", the phrase "the place where this is" is *not* a "description" in R.'s sense. Why not? Because "This is here" = "This is in *this* place".

---

[1] ⟨*Not* in the sense that they are "necessary", but in the sense that "This is not here" understood *not* as the negation of "this is here", but as saying "This exists but is not here", is a contradiction.⟩

[2] [Cf. the preceding footnote.]

25

KÖHLER ON "UP" AND "DOWN", "RIGHT" AND "LEFT"

There is a proper use of "shape" in which A & V, E & Ǝ, not only *are* of the same shape, but *look* of the same shape. But though they look *of the same shape*, they certainly *look different*. It is, of course, possible (no contradiction) that when a baby sees an A & V side by side, they look to him as A & A do to us, or as V & V do to us. But even if this were so it would not prove that the baby's visual space was "homogeneous". Their space is *not* "homogeneous" if there is no contradiction in supposing A & V to look to them as they do to us, even if they never do. And there certainly is no contradiction in this. To say that they have a visual space at all, is to *say* that there is no contradiction in this. In other words what K. is calling a "homogeneous visual space" is a self-contradictory conception. In any space at all there must be *opposite directions*—even in Newton's—& *many* of them.

But why we should single out one direction as "up" another as "to the right" is a different question. There must be something about the direction we call "up", which *differentiates it* from others: what is it? Is it "away from the surface of the earth & at right angles to it"? How do children learn the meaning of "up", & the difference between "above" & "by the side of"?

P. 19.[1] Don't astronomers recognise the difference between a right-hand & a left-hand spiral? though they are of exactly the same *shape*.

Pp. 20 to 21. They were to "choose" an equilateral tri., when shewn both it & another figure. They were trained to do this when the e.t. was in this position △. When it was in this position ◁ they still chose it, but first turned their heads. They wouldn't have done this, says K., unless they had "recognised" it; but also they wouldn't have done it unless it had *looked different* to them (K. says "were accurately aware of its changed orientation"!)

When I look at a T through my legs, the horizontal line still looks to be *above* the vertical, although the retinal image of the horizontal is now above & was formerly below. What is "above"

[1] [W. Köhler, *Dynamics in Psychology* (London, 1942).]

241

in my visual field—*looks above*—does not depend upon the position of my head relatively to the thing. I think "looks above" is
something ultimate: it's just "in *that* direction", and we call
"towards the earth" *down*—say that a thing is falling, only
because in normal circumstances a thing that is falling *looks* to
be moving downwards. It still looks to be moving downwards,
even if I look between my legs. Under what circumstances would
it look to be moving upwards? Under any? Would it if I (not
only my head) were upside down? Is it only that it is *logically
possible* it should?

"That is falling" does *not* normally mean "is moving towards
the earth". It means (perhaps) *would* look to be moving downwards
to a normal person under normal circumstances.

Does "my *right* hand" mean the hand which to a person looking
at my front, normally *looks* to be to the *left* of the other? Or does
it mean that one of my hands which is joined to the arm which is
felt by me to be to the right of the other? *Could* my right arm feel
to me to be to the right of the left? And how is "being felt to
be to the right" connected with "looking to be to the right"?
My right hand *now* looks to me to be to the right of the left; and
the sensation of pressure which I get from its touching this page
is *felt* to be to the right of that which I get from the left hand's
touching the opposite page. Is this because the right-hand pressure
is *felt* to be *adjacent* to the visual sense-datum of my right, and
the left-hand pressure is felt to be *adjacent* to the visual sense-
datum of my left? When a blind man feels "This pressure is to
the right of that" does he mean the *same* by "to the right of", as *I*
mean by "This visual sense-datum is to the right of that"?

It is certain, I think, that sensations of pressure (or touch?),
sounds, smells, bodily pains have a *felt spatial* relation to visual
sense-data: it is not true, as, e.g., Berkeley supposed, that the
only *felt* relations between them are *temporal* relations, and that
the rest is due to association. Here "felt" = "directly apprehended" ⟨or perceived⟩: I can't "*see*" a visual sense-datum to
be *near* a sensation of pressure; & no more can I *feel* a sensation
of pressure to be *near* a visual sense-datum, in the sense in which
I can *feel* one pressure to be near another. There is a *coenaesthesis*,
by which *spatial* relations are apprehended between data of
different senses; and not only *temporal* relations.

26

"IMAGINARY" AND "THERE ARE"

There is a temptation to say "There are no imaginary objects";
"there is nothing of which it can be said with truth that it is an
imaginary object".

But Pickwick is an imaginary person; the unicorn in Alice in
Wonderland is an imaginary unicorn.

(1) One important point is: Nothing which *is* (is now, has
been, or will be) perceived or which could be perceived (= is of the
same kind as anything which is perceived = is now, has been, or
will be), is an imaginary object.

But here it is important to say that we are so using "perceived",
that images, including dream-images, are "perceived"; and they
are, in a sense, "objects of sense". And we *can* say that any visual
image which I had in a dream was "seen" by me, any auditory
was "heard" (Revelation: "I heard a great voice out of heaven,
saying"). I saw such images *in a dream*; and here "saw in a
dream" entails "saw"; whereas "I saw Russell in a dream" does
not entail "saw Russell"; nor does "saw a unicorn in a dream"
entail "saw a unicorn".

No object which is or could be *perceived* is an imaginary object.

You can say: Imaginary objects can be *conceived*, but they
can't be perceived. But this isn't all: you can say "Nothing is an
imag. object".

This seems like saying: Nothing is real but what can be perceived. But one doesn't want to say this. The number "1000" is
real, but can't be perceived: you can't even perceive the number 2,
as you can perceive a shade of red. You can even say: "I saw the
colour "red" ", as well as "I saw a red colour". Also electrons
are real but not perceptible.

(2) Another important point is that: "These are imaginary
unicorns" does not entail "These are unicorns", does not therefore entail "These are things of which it can truly be said that
they are both imaginary & unicorns". The imaginary unicorn in
Alice was an imaginary unicorn, but was not a unicorn. This
seems like a contradiction. But from "Lewis Carroll imagined a
unicorn" there does not follow "There is something which was a

unicorn & was imagined by L.C.". He imagined that there was a unicorn, but there was no unicorn with regard to which he imagined that it was a unicorn.

(3) "There are illusions", does not mean "There are at least two objects each of which can be truly said to be an illusion". It means, we can say, "There have been at least two different *cases*, which were cases of some living being having an illusion" or "2 different occasions on which some living being had an illusion".

There are several imaginary unicorns = Several people have told stories each of which was about a particular unicorn. We can then talk of "the" unicorn about which a story is told in Alice; and everybody who reads Alice becomes acquainted with that particular unicorn. But there isn't & never was anything of which it can or could have been said with truth that it is or was the unicorn about which a story is told in Alice. There isn't & never was anything which is *the* unicorn about which a story is told in Alice. And this doesn't mean merely that there isn't & never was any *perceptible* object of which this is true. Electrons are not *perceptible* objects, but there are & have been things of which it could be said with truth that they are electrons. Is there anything of which it can be said with truth that it is the number 2?

Pickwick is an imaginary person = There is a well-known story about a man, whom the writer pretends to have been called "Pickwick"; but there is not & never was a man, of whom it could be said with truth that the person who told the story was telling it about that man. He merely conceived that there was a man about whom many different things were true, & whose name was Pickwick.

"There are", in all its uses, does not stand for a predicate. There are *sorts* of things, such that of each *sort* it is true that *there are* things of that sort. "There is at least one cat" makes sense, but "There is at least one this cat" makes none, nor does "There is at least one the sun". Consider "There are things of which it is true that there are": this is nonsense. But is it nonsense to say: "There are things of each of which it is true that there is such a thing as that"? Betsy Prig says "There ain't no sich a person". But this doesn't mean "There's no person of which the things are true which Mrs Gamp pretends to have been true of Mrs Harris", except that it does mean that when, e.g., Gamp says "Mrs Harris said to me so-&-so", nobody ever did say those things to Gamp. Prig is saying "Mrs Harris is a fiction of yours" = you are pretending that there is a person, called "Mrs Harris", who said those things to you. Gamp uses "Mrs Harris" as a proper name, but there is no "bearer" of that name. But also Gamp *doesn't*: there never was any such person as Gamp. Dickens was pretending that there was a person called "Gamp" who pretended that there was one called "Harris"; & is not pretending that there was one called "Harris". We can say Gamp is *supposed* to be a real person, Harris is not (by Dickens): but Dickens supposes that a real person called "Gamp" supposed that there was a real person called Harris. Lean says we can express this by: Gamp is a *real* character in "Martin Chuzzlewit", but Harris is an imaginary one. Perhaps we could: but I don't feel we should naturally. Similarly in "Alice", Alice is supposed to be a real person, but Humpty Dumpty is only supposed to be an imaginary person of whom Alice dreams. Lewis Carroll imagined that Alice dreamt of a unicorn: did he imagine the unicorn of which he imagined Alice to dream? Yes; in a sense.

It is said that there was a real little girl who "was" Alice. Does this mean that Carroll was imagining *that* girl to have had the experiences which he imagined Alice to have had? Certainly not all the time. He was not using "Alice" as a proper name for that little girl, but for a fictitious little girl. And when you use a name (as Gamp is supposed to have used "Mrs Harris") as a proper name for a fictitious character, you are not, in all respects, using it in the same way as when you use it as a proper name for a real person. But you may also use it as a proper name for a person whom you believe to be real, but who is not. The writers in the Old Testament supposed Jehovah to be a real person, though he wasn't. They didn't use "Jehovah" in the same way either (1) as that in which Dickens used "Mrs Gamp" or (2) that in which I use "Dickens". Or didn't they the latter? "Jehovah" wasn't the name of a real person, whereas "Dickens" is: but does that make any difference to the use?

27

[NO TITLE]

The fact that we can say " "Socrates was a man" is a proposition", though it entails "There are propositions", does not entail "There are objects of each of which it could be truly said that it is a proposition": it is consistent with "There is nothing which is a prop.".

"There are no such things as props." is ambiguous: it may mean something true, it may mean something false.

It is quite right to say "A question is not a prop.; a command is not a prop.": = to ask a question is not to make a prop.; to give a command is not. But isn't it also right to say that when you ask *the sort of* question which can be answered by "Yes" or "No", & when you give a command you are *contemplating* a prop.? *What* you ask is whether a certain prop. is true; & *what* you command is that a certain prop. should become true.

In the case of questions which can't be answered by "Yes" or "No" the case is different: there is no prop. with regard to which you're asking whether it is true. You are asking with regard to a certain propl. function *what value* of it is true.

"EXIST" AND "REAL"

(1) Randall, J. of P., 1920, p. 340[1] suggests " "real" is essentially a category of laudation".

This is absurd. It certainly is not *always*. But there *are* uses in which it is: e.g. "That's what I call a real man!" Perhaps also we might say in: "You shall have a real live pony" as opposed to a mere toy-pony. Perhaps also: "Now I'll shew you a real snake" (to a man seeing snakes in d.t.).

These are attributive uses of "real", with a noun following; & in these uses "real" $\neq$ "existing".

(2) People do use "real" as if it meant something capable of degree, e.g. Shelley

> But of these create he can
> Forms (?) more real than living man.

"Exist" is not so used.

(3) "Cats exist" = "Cats are real".

(4) Alice: "I *am* real" = I am a real person = I exist.

---

[1] [J. H. Randall, Jr., "The Really Real", *The Journal of Philosophy*, vol. XVII, 1920.]

PROPER NAMES

My name is "George Edward Moore", but I am rarely *called* by that name. I can also say that my name is "G. E. Moore", & also that it is "Moore"; and I am pretty often *called* both of them, but much more often by the latter.

I used to be called "Jumbo"; & used to be called "Tommy"; also "Georgie"; & still am called (by my brothers & sisters) "George"; by Dorothy & others I am called "Bill", but that is decidedly *not* my name, nor even *a* name of mine, as "George" is.

What is meant by saying that D. *calls me* "Bill"? Uses "Bill" to refer to me: but in what does "using "Bill" to refer to me" consist? When she writes to Tim "Bill had an operation", what is meant by saying she is "referring" to me? We can't say she is referring to me by the description "The person you & I *call* "Bill" ", because the question then arises what is meant by saying that she & T. "call" me "Bill". They *habitually* use "Bill" as a proper name for me. And this seems to imply that they *could* have used "Bill" as a proper name for me on one or two occasions, but *not* habitually. When a person says to a strange boy: "Now, Tommy, hand me that spanner" is he using "Tommy" as a proper name for that boy on that one occasion? Perhaps; but an *habitual* use must include not only cases where the name is used in addressing the person in question, but cases where it is used in narrative, in the *absence* of that person. There must have been a *first* occasion when D. used "Bill" as a proper name for me in *narrative* in my absence. In *what* did the fact that she was doing so consist? She certainly didn't mean "The person I am calling "Bill" ". Suppose she said to T.: "Go & fetch Bill". This is not in narrative; & she wouldn't have been understood, unless T. had become accustomed to hearing her call me "Bill". This, therefore, couldn't have been the *first* occasion.

30

CONTRADICTIONS

It is by experience we learn what words & sentences mean.

It is by experience we learn that "Some dogs bark sometimes" means "Some dogs bark sometimes", & that "It's not true that some dogs bark sometimes" means "It's not true that . . .".

But it's not by experience we learn that "Some dogs bark sometimes & It's not true . . ." is a contradiction; nor yet that a prop. which is a contradiction is not true.

That a sentence of form "p . ~ p" *expresses* a contradiction is learnt *partly* by experience, *partly* otherwise: by experience that the sentence used expresses the prop. it does, otherwise that the prop. in question is a contradiction.

31

"EITHER . . . OR"

Exclusive use: "He's going to buy either this one or that one." Everybody would understand this to mean: "He's not going to buy both", although there is no *impossibility* in his buying both. Examples in which it is *impossible* that both should be true don't (as Johnson says) shew that the use is exclusive: e.g. "He was either first or second".

"x & y had at least one common parent" = "*Either* x & y had the same father *or* x & y had the same mother *or* x & y had both the same father & the same mother".

The addition of the last "or"-clause would be redundant, if "either . . . or" had no exclusive use; i.e. if "either had the same father or had the same mother" meant merely "it is not the case that x & y both didn't have the same father & also didn't have the same mother".

But this would not be so, if "either had the same father or had the same mother" = "either had the same father but *not* the same mother, or had the same mother but not the same father".

32

P ⊃ Q

To shew that p ⊃ q does not mean the same as "if p, then q".

"If it's false that cats don't mew, then ∼ cats mew ⊃ cats mew" is a true prop.: it follows from: if p is false, whatever p may be, then p ⊃ q, whatever q may be.

But the prop. "If it's false that cats don't mew, then *if* cats don't mew, they do mew" is *not* a true prop. It is = "If cats do mew, then if they don't they do."

NOTEBOOK VI

(Begun Feb. 1, 1944)

1

ANALYSIS AND "ANALYTIC"

Nagel (*Mind*, Jan. 44, p. 64)[1] says the connexion between A. "x is a cube" & B. "x has 12 edges", *in virtue of which* the second *follows from* the first, is *entirely an analytic one*.

He asserts that B does *follow* from A; but follows in virtue of "*an analytic connexion*" between the 2. This must mean that there is *some* analytic connexion, such that from the fact that it holds between A & B it *follows* that B follows from A. Nagel implies that the assertion that B follows from A is not *identical* with the assertion of a particular analytic connexion between them.

What does he mean by an "analytic connexion"? He apparently holds that to say there is an "analytic connexion" between A & B means that B is "analytically *contained*" in A, or "logically *contained*".

But what is meant by "contained" (= "included")?

There is *one* obvious meaning of "*q* is contained in *p*", viz. that *p* is a conjunction of which *q* is one of the conjuncts; and *another* in which every prop. of form $(\exists x) . \phi x . \chi x$ *contains* the corresponding prop. of forms $(\exists x) . \phi x \, \& \, (\exists x) . \chi x$.

In Kant's use of "analytic": "Every body is extended" is analytic: $= \sim (\exists x) . x$ is a body $. \sim (x$ is extended), which is like $\sim (\exists x) . x$ is a brother $. \sim (x$ is male$) = \sim (\exists x) . x$ is male & a sibling $. \sim (x$ is male). And here though $(\exists x) . x$ is male $. x$ is a sibling does *contain* $(\exists x) . x$ is male, it is *not* a *conjunction* of $(\exists x) . x$ is male & $(\exists x) . x$ is a sibling.

But I think Nagel would wish to say that

(a) D. "$\sim (\sim$ (cats mew) $. \sim$ (dogs bark))" is "logically contained" in C. "cats mew." Certainly D "logically follows" from C. But is D, & all the other props. of the form $\sim (\sim$(cats mew) $. \sim (q)$) which follow from "cats mew", *contained* in "cats mew"? If so, in what sense? certainly not in any *natural* sense; *not* in conjunctive senses.

(b) "Socrates was mortal" is *contained* in "$\sim (\exists x) . x$ is a

[1] [E. Nagel, Critical Notice of P. A. Schilpp (ed.), *The Philosophy of G. E. Moore*, *Mind*, vol. LIII, 1944.]

man . ∼ (x is mortal) . Socrates was man". If so, in what sense?
Not in conjunctive senses.

(c) "This tie is red" & "This tie is not green" are *contained* in
"This tie is scarlet". In what sense? *Not* that of conjunction.

If q is "contained" in p, you can also say that "q is *part* of
what you assert in asserting p".

This holds in the conjunctive cases, but does *not* hold for
(a), (b) & (c).

Analysis

In G. E. M.[1] I give 5 conditions, each of which I take to be a
necessary condition if a man is to be said to have given an analysis
of a given concept.

I *think* it is true that not only I, but everybody else, when
speaking correctly, only says that a person has given an *analysis*
of a concept when these 5 conditions are fulfilled.

But I do *not* say that I *intend* to use it in that way: I say, I
think I both used & intend*ed* so to use it.

P. 666. I say you can't be *properly said* to be "giving an analysis"
of a *concept* unless (1) you use 2 different expressions each of
which expresses the *same* (in some sense) concept, (2) the one
expression *explicitly mentions* concepts not explicitly mentioned
by the other and also *mentions* ⟨?⟩ the way in which these are
combined.

The 3 conditions on p. 663 are (as regards (a) & (b)) conditions
for distinguishing the *sense* in which the concept mentioned must
be the *same*—i.e. the sense in which the two expressions must be
synonymous.

I do not say these conditions are *sufficient*: e.g. " "cats mew"
is the same prop. as "∼ (∼ (cats mew))" " seems to fulfil them,
but, in saying this, no-one would say you are giving an *analysis*
of "cats mew"; and " "cats mew" is the same prop. as "it's true
that cats mew" " also gives no *analysis* of "cats mew". On the
other hand "Most cats on this earth mew" does give an analysis
of *one* prop. that is meant by "cats mew"; and this in its turn is
further analysed by saying it is the same prop. as "There are
many cats on this earth, and there are more cats on this earth
which mew than there are which don't".

[1] [P. A. Schilpp (ed.), *The Philosophy of G. E. Moore* (Evanston and Chicago,
1942).]

Another example of analysis is Langford's " "That is a small elephant" is the same prop. as "That is an elephant & that is smaller than most elephants" ". And this is enlightening because it shews that to say it's identical with "That is an elephant, & that is small" does *not* give a correct analysis.

Similarly to say "($\exists$ x). ϕx. χx" is the *same* prop. as "($\exists$ x). ϕx. ($\exists$ x). χx" is to give an *incorrect* analysis; and this is an example in which no *complete* analysis is possible. You are giving a correct *partial* analysis if you say it asserts ($\exists$ x). ϕx & also asserts ($\exists$ x). χx; but though it says *more* than these 2 things, it is not a *conjunction* of these 2 props. with any third.

To say the prop. "cats mew" contains as a part $\sim$ ($\sim$ (cats mew). $\sim$ (dogs bark)), i.e. (cats mew v dogs bark), is to give a false *partial* analysis of "cats mew"; since this, though it logically follows from "cats mew", is *not* "a part of", "contained in", "included in" the prop. "cats mew".

Similarly to say, as Hempel does, that ($\exists$ x). ϕx is the *same proposition* as ($\exists$ x). ϕx. $\sim$ (ϕx. $\sim$ ϕx) is incorrect, because the latter does *contain* ($\exists$ x). $\sim$ (ϕx. $\sim$ ϕx) whereas the former does not. If the former *is* the same as the latter it is also the same as ($\exists$ x). ϕx. $\sim$ (χx. $\sim$ χx) or ($\exists$ x). ϕx. $\sim$ (ψx. $\sim$ ψx): and hence also ($\exists$ x). $\sim$ (ϕx. $\sim$ ϕx) must be the same as ($\exists$ x). $\sim$ (χx. $\sim$ χx) etc. That is to say, he is committed to the view that every tautology is the same as every *other* tautology (a contradiction);—*every contradiction the same as every other contradiction.* (He thinks that $\sim$ ($\exists$ x). $\sim$ (ϕx. $\sim$ ϕx) is a contradiction, & therefore ($\exists$ x). $\sim$ (ϕx. $\sim$ ϕx) a tautology; but both seem doubtful).

Even if $\sim$ ($\exists$ x). $\sim$ (ϕx. $\sim$ ϕx) is the same as $\sim$ ($\exists$ x). $\sim$ (χx. $\sim$ χx), it seems clear that ($\exists$ x). ϕx. χx. $\sim$ χx, though a contradiction, is *not* the same as ($\exists$ x). ψx. χx. $\sim$ χx, which is also a contradiction.

2

SYNTAX AND ENTAILMENT

Hempel says (p. 38):[1] "With respect to language systems with a precisely determined logical structure, deductive logic has succeeded in establishing purely formal, or syntactical, CRITERIA of consequence", & refers *especially* to Carnap's *Logical Syntax*, § 72 & *Introd. to Semantics*, p. 250.[2]

Acc. he speaks (p. 38) of the *sentences* "Swan(a)" and "White(a)" being able to be *inferred* or *deduced* from the sentence "$\sim (\exists x)$. Swan(x) . $\sim$ white(x)".

To talk of *deducing* one sentence from another sentence is not English. What these people must mean is deducing *what is expressed by* one sentence from *what is expressed* by another.

With this sense of "S_2 can be deduced from (is a consequence of) S_1" whether this relation holds between S_1 & S_2 depends on whether *what is expressed by* S_2 can be deduced (in ordinary sense) from *what is expressed by* S_1. E.g. [the truth of the proposition] "the *sentence* "Swans exist" can be deduced from the sentence "White swans exist" *in English*" depends on whether it is true that the proposition that swans exist can be deduced from the proposition that white swans exist, since the sentence "swans exist" *in English* expresses the prop. that swans exist, and the sentence "white swans exist" *in English* expresses the prop. that white swans exist. If it were not true *both* that the prop. that swans exist can be deduced from the prop. that white swans exist, & *also true* that the sentences "swans exist" & "white swans exist" do *in English* express these 2 props., it would not necessarily be true that the first sentence can *in English* be deduced from the second. The sentences *might* have been used in English in such a sense that the first did not "follow" from the second.

Now there *might* be rules of English syntax (?) such that from

---

[1] [I think that this is a reference to the typescript of C. G. Hempel's "Studies in the Logic of Confirmation" which Moore must have read, as editor of *Mind*, in 1944. The article was published in the following year (*Mind*, vol. LIV, 1945), and a passage very similar to the one quoted above occurs there on p. 29.]

[2] [R. Carnap, *The Logical Syntax of Language* (London, 1937); R. Carnap, *Introduction to Semantics* (Cambridge, Mass., 1942).]

the construction of the two sentences, if you knew they were correctly formed English sentences, you might be able to tell that the first "followed" from the second, without knowing what they meant. But this could only be the case if the rules were such that 2 sentences related in that way were never used except with such meanings that the first *meaning* followed from the second: and you would have to know this in order to know that the first sentence "followed" from the second. And I suppose that by "a language system with a precisely determined logical structure" is meant simply a language which is such that any pair of sentences which express a pair of props. of which the first follows from the second are structurally related in a way in which no other pairs of sentences are. If this be the meaning, then Hempel's statement becomes a tautology, in so far as it states that in any such language there will be syntactical *criteria* for "following" between sentences. Certain relations of structure between sentences will be such that in the case of every pair which exhibits them the prop. conveyed by the first will entail that conveyed by the second; and also whenever the prop. conveyed by one sentence entails that conveyed by another the 2 sentences will exhibit these relations of structure. They will be "criteria" in the sense in which if men were the only featherless bipeds & there are no feathered men, being a featherless biped would be a "criterion" of being a man. But it wouldn't be true that *why* sentences with that relation "entailed" one another, was because they were of that structure; any more than it would be true that why a person was a man was because he was a featherless biped.

What Carnap, Hempel, etc. imagine, I am afraid, is that there might be a language having rules (rules of transformation?) such that from the structure of 2 sentences, S_1 & S_2, it would *follow* that the prop. expressed by S_2 *followed* from that expressed by S_1, & that there were syntactical *criteria*, not in the *empirical* sense of "criterion" just explained, but in the sense in which a man's being a male sibling is a *criterion* for his being a brother; i.e. that from the 2 props. that the rules were such & such & that S_1 & S_2 had the structure mentioned in the rules, it would *follow* that S_2 "followed" from S_1.

I do not believe that any linguistic rules can be criteria in this sense. It is natural to say that from the fact that "brother" in English *means* "male sibling" (a semantical rule) it *follows* that "x is a brother" entails "x is male". But all that really follows from this semantical rule is that the expression I've just used (i.e. " "x is a brother" entails "x is male" ") is a correct way of expressing in English an entailment which holds—namely that a prop. of the form "x is a male sibling" *entails* "x is male".

Suppose it were a syntactical rule in English that every sentence of the form "It is not the case that it's not the case that *p*" *meant the same as* the corresponding sentence of the form *p* (a rule of transformation). It would then follow from this rule (1), together with the prop. (2) that "cats mew" is an English sentence, that "cats mew" in English means the same as "It's not the case that it's not the case that cats mew" means in English. But from this prop. it would *not* follow (3) that the *prop.* "cats mew" entails & is entailed by the *prop.* "It's not the case that it's not the case that cats mew". In order to get *this* consequence (3), we shall certainly need in addition (4) the prop. that "cats mew" in English means that cats mew. But will (3) follow from the conjunction of (1), (2) & (4)? *No*, because (1), (2) & (4) would only yield the consequence (5) that the sentence "It's not the case that it's not the case that cats mew" means that cats mew. It would not throw any light on *the difference* between the prop. "cats mew" and the prop. "it's false that it's false that cats mew". There *is* a difference because understanding the latter sentence involves understanding the sentence "it's not the case (or it's false) that cats mew" or "∼ (cats mew)". We could say: There's a *synthetic* necessary connection between "Cats mew" & "∼ (∼ (cats mew))": the latter is not "included" or "contained" in the first.

3

LOGICAL CONSEQUENCE

q *follows logically from* p, may be used in 2 different ways.

From A. "Russell is bald" (a false prop.) there *follows logically* B. "It's not the case that it's not the case that R. is bald".

And C. "B follows logically from A" *follows logically* from D. "∼(∼p) follows logically from p".

D may be said to be "a prop. of pure logic", though it is not the same prop. as "p ⊃ ∼(∼p)" which is also a prop. of pure logic; & C may be said to be an *instance* of the generalisation D.

But that C follows logically from D is not an instance of any prop. of pure logic: it is only an instance of the generalisation ⟨Is it?⟩ "any instance of a prop. of pure logic is true".

(a) If a prop. of the form "p ⊃ q" is an instance of a prop. of pure logic, then q may be said to "follow logically" from p. And perhaps we can say that when B is said to follow logically from A, it is meant that A ⊃ B is an instance of a prop. of pure logic.

(b) But when it is said that C follows logically from D, it is not meant that D ⊃ C is an instance of a prop. of pure logic. D ⊃ C is not an instance of any prop. of pure logic: it is only an instance ⟨Is it?⟩ of the prop. "any prop. of pure logic ⊃ any of its instances".

4

(x) . φx AND φa

$(x) . \phi x = \sim (\exists x) . \sim \phi x.$

$(x) . \phi x \supset \chi x = \sim (\exists x) . \phi x . \sim \chi x.$

Take A. $\sim (\exists x)$. x is a man . $\sim$ x is not mortal.

Does there follow from this B. "It's not the case that *I* am a man & not mortal"?

From *negation* of B *negation* of A seems to follow: for, if I am a man & immortal, it follows that there is at least one immortal man.

But from A it does not follow that there is any such person as me; and B can't be true unless there is: ∴ B does *not* follow from A.

∴ $\sim$ A does not follow from $\sim$ B; i.e. "I am a man & immortal" is *not* the negation of B. Its negation is: "It's not the case *both* that I exist & that I am a man & not mortal".

(1) "I don't weigh 200 lbs." → (2) $(\exists x) . \sim$ (x weighs 200 lbs.). But (3) $\sim (\exists x) . \sim$ (x weighs 200 lbs.) ↛ (4) I weigh 200 lbs. (2) follows from (1), only because (1) entails "I exist". From "Ariel didn't weigh 200 lbs.", there does not follow $(\exists x) . \sim$ (x weighed 200 lbs.).

But (3) does *not* entail "I exist" whereas (4) does, & that is why (3) does not entail (4).

From (3) there does follow "Either I don't exist or I weigh 200 lbs.", which (& *not* 4) is the contradictory of (1). Does (1) = I *both* exist & don't weigh 200 lbs.?

(1) & (4) are not each other's contradictories, because both entail "I exist".

A prop. *of the form* "$\sim \phi a$" is ambiguous: it may mean "a exists & hasn't ϕ" or "it's not the case that a *both* exists & has ϕ".

From (3) there doesn't follow that there *is* any prop. of the form "x weighs 200 lbs.": it only says that, *if* there is, it's true.

5

IDENTITY

A. The word "white" is not identical with the word "black". This seems to be a true prop., but a *necessary* one; i.e. its negation self-contradictory.

Hence it would seem to follow that B. "The word "white" *is* identical with the word "black"" is a prop., but a self-contradictory & therefore false one.

But have (1) the word "black" is identical with the word "black" & (2) the word "black" is *not* identical with the word "black", any meaning at all?

The latter sentence seems to express a self-contradictory prop., & if so its negation would seem to express a necess. prop. Yet I feel it expresses no prop. at all: is nonsense.

A sentence of the form "— is identical with—" *never* expresses a prop. unless the word or phrase preceding "is identical with" is different from that which follows it.

This would seem to explain why (1) & (2) have no meaning, though A & B *have*.

I can utter the word "black" twice over; and the sound I make on each occasion may be the same. Yet I have made 2 sounds. ∴ the first was not identical with the second; it may have been identical *in quality* = exactly similar, and that is what I mean by saying I made the same sound on each occasion—twice over. But the second sound was not *numerically* identical with the first; since, if it were, it would not be true that I made 2 sounds. Yet it might be said that, in this case, "I made 2 sounds" means only "I caused the same sound to be simultaneous with 2 things, x & y, which were not simultaneous with one another." The fact that it was simultaneous with x was of course a different fact from the fact that it was simultaneous with y.

6

(x) φx AND φa

(1) "Stace is 6 ft. high" → (2) (∃ x) . x is 6 ft. high. (*Not*, perhaps, if we are using (∃ x) . φx as P.M.[1] intends to use it. For this asserts: "at least one prop. of the form "φx" is true"; but (a) perhaps props. of the form "x is 6 ft. high" are *not* of the form "φx" & (b), even if they are, perhaps "Stace is 6 ft. high" is not of the form "x is 6 ft. high", just as R. would say that "The King of France is 6 ft. high" is not of the form "x is 6 ft. high". What props. are of the form "φx" is never explained in P.M.)

But does the negation of (2) entail the negation of (1)?

The conjunction of (1) with ∼ (2) is certainly a contradiction. But does ∼ (1) *follow* from ∼ (2)?

It is certain that a person who knew ∼ (2) would not necessarily be able to *infer* ∼ (1). He would not if he didn't know that there was any such person as Stace. I know that there are no people a mile high, but I can't infer with regard to any person I've never heard of, the prop. that he isn't a mile high.

Moreover, if there were no such person as Stace, there would be no such prop. as (1). And from ∼ (2) it doesn't follow that there is such a prop.: only that, *if* there is, it isn't true. ∼ (2) only says: "No prop. of the form "x is 6 ft. high" is true". And from this it doesn't follow that there are any props. of that form. If nothing existed, there would be none; and there seems no contradiction in supposing that nothing exists. "Pickwick was 6 ft. high" is *not* of the form "x was 6 ft. high" bec. it does *not* entail "There was such a person as Pickwick": any prop. of the form "x is 6 ft. high" entails "There is such a person as x", just as "Stace is 6 ft. high" entails "There is such a person as Stace".

(1) *is* a prop. of the form "x is 6 ft. high"; & from this premiss *together with* ∼ (2), it follows that (1) is false. But that (1) is false does *not* follow from ∼ (2) *alone*.

[1] [*Principia Mathematica.*]

7

"INSTANCE"

(1) When I point at a thing & say "This is an instance of a lion", "a specimen", "an example", this is logically equivalent to "this *is* a lion": it can't be true unless the thing pointed at *is* a lion, & *must* be if it is. So "this is an instance of a female rhyme" "an instance of an anacoluthon" "an instance of a prop. of the form $(\exists x) . \phi x . \chi x$", etc. etc.

(2) But when I say "The fact that this is a crow & is not black" is an *instance* of the *truth* or *fact* that "not all crows are black", this is an entirely different use of "instance"; for I do not mean that fact (1) *is* fact (2). Fact (2) here *follows* from fact (1); but fact (1) doesn't follow from fact (2).

(3) Can I say that A. $\sim$ (cats mew . $\sim$ cats mew) is an "instance" of B. the law of contradiction, i.e. $\sim (p . \sim p)$? Here A follows from B, & *not* vice versa.

I can say "The fact that this [white] tom-cat with blue eyes is deaf" is an instance of the fact reported by Darwin that all white tom-cats with blue eyes are deaf. But I don't think we should say this, if we knew D.'s prop. to be false. We shouldn't say "The fact that this swan is white" is an instance of the prop. "All swans are white". We could say the prop. "all swans are white" was generalised *from* instances like this. They are instances of facts corresponding to the kind of prop., of which the generalisation asserts that all props. of that kind are true.

In this third sense, as in (2), it is not one *prop.* which is an instance of another *prop.* (we can *never* say this), but one *fact* which is an instance of a universal *truth*.

8

SYNTHETIC NECESSARY PROPOSITIONS

Any prop. of the form
"A. a began before b & b began before c : ⊃ : B. a began before c",
is necessary: i.e. it is a contradiction to assert "a began before b,
& b before c, but a did not begin before c."

But this is not an *explicit* contradiction and (1) B is not contained in A, in any proper sense; & also (2) it is not the case that
there is any necessary prop., which can be expressed without the
use of any constants but logical constants from which it *follows*
that A ⊃ B.

The prop.: (x, y, z) : x began before y . y began before z . ⊃ . x
began before z, from which any such prop. does follow, and of
which the corresponding fact is an "instance" (there always is
one, because every such prop. is *true*), is of course not a "purely
formal truth" or a "prop. of pure logic".

Let us define "purely formal truth" or "prop. of pure logic"
as: necessary truth which can be expressed without the use of any
constants but logical constants.

(∃ p) . p . ∼ p is a "purely formal *prop.*", but is not true &
hence is *not* a purely formal *truth*, nor a "prop. of pure logic".

9

I AND MY BODY

"Mine eyes have seen . . ." "Eye hath not seen, nor ear heard . . ."

We *can* therefore say that *eyes* see, *ears* hear, *noses* smell; but if I say that *my eyes are seeing* the words I am writing, that is only another way of saying that I am seeing them *with* my eyes—*by means of* my eyes.

And the sense in which I see *with* my eyes, & hear *with* my ears, differs in an important way from that in which I walk *with* my legs or write *with* my hand.

Walking & writing are processes which are *logically* dependent upon a movement of some part of my body; but seeing & hearing are only *causally* dependent upon changes in some part of my body. To say that walking or writing are taking place is to say that physical changes of a certain kind are taking place in the physical universe; but to say that seeing or hearing or thinking are taking place is *not* to say that any physical changes are taking place.

Even, therefore, if it is logically impossible that *I* should exist without a body, & hence the prop. that I am seeing at a given time & not at another *entails* the prop. that something is true of a body at the first which is not true of it at the second, the prop. that I first see & then cease to see, does not *entail* that any *physical* change has taken place, although we should have to say it does *entail* that something was first true of a *physical* object & then ceased to be true.

To say that I see *with* my eyes & hear *with* my ears, means only that my eyes & ears are *causally necessary* conditions for my seeing & hearing; but to say that I walk *with* my legs or write *with* my hand is *not* merely to say this: walking with my legs is *logically* dependent upon the existence of my legs. Some men can walk upon their hands; but walking *logically* involves some movement of a material thing; whereas seeing does not.

But what is a *physical* change? If my eyes first see a word & then cease to see it, why should we not say that they have undergone a *physical* change?

A *physical* change is a change of such a sort that from the fact that a change of that sort occurred during a certain period it does not follow that anyone was conscious during that period. But during a period in which my eyes first see a word & then cease to see it, somebody must have been *conscious* while they saw it, since to say that my eyes saw it is to say that I saw it *with* my eyes.

But *physical* does not mean merely "*not* involving consciousness". What does it mean positively?

For each one of us "physical space" means *the* space in which some object *of a certain kind* which he is perceiving at the moment or remembers having perceived in the past *is* or *was* situated. My body is an object of *the kind* in question; so are its parts—my hand, head, etc.; so are trees, stones, buildings, coins, loaves, trousers, etc. etc., the sun & the moon. One thing common to all such objects is that they are 3-dimensionally extended in a certain *sense*—*the* sense in which a penny is: we have to analyse what is meant by saying that a penny is 3-dimensionally extended—has a finite length, breadth & thickness—is a solid body. But the mere fact that a thing is or was a solid body in this sense, would not entail that it is or was in *physical space*. That it was or is also *entails* that it is or was *in the same space in* which *this* solid body which I am or was perceiving *is*. 2 people who are perceiving the same object at the same time, or who are remembering some object (e.g. St Paul's) which they both perceived in the past, may be using the same "description" for physical space—viz. the space in which *this* (perceived or remembered) solid body *is* or *was*. But 2 people who are doing neither only mean the same by "physical space" in the sense that they use different descriptions which apply to the same space: only because the object by reference to which the one is describing physical space is or was in fact *in the same space* in which the object by reference to which the other is describing it is or was. Each always means "*the* space in which *this* object is or was" (*this* object being a different object in the case of each).

(N.B. there is a sense of "solid body" in which the sun is *not* a solid body, nor any part of it, if it is gaseous throughout, though the moon is. I have been using "solid body" = 3-dimensionally extended, in *the* sense in which a penny is so.)

But what is meant by saying (a) that the sun is *now in the same space in which* my body is? and (b) that Napoleon's body *was in the same space in which* my body is? or (c) that the sun, ever since it existed, has been *in the same space in* which it is now?

(a) It is *now* in the same space if there are 2 different "distances", d_1 & d_2, (e.g. 100,000,000 miles & 80,000,000 miles) such that it can be said with truth that it is $<d_1$ & $>d_2$ *distant* from my body —where "distant" is used in the sense in which my piano is now more distant (further) from my body than this sheet of paper is. And any object, *even* if it is not *a solid body*, e.g. a rainbow or a reflection, can be said to be *in physical space* now, if this can be said of it with truth.

(b) *Nap.'s* body *was* in the same space in which my body *is* if either (α) it can be said with truth that any part of Nap.'s body was, at any time, *in the same* PLACE, in which some part of my body *is* or (β) there is any 3rd solid body (e.g. the sun, or the moon, or the Great Pyramid) such that at every time at which Nap.'s body existed there were a pair of distances d_1 & d_2 such that Nap.'s body could have been said with truth to be $>d_1$ & $<d_2$ from that body at that time, & there are a pair of distances d_1 & d_2 such that it can be said with truth that my body is $>d_1$ & $<d_2$ from that same body or (γ) it might have been, if neither (α) not (β) was fulfilled ((β) would not be fulfilled, if there happened to be no solid body which both exists now & existed at every time at which Nap.'s body existed). What would be meant then by saying it *was* (at *every* time when it existed) in the same space in which mine is? That it *might* have moved in such a way that some part of it was in *the same place* in which some part of mine *is*?

(c) It has been assumed above (in b) that any body which is in physical space *now* must have been in physical space ever since it began to exist. We don't call it the same body unless it was. It must have been in some place which was either the same as that in which it now is, or at some distance from that in which it now is. What do we mean by saying that a body is in *the same place* at one time as at another? (α) If it has been at rest during the whole period between the 2 times, including them, (β) if, though not at rest but rotating during the period it has undergone no translatory motion, (γ) if, though it has undergone translatory motion, it has *returned* to the same place. But is there any meaning in "absolutely at rest"? Certainly there is with regard to *sense-data*: we can say that a sense-datum is moving, or isn't moving. But in the case of physical objects we seem to have no means of finding out more than that one body has undergone or is undergoing a translatory motion *relatively to another*, or has not & is not.

10

COLOURS

What does Broad mean by "*literally* coloured"?

I think we can define it by saying: "coloured" in that sense of "coloured" which is such that there's no contradiction in saying "Something coloured exists now, but no material thing exists now". Images which I see in dreams & after-images which I see with closed eyes are "coloured" in this sense. There is a contradiction in saying: "I have an after-image, but no material thing ever existed", because to say of so & so that it *is* an after-image is to say that it is an image of a material thing seen before. And perhaps there is a contradiction in "I had a coloured image in a dream last night, but no material thing existed last night", because it may be that to say I was dreaming is to say that my body was asleep. But there is no contradiction in saying of a thing which *is* an after-image or a dream-image, that it might have existed without being an after-image or a dream-image.

11

"IF P, THEN Q"

If p then q = There is some true prop., satisfying the 3 conditions (a) that it is logically independent both of p & of q, (b) that it is *not* a conjunction of p ⊃ q with some other true prop., & (c) that p ⊃ q follows from it.

It follows that "if p then q" entails "p ⊃ q", but *not* vice versa; since p ⊃ q is *not* logically independent either of p or q, since ∼p entails p ⊃ q, & q also entails p ⊃ q. ∼p does *not* entail "if p, then q", nor does q.

Props. satisfying these 3 conditions may be of any of the 4 following kinds (possibly others as well).

(a) *Logically necessary props.*, either (α) props. of pure logic like ∼(p . ∼p), i.e. props. that can be expressed without the use of any constants but logical constants or (β) props. of pure mathematics, like 7 > 3 or (γ) universal props. that can only be expressed by the use of material constants, e.g. (x, y, z) : x began before y . y began before z . ⊃ . x began before z.

But we can cover all cases of this kind by saying that they are cases in which ∼(p ⊃ q) is a contradiction; i.e. ∼(∼(p . ∼q)) is a contradiction = p . ∼q is a contradiction, for *some other reason* than that p is a contr. or that ∼q is a contradiction.

E.g. if x was a brother, he was male; if there were 7 men in the room, there were more than 3; if you had breakfast before lunch & lunch before dinner, you had breakfast before dinner.

(b) Causal generalisations, e.g. being shot through the heart causes death.

If he was shot through the heart, he is dead ("must be").

(c) Empirical generalisations, e.g. All white tom-cats with blue eyes are deaf.

If that white cat over there is a tom & has blue eyes, it's deaf.

(d) Props. like

"My pass-book & passport are in the same drawer", "Hitler's invasion of Poland & England's declaration of war on Germany took place in the same month", "Chas. V & Don John of Austria had the same father".

"If my pass-book is in that drawer, so is my passport", "If H.

invaded in Sept., England declared in Sept.", "If Philip was Chas' father, he was Don John's father".

Such a sentence as "If H.'s invasion *had been* in Aug., E.'s decl. *would have been* in Aug." may have 2 different meanings, viz.

(a) $(\exists\, x, y)$. H. invaded in x & only in x . E. decl. in y & only in y . if x had been in Aug., y would have been in Aug.

(b) If H. had invaded in Aug., E. would have declared in Aug.

The truth of (a) follows from "It was in the *same* month that H.'s only invasion & E.'s only declaration occurred"; but the truth of (b) by no means so follows.

12

"IMMEDIATE INFERENCE"

An inference of q from p is said to be "mediate", if either (a) there is some 3rd prop., r, such that the person first infers r from p, & then q from r or (b) p is a conjunction & q is a prop. which is not one of the conjuncts in p.

"Immediate" = not mediate.

13

CONTRADICTION

For that use of "a contradiction" in which "that is a contradiction" = "that is a self-contradictory prop.", there are the following *species*:

1. Any prop. which is a conjunction of some prop. with its contradictory. E.g. "Some dogs sometimes bark and it is not the case that some dogs sometimes bark"; "This book is red and it is not the case that this book is red".

2. Any prop. which is a conjunction in which some prop. & its contradictory are 2 of the conjuncts but in which there are one or more other conjuncts as well. E.g. "Geo. VI is male & is a sibling, but it is not the case that Geo. VI is male"; "Geo. VI is both tall & fat, but Geo. VI is not tall".

3. Any prop. which *entails* both some prop. & its contradictory, but which is not a conjunction in which they are conjuncts. E.g. "This book is red, but it is not the case that this book is coloured", which entails "This book is coloured, but it is not the case that this book is coloured"; "There were 7 people in the room, but there were not more than 3 in it", which entails "There were more than 3 in it, but it is not the case that there were more than 3 in it".

4. Any positive existential prop. which entails that at least one prop. of kind 1 or kind 2 or kind 3 is true, though it is not itself of any of these kinds. E.g. $(\exists p) . p . \sim p$ (the contradictory of the Law of Contradiction); There are some books of each of which it is true both that it is red & that it is not the case that it is red; There are some people of each of whom it is true that the person in question is both male & a sibling, & also that it is not the case that the person in question is male; There are some books of each of which it is true that it is red, and also that it is not the case that it is coloured. I.e. props. *of the form* $(\exists x) . \phi x . \sim \phi x$; or $(\exists x) . \phi x . \chi x . \sim \phi x$; or $(\exists x) . \phi x . \sim \chi x$, where $(x) . \phi x \rightarrow \chi x$ is true.

14

INTERNAL PROPERTIES AND
CONTRADICTION

It seems as if "being a man", "being a tiger", "being a chair", etc., are internal properties of anything which possesses them. Any object which is a human being *could not have failed* to be one: whether an object is a human being or not depends upon *its internal constitution*; and an object with a different internal constitution would not have been *that* object.

It would seem to follow that to say of an object which is a man "That is not a man", is to say something *necessarily* false: but this is certainly not the case. A person who says of a man on a distant hill-side "That's not a man, it's a rock" is making a prop. which *might have been* true—a contingent, not a necessary, prop.

So far as I can see when we talk of "*describing*" a person or thing, we always mean mentioning *internal* properties of the person or thing in question; so that R.'s use of the term "description" is contrary to ordinary usage. If I say of G.M.T. that he is "the present Master of Trin." I am not by saying this *describing* him *at all*, either definitely or indefinitely. If I say that a man is 6 ft. in height, this would be called *part* of a "description" of him. And yet to be 6 ft. high does not seem to be an "internal" property of anything. *His height* is an internal property of a man, but what does it mean to say that this height is 6 ft.? People may say it involves a reference to the standard yard in Westminster Hall; but no-one is saying anything about this piece of metal when they say a man is 6 ft. high. To find out whether he is they would use an ordinary measuring rod or tape-measure or measuring instrument; but they would admit that any particular instrument might not be quite accurate, & they are not asserting a relation to any particular instrument. A most important element in what is *meant*, is that it tells you what he *would look like*, under ordinary circumstances. This is not so when we are told that the earth's diameter is 7918 miles.

I write the sentence "Dogs bark". The *token*-sentence I have written has for an internal property that it contains the word "dogs", & also that it contains the particular *specimen* (token) of that word which occurs in it. But that that token-sentence contains these is *not* a *necess.* prop., because it (the token-sentence) might not have *existed*. What is necess. is only that it could not have existed without containing that specimen. But that specimen might have existed without being contained in the token: it is an external property of the specimen that it is contained in that token.

But it is an internal property of *the sentence* (a type) "Dogs bark" that *the word* (a type) "dogs" occurs in it. And this *is* a necessary prop., since it only says that any specimen of that sentence *would* contain a specimen of the word "dogs": it does not assert that any specimen of either exists, although we cannot make the prop. without using a specimen. But though it is a necessary prop. it *does not seem* ⟨doesn't it?⟩ that its denial, i.e. "The sentence "dogs bark" does *not* contain the word "dogs" " is *a contradiction*. It is true that any sentence which did *not* contain "dogs" could not be identical with the sentence "dogs bark". But "The sentence "dogs bark" is not identical with the sentence "dogs bark" " is not a contradiction. ⟨Isn't it?⟩

15

"IT'S CERTAIN THAT"

Lewy tells me (Aug. 26/44) that in my Howison [Lecture][1] I assert both (a) that "It is certain that p" → "I know that p", & (b) that "I don't know that p" ↛ "It's not certain that p".

He says that this conjunction is inconsistent with "the principle of contraposition", & suggests that therefore (a) & (b) can't both be true.

I think that (a) entails that (b) is false, & (b) that (a) is false; & that hence to assert both (a) & (b) is a contradiction.

Which is false? or are both false?

(b) seems to be true, bec. it doesn't seem absurd to say: "*I* don't know that p is true, but yet I think very likely it is *certain*"; & also, if you ask "Is that certain?" you are not asking "Do I know that?" You may know that you don't know it, & yet be uncertain whether it isn't certain. "Many things which I don't know are certain" is not a contradiction. Hence (a) is false. Why I thought it true was because it is certainly absurd, & seems like a contradiction, to say "It's certain that dogs bark, but I don't know that they do". But this, I think, is only absurd for the same reason for which "Dogs bark, but I don't know that they do" is so; i.e. because by asserting p positively you *imply*, though you don't assert, that you know that p. "I know that it's certain that dogs bark, but I don't know that dogs bark" *is* a contradiction, just as "I know that dogs bark, but I don't know that they do" *is*.

"I don't know whether — is due to a virus or bacteria" ↛ "It's not yet certain whether — is due to a virus or to bacteria". This, I think, is quite conclusive against "It's certain that p" → "I know p", for at least *one* use of "certain". This use of "certain", so far as I can see, = "some human being knows that p"; though I think it is usually confined to cases where the knowledge in question has been obtained by proof or by inference. It is usually confined to universal props. such as scientific generalisations & math. theorems.

But that this isn't the *only* proper use of "certain", is shewn

[1] ["Certainty." Published for the first time in G. E. Moore, *Philosophical Papers* (London, 1959).]

by the fact that though I know at this moment that I am still alive, my friends in America would be expressing a true prop. correctly if they said at this moment "It's not certain that Moore is still alive". If by this they meant "No human being knows that M. is still alive", the prop. they expressed would be false; but it is clear that they wouldn't mean this, & that though they didn't they would be using language correctly. Here, I think, "It's certain that p" refers to a limited group of human beings, always including the speaker & those whom he addresses, & says only "Some*one* of this group knows that p"; so that "It's *not* certain that p" = "None of this group knows that p". But here again "It's certain that p" $\nrightarrow$ "I know that p", though, as in the other case, "I know that p" entails "It's certain that p": "I don't know that p, but it's certain that p" is not a contradiction.

For the truth of "It's certain that p", "I know that p" is sufficient, but not necessary. "Somebody knows that p" is necessary, but not sufficient, since "It's not certain that Hitler is still alive" may be true in spite of somebody (e.g. himself) knowing that he is.

Under what conditions is "It's not certain" false? In speaking, if any of the people you are talking to knows that p: e.g. if you say "It's not certain that they're married yet" & someone present says: "Oh yes, it is; I was present at the ceremony yesterday", that proves you were wrong. But you may be wrong even if nobody present knows the contrary. E.g. in the case of a mathematical theorem, if any mathematician has proved it, you will be wrong in saying it's not certain.

We are always referring to *human* knowledge: a thing is certain, only if some *human being* now living on the earth knows it. But the Hitler case shews that for *some* human being to know it, is *in some cases* not sufficient for it to be true that it is certain. Perhaps *in some cases*, e.g. of a mathematical theorem, this *is* sufficient as well as necessary. I think this is the case; i.e. "it's certain that p" *means different things* according as p is of one sort or another sort. If p is of a sort illustrated by the Hitler case, it is *necessary* that some human being *belonging to a certain group* should know p (i.e. that p is true); & perhaps the group referred to is different in different cases. It seems obviously to be the case that, in the case of one & the same prop. p, one set of people can say with truth "p is not certain", while another set can say "p is certain": Hitler can perhaps say with truth "It's certain that I'm alive", when we can say with truth "It's not certain that H. is alive".

It seems fair to say that "It's not certain that p" is used in 2 different ways: (1) = "None of this group either knows that p or knows anything from which p follows" = where "this group" includes the speaker & those he is addressing; & (2) = "No human being either knows that p or knows anything from which p follows".

The 2 corresponding uses of "It's certain that" should be (1) = Some one of this group knows that & (2) = Some human being knows that. But perhaps sometimes it means rather (3) "It's a matter of common knowledge that". If so, it seems that this is a use of "it's certain that" to which no use of "It's *not* certain that" corresponds.

The first use of "not certain" = "None of *this* group knows" is, of course, not *one* use but several different ones—"it's not certain that" means something different in the case of different speakers, though not in the case of *every* different speaker. But a speaker who does *not* belong to the group to which one speaker refers, will mean something different from what is meant by *that* speaker.

There is a use of "*possible*" in which "It's possible that p" = "It's not certain that $\sim p$"; & hence in this *use*, "possible" has at least 2 different *senses*, both different from that sense of "possible" in which "possible" = not self-contradictory. Hence the 2 senses are: (1) "No man *in this group* knows that $\sim p$ *or knows anything from which $\sim p$ follows*"; (2) "No human being knows that $\sim p$ or *knows anything from which $\sim p$ follows*". (The second clause will hardly do, bec. we can say it's possible a math. theorem is true, provided no human being knows it's not true, even though someone does know a set of truths from which it follows that it's not true, provided he hasn't seen that it follows.)

16

COMMON SENSE

I use the phrase the "Common Sense view of the world", & say
that my belief in (2) amounts to saying that this view is "in
certain fundamental features" wholly true.[1]

What is meant by saying that so-and-so is a feature or item in
"the Common Sense view of the world"?

Something like this: That it is a thing which every or very
nearly every sane adult, who has the use of all his senses (e.g. was
not born blind or deaf), believes or knows (where "believes" &
"knows" are used dispositionally). Does one need to add: And of
which, for many centuries, it would have been true to say this?

But now, we use "a thing which everybody knows or believes"
in such a way that we can say "That he was born is a thing which
everybody knows", although of course what I believe when I
believe that *I* was born is *not* the same thing as what you believe
when you believe that *you* were; & similarly that the existence of
other minds is a thing in which both A & B believe, although, of
course, what is meant is that A believes in the existence of minds
other than A's, & B in the existence of minds other than B's.
Thus "the Common Sense view" is not a collection of *props.*
every one of which is believed or known by every sane adult.

[1] ["A Defence of Common Sense", in J. H. Muirhead (ed.), *Contemporary
British Philosophy* (2nd series) (London, 1925). Reprinted in G. E. Moore,
Philosophical Papers (London, 1959). Cf. in particular p. 34 and pp. 44–45.]

17

IF

(1) "A's father was called P, but B's was not" → (2) ∼ (A & B had the same father).

Hence ∼ (2) → ∼ (1), & (∼ 2) = A & B had the same father.

But now take (3) "C & D are in the same drawer". Does this entail (4) "It's not true that C is in this drawer & D isn't"? We should certainly *say* that (4) *follows* from (3); but yet (3) certainly doesn't entail that there is any such drawer as "this drawer".

(5) "C is in this drawer & D isn't" → ∼ (3); & therefore (3) entails ∼ (5); and it's easy to confuse ∼ (5) with (4). But ∼ (5) must be understood as something which would have been true even if there had been no such drawer as this one, being the *contradictory* of (5). (5) *does* entail that there is such a drawer as this one, & hence, if there had been no such drawer, ∼ (5) would have been true.

If there had been no such thing as this drawer, (5) would have been false; ∴ (5) entails that there is such a thing as this drawer.

18

"TRUTH-POSSIBILITIES"
(WITTGENSTEIN, 4.28–4.31)[1]

It is possible for a pair of props. to be (1) both true, (2) the first false & second true, (3) the first true & second false, (4) both false.

What does it mean to say that these 4 things are *possible*?

A. There *are* pairs of which (1) is true, pairs of which (2), pairs of which (3), & pairs of which (4).

B. And since there are, it follows that the prop. "There are pairs of which (1) is true" *is not self-contradictory*, & similarly for (2), (3), (4).

But we must be careful not to suppose that we can say with truth: *Whatever pair you take*, there will be no contradiction in supposing (1) to be true of it, nor in supposing (2) or (3) or (4). On the contrary, (a) if either of the pair is self-contradictory, there *will be* a contradiction in supposing (1) to be true of it; & there will also be a contradiction (b) if the 2 are incompatible. So with (2), there will be a contr. (a) if p is necess. (= its negation self-contradictory); or (b) if q is self-contradictory; or (c) if $\sim$ p is incompatible with q. Similarly with (3), interchanging p & q. And with (4), there will be a contradiction if (a) either p or q is necessary, or (b) if $\sim$ p is incompatible with $\sim$ q.

But it is true that these are *exhaustive* possibilities, in the sense that *whatever* pair you take, *one* of the 4 must be true of it; and this, I think, is what W. meant.

⟨Yes; this is certainly what was meant—that they are the *only* possibilities, i.e. that it *must* be the case that *either* (1) or (2) or (3) or (4) is true of any pair—that if (1) isn't true, then either (2) or (3) or (4) must be; that if (1), (2) & (3) are all false, (4) must be true etc.; where the "*if . . . then*" is a case of *following*: to suppose all 4 false is *self-contradictory*.⟩

And it is also true that they are *mutually exclusive*: it is a contradiction, in the case of any pair whatever, to suppose

[1] [L. Wittgenstein, *Tractatus Logico-Philosophicus* (London, 1922).]

any 2 of these 4 things to be *both* true of it. E.g. the prop. $(p, q) : p \cdot q \cdot \supset \cdot \sim (p \cdot \sim q)$ is itself a *necess.* prop., but is apparently *not* a tautology in W.'s sense: or is it? It is something which will be true of p & q, no matter whether (1) or (2) or (3) or (4) is true of them.

19

WITTGENSTEIN'S SENSE OF "TAUTOLOGY"

How does W. use "tautology"?

He talks as if it were *sentences*, not *props.*, which were "tautologies"; & as if it were *sentences*, not *props.*, of which the "truth-possibilities" are given in the truth-tables (4.31).[1] Does he ever explain what he supposes to be meant by saying that an "elementary" *sentence* is "true"? Suppose the sentence "The moon is round" were an "elementary" sentence (it can't be, if he's right in saying that no elementary sentence can contradict another; for "M. is round" contradicts (is incomp. with) "M. is square"; also doesn't "round" = "of *some* round shape"?). He tells us (4.25) that "*the* state of affairs" (meaning, appar., *the* one meant by the sentence) "besteht", if the sentence is true, "besteht nicht" if it is false. If so, in saying that the sentence is true, you must be saying *what prop.* it expresses, & that this prop. is true: you can't be merely saying "expresses *some* true prop." nor "*the* prop. it expresses is true": that is to say, this is so if from "The sentence "M. is round" is true" it is to *follow* that the moon is round.

He says (4.431) that the expression "WWFW" (in case of 2 elementary sentences) expresses "the truth-conditions" of the sentence. *Which* sentence? p ⊃ q is fully expressed by "WF is false". But it is a *condition* for the falsehood of WF, that *either* WW, *or* FW, *or* FF should be true: on the other hand WF is *not* a condition for the truth of ∼ (WF).

In 4.46, in case of WWWW he says the *Wahrheitsbedingungen* are "tautologisch"; & that there "the sentence" is a "Tautologie".

⟨Of the "W"'s which W. puts to the right of the first 2 & the 4th "truth-possibs." in 4.442, he says (4.43) they express the "agreement" of a prop. with the "truth-poss." against wh. they are put; & of the absense of the W or (later, 4.431) presence of an F that it expresses the lack of agreement (disagreement) with the truth-poss. against wh. it is put.

Here it seems as if "agreement" must mean "consistency": it certainly can't mean that the truth-poss. is *true*, although in 4.43 he puts "wahr" in brackets after W.

Here it seems as if, when he says, in 5.101, that WWFW

---

[1] [L. Wittgenstein, *Tractatus Logico-Philosophicus* (London, 1922).]

expresses the same prop. as p ⊃ q, he must be saying that p ⊃ q is the *only* prop. which is *both* consistent with (1), (2) & (4), & inconsistent with (3).

But it certainly isn't since any prop. of the form "p ⊃ q . r", provided r is not inconsistent with p ⊃ q nor self-contradictory, will be consistent & inconsistent with the same.

But suppose we take W to mean "follows from", & F to mean "is inconsistent with"; then: Is it true that p ⊃ q is the only prop. which *both* follows from each of the 3, (1), (2) & (4), & is inconsistent with (3)?

p ⊃ q is the negation of (3) & is therefore inconsistent with (3); but ∼p, q, & the conjunction of p ⊃ q with any other prop. whatever, are also inconsistent with (3). None of these, however, follows from *each* of the 3, (1), (2) & (4); & therefore, so far as I can see p ⊃ q does fulfil this condition.[1] But it does so, only if "p ⊃ q" is the same prop. as "∼(∼1 . ∼2 . ∼4)", for this prop. also follows from each of the 3, & is inconsistent with (3), since (1), (2), (3) & (4) are all mutually inconsistent.⟩

In W.'s symbols WWFW etc. (4.442 & 5.101), the W does not stand for "is true" but only for "is consistent with" (übereinstimmt): e.g. (WWFW) (p, q) = p ⊃ q; & this, of course, does not state that p & q are both true, or that they're both false, or that p is false & q true, it only states something which *follows* from each of them separately. It is, of course, *impossible* that (1), (2) & (4) should all be *true* together: but each of them separately is a *sufficient* condition, though not a necess. one, for the falsehood of (3). The F on the contrary does seem to say that (3) is false: indeed the whole expression (WWFW) (p, q) is merely another way of saying "It's false that (3)"; and it seems doubtful whether in saying this you are saying anything about (1), (2) & (4) at all, although what you are saying is in fact not only consistent with each, but would follow from each separately.

But now in WFFF = p . q, W does seem to mean that (1) is *true*; not merely that p . q is *consistent with* or *follows from* (1), which *is* p . q. And here again the Fs can be taken to mean "is false".

Taking the 16 given in 5.101:

In (2), (3), (4), (5), (6), (7), (8), (9), (10), (11) the F means "false", the W only "consistent with" or "follows from".

---

[1] [I.e. the condition stated in the preceding paragraph.]

But in (12), (13), (14) & (15) the W means "is true", while the Fs still mean "is false".

It seems doubtful whether (1) & (16) can be properly called "truth-functions" of p & q; they certainly are not if we define "truth-function" = prop. whose truth or falsehood depends only on the truth & falsehood of the props. which are its arguments, since neither (1) nor (16) depends at all on this.

In (1) W certainly means only "is consistent with"; & in (16) F for the first time seems to mean only "is inconsistent with", *not* "is false"; since "p . ∼ p . q . ∼ q" certainly does not seem to be identical with the statement that (1), (2), (3), (4) are all false.

In what sense are (1), (2), (3) & (4) "conditions", as W. seems to say they are (4.41) of the truth & falsehood of "*the* propositions" or "props."?

Is a conjunction a "prop."?

Then (1) is not a *condition* of the truth of p . q but *identical* with it. Each of (2), (3) & (4) is a *sufficient* but not a necessary condition for the falsehood of p . q; & that *one or other* of the 3 should be true is both a sufficient & necessary condition for its falsehood. Moreover, *not* (2), (3) & (4) themselves, but *that they should all be false* is both a necessary & a sufficient condition for the truth of (1), i.e. of p . q.—In 4.442 W. says that *his last column* expresses the "truth-condition". In the case of p . q the last column is WFFF. And what this tells us is that (1) is true, & (2), (3), (4) false. In telling us this is it expressing the truth-conditions of (1)?

[*Later addition*]

Both von Wright & Lewy suppose that what WWFW means is that (1), (2) & (4) are not *all* false (this they call saying that *either* (1), *or* (2), *or* (4) is true), & that this is the *same* prop. as that (3) is false: so that WWFW is saying the same thing twice over in different words.

If so WWWW (i.e. the tautology of any 2 props.) should mean that (1), (2), (3) & (4) are not all false. Now W. 5.101 says it means ∼ (p . ∼ p) & ∼ (q . ∼ q). Is this the same prop.?

20

INTERNAL QUALITIES

When I say of a sense-datum that it *is red*, I am saying either (1) that it is of some absolutely specific shade of red all over or (2) that it's of shades of red which vary continuously or (3) that it has a set of parts, each of which is either of some a.s. shade all over, or is of shades of red which vary continuously.

But any absolutely specific shade, or any continuum of shades which it is of, is *related* to it in a certain manner: to say that it is *of* that shade is to assert that it is *related* to that shade, since *it* consists in the occupation of a place by that shade, & *occupation* is a relation: so that a shade of red is not a "universal" in the sense that it can be predicated of anything: what can be predicated of a sense-datum is that it is *of* that shade, i.e. is related to it in a certain manner.

But to say of a *place* that it is *of* a certain *shape* is *not* to say that it is *related* to that shape; or to say of a shade of red that it is a shade of red is *not* to say that it is *related* to anything.

How about saying of a sense-datum that it is *extended*? This again doesn't seem to be saying that it is *related* to anything.

To say of a sound that it is soft, or high in pitch, doesn't seem to be saying that it is *related* to anything.

When you say of a shade of red that it *is* a shade of red, what you are asserting of it is *not* a relational property; but when you say of a sense-datum that it is red what you are asserting of it *is* a relational property. But when you assert that a sense-datum is round or square or triangular, I don't think that what you're asserting of it is a relational property.

But whether relational properties or "qualities", all these are *internal* properties of any sense-datum which possesses them, i.e. any sense-datum which didn't possess them wouldn't have been *that* sense-datum.

Of a physical sound it's perfectly sensible to say that it would have *sounded louder* to me if I'd not had wool in my ears; but of a soft sense-datum as short as a tick it's absurd to say that *it* might have been louder.

But how about a sound which lasts a considerable time? *It*

may *change* in quality, become softer or louder, higher or lower. Of the *whole* sense-datum which thus changes it's absurd to say that *it* might not have changed. But of an early part of it it's not absurd to say that *it* might not have changed—might have remained at the same pitch or intensity. But a sound has *early* parts; whereas an after-image hasn't. This is the business of phases.

But to return:—

Suppose I have an after-image which *is* (1) extended, (2) triangular, (3) red. Does "is" mean the same thing in all 3 cases?

Is extended = is of *some* (large or small) size; is tri. = is of *some* triangular shape; is red = is either (a) *of* some one absolutely specific shade of red all over or (b) is *of* some abs. specific continuum of shades of red or (c) has a set of parts such that each part is either *of* some a.s. shade or is *of* some a.s. continuum of shades.

21

"IF . . . THEN . . ."

Consider: If (1) "There were 5 last night" entails "There were more than 3", then (2) "There were 7" entails "There were more than 3".

This is certainly true. What true prop. is there which entails "(1) parules (parates) (2)[1]"?

Lewy says it doesn't seem that (1) *by itself* entails (2). An extra premiss is required, viz. "7 > 5". ∴ the true prop. is *not* (1) entails (2). Whereas in "If there were 5, there were more than 3" the true prop. which entails "There were 5" ⊃ "There were more than 3" *is perhaps* "There were 5" entails "There were more than 3". But isn't it rather: (ϕ) . There were $5\phi \to$ There were more than 3ϕ? In any case there is *a* true prop. which entails "There were 5" ⊃ "There were more than 3".

But in our case is there? *What* prop.?

Is it the *conjunction*: (a) $7 > 5$, (b) (n) :. there were $n\phi \to$ there were more than $3\phi : \to :$ there were more than $n\phi \to$ there were more than 3ϕ?

---

[1] ⟨"parules" was my suggestion as English for "⊃", in order to avoid "implies" or "materially implies".

p parules q = def. $\sim (p . \sim q)$

But "parates" would be better, since you need a verbal noun, corresponding to "implication", & this gives "paration".⟩

IS TRUE

It is true *now* that I'm sitting in a chair but it won't be true this afternoon & wasn't true last night.

"It's true now that I'm sitting" = "I'm sitting now". That I'm sitting now is true; but is it *true now*?

(1) If at any time *the prop. that an import duty is paying* is true, then *the prop. that* that *duty is not protecting* is also true.

If at any time & place *the prop. that it's raining* is true, then at that time & place *the prop. that there are clouds overhead* is also true.

(2) If at any time the prop. that an import duty is paying is true, then *at that time* the prop. that an import duty is not protecting is also true.

(1) & (2) are quite different props.

(1) might be expressed by: "If it's true that an import duty is paying, it is also true that *that* i.d. is [not] protecting".

RAMSEY ON "THE LIAR"

Ramsey says[1]: "I am lying" is to be analysed as "($\exists$ "p", p) : I am saying "p" . "p" means p . $\sim$ p".

This won't quite do, even for "I am making a false assertion" because, e.g., while *saying* "I am making a false assertion", a man might be *writing* a sentence which expressed a false prop., e.g. "I did not steal that bicycle", in which case what he *said* would be true, & no even apparent contradiction would result. It is only if the *only* assertion he is making at the time is that which he makes by saying the words "I am making a false assertion", that an apparent contradiction results.

"I am making a false assertion" certainly *could* mean "($\exists$ "p", p) : I am saying *or writing* "p" . "p" means p . $\sim$ p" which would be true if, while he said "I am making a false assertion", he were writing "I did not steal that bicycle" & in fact he did steal it.

("*You* are lying" = "You are making an assertion which you *believe* or know to be false", i.e. it does not entail "You are making an assertion which *is* false": for there is no contradiction in "You are lying, though what you are saying is *not* false", because there's none in "You are saying something which you believe to be false, though in fact it isn't." But there is an absurdity in "*I* am making an assertion which I believe to be false, but which isn't false", just as there is in "I believe it's raining, but it isn't", *though* both *might* be true. Hence though "I am making an assertion which I know or believe to be false" does not *entail* "I am making a false assertion", yet by saying the former a person does *imply* that he is making a false assertion, though *what* he asserts does not *entail* that he is. For this reason it's not important to distinguish between "*I* am lying" & "I am making a false assertion", though it *is* important to distinguish between "I *was* lying" & "I *was* making a false assertion", since it may turn out that though you were lying when you asserted p, p was in fact true.)

Let us take "This sentence which I am now uttering

[1] [F. P. Ramsey, *The Foundations of Mathematics* (London, 1931).]

expresses a false proposition". This is (∃ p) : this sentence expresses p . ~ p.

Why not take "This prop. which I'm now asserting is false"?

Bec. "*this* prop." will only lead to the difficulty if it means "the prop. which *this* sentence expresses is false"?

NOTEBOOK VII

(Begun Feb. 9/46)

1

"IF P, THEN Q" AND "P ⊃ Q"

I propose to use the expression (which I will call "A") "sentence of the form "If it is true that p, it is also true that q" " as short for the expression "sentence which can be obtained from the expression "If it is true that p, it is also true that q" by substituting for each of the two letters "p" & "q" some English sentence such that the sentence formed by adding "it is true that" before the sentence in question is grammatically correct"; and, similarly, to use the expression (which I will call "B") "sentence of the form "The two propositions "p" & "$\sim q$" are not both true" " as short for "sentence which can be obtained from the expression "The two props. "p" & "$\sim q$" are not both true" by substituting for the letter "p" some English sentence, such that the sentence obtained by adding before it the words "it is true that" is grammatically correct, & for the symbol "$\sim q$" some Eng. sentence consisting of the words "it is not the case that" followed by some sentence such that the sentence obtained by adding before it the words "it is true that" is grammatically correct." Thus I shall be so using A, that the sentence "If it is true that it is raining, it is also true that there are clouds overhead" is unquestionably a sentence of the form "If it is true that p, it is also true that q", since it can be obtained from this expression by substituting for "p" the sentence "it is raining" & for "q" the different sentence "there are clouds overhead", & since each of these two sentences satisfies the condition, that, when it is preceded by "it is true that" the whole thus formed is in English grammatically correct; and similarly, I shall be so using B, that the sentence "The two props. "It is raining" & "It is not the case that it is raining" are not both true" is unquestionably a sentence of the form "The two props. "p" & "q" are not both true".

Now *some* sentences of the form "If it is true that p, it is also true that q" can, it seems to me, be properly used in English in two very different ways. The sentence "If it is true that it is raining, it is also true that there are clouds overhead" is an example of such a sentence. It may express what Keynes calls a "conditional" prop., viz. when it means the same as "*Whenever* it is true that it is raining, it is also true that there are clouds overhead." But it may express what he calls a hypothetical or "pure hypothetical", viz. when it means "If it is raining *now*, there are clouds overhead *now*".

It is only with the latter I am now concerned: and I want (1) to shew that such a proposition is *never* identical with *the corresponding* prop. of the form "It is not the case that p & ~ q are both true": i.e. "If it's raining now, there are clouds overhead now" is *not* identical with "The two props. that it is raining now & that it is not the case that there are clouds overhead now are not both true". (2) To enquire *how* a "hypothetical" prop. of the form "If p, then q," differs from the corresponding prop. of the form ~ (p . ~ q). For it is certain that the truth of ~ (p . ~ q) is a *necessary* condition for the truth of "If p, then q": but it is not *sufficient*. What else is necessary?

I'm sitting down, & *consequently* if I'm standing up, every other prop. is both true & false.

Absurd!

If I'm both sitting down & not sitting down, every other prop. is both true & false.

No!

I'm sitting down, & *consequently* the 2 props. "I'm not sitting down" & " ~ (The moon both is & is not made of green cheese)" are not both true.

And *consequently* if the former *is* true, the moon is both made & not made of green cheese.

I know quite well that I'm sitting down, & consequently I know quite well that if I'm not, the moon is made of green cheese & also the moon is not made of green cheese.

Absurd!

If I know that ~ (p . ~ q) *&* *don't* know that ~ p *&* *don't* know that q, then I can infer that "If p, then q".

But I can only know that ~ (p . ~ q) without knowing either ~ p or q, if I know something *other* than ~ p & than q, & which does not entail these, from which ~ (p . ~ q) follows.

But "If A. ~ (p . ~ q) is *true*, it follows that B. if p is true, ~ q is false".

You *can't* have A true & B false.

Yes, you can! If the first is true, the second is nevertheless false, if *you know* that ~ p.

I.e. "If p, then q" entails "I don't know that ∼ p".

A man who says "∼ (p . ∼ q), but it's not the case that if p, then q" is not contradicting himself.

Why not?

Because, if he *knows* that ∼ p, he is right in saying "∼ (if p, then q)".

Why?

Because by saying "if p, then q" he would *imply* "I don't know that ∼ p"? Or because "if p, then q" *entails* "I don't know that ∼ p"?

Is "I know that ∼ p, but nevertheless if p, then q" a contradiction?

Is "p is false, but *if* p is true, q is true too" a contradiction?

(1) "p is false" *and* (2) "p & ∼ q are not both true" is certainly *not* a contradiction; on the contrary (2) follows from (1).

If p & ∼ q are not both true it *follows* that if p is true ∼ q must be false

      seems merely another way of saying

If p & ∼ q are not both true it *follows* that the conjunction of p with ∼ q is false,

      which is certainly the case.

"The conjunction of my uncle's coming & his not bringing me a present *won't happen*, but I'm not at all sure he won't come" implies "My reason for asserting that the conjunction won't happen is not that I feel sure he won't come".

Is "If p & ∼ q are not both true, then if p is true ∼ q is not true" sometimes merely another way of saying "If p & ∼ q are not both true & p is true, then ∼ q is not true"?

If so, there is no objection to it.

(∼ (p . ∼ q) and p) certainly does entail ∼ (∼ q) = q.

But ∼ (p . ∼ q) does not entail "if p, then q".

To put it otherwise

(1) "If a man knows that ∼ (p . ∼ q) & also that p, he can be sure (infer) that q" *is true*;

but (2) "if a man knows that ∼ (p . ∼ q) he can be sure (infer) that if p then q" *is false*.

In other words "If p & ∼ q are not both true, then if p is true ∼ q is not true" can be used in two different ways: it may mean (1) & then is true, it may mean (2) & then is false.

(2) is false because a man who knows that ∼ (p . ∼ q) (a) may

also know that ~ p, in which case he could not correctly say "if p *is* true, q is true", because by using this expression a man implies "I don't know for certain that ~ p"; and because it is absurd to say "Since ~ p, if p is true q is true" or "If ~ p, if p is true q is true"? (b) may also know that q, in which case he could not correctly say "if p is true, q is true", because by using this expression one implies "It is not the case that if p is not true, q is true", "It is not the case that q is true, whether p is true or not"? Moreover ~ (p . ~ q) follows from q, but "If p, then q" does *not*.

2

AUTONYMOUS

Carnap (*Syntax*, p. 16)[1] defines "autonym" as what we call a "Zeichen" which occurs as a name for itself "(or, more accurately: for its own form)", or which *serves* as a name for itself. (He says he will use '(' as a "syntactic name" for '(' in the "object-language", so that it is short for "opening limb of a bracket"; & that it then "occurs autonymously".)

On p. 109, he illustrates by contrasting (3) "Omega is a letter", with (4) " 'Omega' is not a letter but a word consisting of 5 letters". And goes on to say that (4) does not "deal with" Omega but with 'Omega', & that hence while we can say that the word 'Omega' *appears in the subject-place* in (3), we must not say that it does in (4) but must say that what occurs in the subject-place in (4) is the expression " 'Omega' " (i.e. the expression formed of the word 'Omega' together with single quotes).

Carnap seems to suppose that in (4) you are *not* using the word "Omega" as a name for itself, but are only using the expression " 'Omega' " as a name for that word. But why should we not say you are using it as a name for itself, & that the single quotes don't form part of an expression which you are using as a name for it, but only serve to indicate that you are using it as a name for itself?

He may quite properly, as he has chosen to do, say that what "stands in the subject-position" in (4) is *not* the word "Omega", but an expression of which this word forms a part, viz. " 'Omega' ". And he would apparently say that in (4) the word "Omega" is *not* being used autonymously at all. And he is, of course, entitled to use "autonymously" in such a way that this is true. But in that case "used autonymously" does *not* mean the same as "used as a name for itself"; for in (4) the word "Omega" certainly is used as a name for itself, even if you can also truly say that an expression of which it is only a part, viz. " 'Omega' ", is *also* being used as a name for it.

"Autonymous" does not occur in O.E.D. Is it an invention

[1] [R. Carnap, *Logische Syntax der Sprache* (Wien, 1934). Eng. trans. *The Logical Syntax of Language* (London, 1937).]

of Carnap's? In that case we should adopt his usage, & not use "used autonymously" = "used as a name for itself".

On p. 195[1] I say that I will *call* the sentence "The King of France is wise" "T" & that I will call the sentence "at least one person is K. of F., at most . . ." "U".

I.e. I say that I shall use the capital letter "T" as a *name* for the sentence "The King of France is wise".

But when, on p. 198, I say "I was using T merely as a name for itself" I am using "T" *as short for* the expression "the sentence "The King of France is wise" "—in such a way that this expression might be substituted for "T" without changing the meaning.

Can it possibly be true that where I am using "T" as *short* for the expression "the sentence "The King of France is wise" ", I am *also* using it as a *name* for that sentence? Carnap (p. 110) points out, quite justly, that to use one expression as a *name* (Bezeichnung) for another is quite a different thing from using it as *short* for that other. He says "An abbreviation does not "bedeuten" the expression of which it is an abbreviation, but "bedeutet" that which the latter bedeutet", where we can suppose that whatever is *a name* for anything "bedeutet" the thing in question.

The expression "the word 'Chicago' " is used as a name for the word 'Chicago'. And similarly the expression 'the sentence "The K. of F. is wise" ' is used as a name for that sentence. Hence if T can be substituted for this expression it *is* a name for the sentence in question though short for "the sentence "The K of F. is wise" ".

What I imply is that when I used the expression "the sentence 'the K. of F. is wise' " I was using a *part* of this expression, viz. the part between the single quotes, as a name for itself. Was I right in this? Carnap would apparently say that I was not using it "autonymously"; and he has a right so to use the word "autonymously" that I was not; but, if I am right, he is wrong in suggesting that what he means by (a) "use autonymously" is the same as what is ordinarily meant by (b) "use as a name for itself": (a) entails (b), but (b) does not entail (a).

What reasons can I give for saying that when I wrote the

[1] ["Russell's 'Theory of Descriptions' ", in P. A. Schilpp (ed.), *The Philosophy of Bertrand Russell* (Evanston and Chicago, 1944). Reprinted in G. E. Moore, *Philosophical Papers* (London, 1959).]

expression "the sentence 'The K. of F. etc.' " I was using the sentence which this expression *names* merely as a name for itself? *Merely* = *not* to express a prop. It can be said that I was using the sentence in question *not* merely as a name for itself, but also as *part* of a name for itself, viz. the expression "the sentence 'The K. of F. . . .' ".

By its use I was certainly indicating *what* sentence I was talking of.

It is like giving an *ostensive* "definition". Whom are you calling "George"? You *point at* the person. Here, instead of pointing, you say or write the sentence in question. You *could* answer by pointing at it. (N.B. when we say "He is called George" it is quite correct *not* to put quotes round "George" or to write it in italics; so that this is an autonymous use in Carnap's sense. George in italics & George in romans are different *expressions*, though they are the same *word*; so that, apparently, if you use italics instead of quotes you *are* in Carnap's sense using the word autonymously, though *not* if you use quotes. This seems very arbitrary & inconvenient.)

Use S autonymously = are making a prop. about S, & in the sentence in wh. you express that prop. are using S to indicate that it is about S you are making it.

3

"THE A. OF W.
MIGHT NOT HAVE BEEN A. OF W."

This is true. But does it mean: "The A. of W. was not A. of W."
is not self-contradictory?

(∃ x) . x alone invented W. . x did not invent W., certainly is a
contradiction.

What is *not* a contradiction is

(∃ x) . x alone invented W. . x might not have invented W.

= (∃ x) . x alone invented W. . the prop. that x did not invent W.
is not a contradiction.

And this, I think, is how we should always use the expression at
the top. We shouldn't use it to mean " "The A. of W. was not
A. of W." is not a contradiction"; for this is false.

"The author of W. *must* have invented W." is true, & therefore
does not contradict "The A. of W. might not have invented W."

So similarly: "The sentence (A) 'The moon is round' means
what it means" = "(∃ p) . A means p : and : (p) . ∼ (A means
p . A does not mean p)".

But (A) might not have meant what it does mean, is perfectly
true, & does not involve the absurdity of saying that "(∃ p) . A
means p & A does not mean p" is not self-contradictory: what it
does say is "(∃ p) . A means p and 'A does *not* mean p' is not
self-contradictory."

4

SENTENCES AND PROPOSITIONS

Suppose a person asks me what "mensa" means, & I say "table". Am I telling him anything about the *word* "table"? If I were to say "There is a table in the next room", it would seem I am *not* telling him anything about the word "table". Why should I be in the other case? And if he believes me, would he necessarily be believing that the word "table" has the same meaning as the word "mensa"? Even if he would, yet if he understands the word "table", won't he be believing something about the word "mensa", which he would not be believing about it, if he did not understand the word "table"? I am answering his question, *only* if (provided he believes me at all) I produce this extra belief in him. But, even if I do, am I necessarily answering his question? No: only if I *intend* to produce this belief in him. Suppose I want to tease him, & answer "τράπεζα", hoping that he won't understand this word, but he does happen to understand it. I shall then have produced the same extra belief in him as if I had said "table", but shall I have "told" him what "mensa" means— have answered his question? In a sense, Yes; but not in the most natural sense. I shall have caused him to believe something which, whether true or false, would be an answer to his question, but if I did not intend to cause any such belief, I have not, in the straightforward sense, told him the thing in question. I have "let the cat out of the bag", by telling him that the two words have the same meaning; but if I thought he hadn't understood "τράπεζα", I might quite rightly say that I hadn't told him what "mensa" meant—that I had *only* told him that "τράπεζα" had the same meaning, had *only* given him an equivalent which he wouldn't understand. The mere fact that he did in fact understand it wouldn't prove that I had told him what "mensa" meant, if I didn't intend to tell him. There is a sense in which you can be said to have asserted, only what you intended to assert?? ⟨No⟩ Certainly you *can* be properly said to have asserted things which you didn't intend to assert. If by a slip you say "Broad" when you mean "Moore", you can be said to have asserted that Broad lectured for 4 terms at Columbia, when all you intended to assert was that Moore did; & you *can* be said to have *told* people that Broad did. This is a case where you weren't *thinking* that Broad did, but only that Moore did: you *said* Broad did, but didn't mean it. "I told him that "mensa" meant τράπεζα; but I didn't tell him what "mensa" meant" is a perfectly sensible thing to say. But can it be true, if he in fact understood "τράπεζα"? It looks as if it couldn't. Is it sensible? It is certainly sensible to say: "I told him that "mensa" meant τράπεζα, but he didn't know what τράπεζα meant, so of course I wasn't answering his question—I didn't succeed in telling him what "mensa" meant". This shews conclusively (?) that to make an assertion of the form " 'mensa' means the same as '——' " is not the same thing as to tell a person what "mensa" means: you will not be telling him what "mensa" means unless he *understands* the word that takes the place of the dash. This is a *necessary* condition; but is it also sufficient?

Suppose one said "I told him that "mensa" meant the same as "tompa", thinking that "tompa" was a mere nonsense word & meaning to tease him; but by an extraordinary coincidence it turned out that "tompa" does mean "table" in Hausa, & he knew it, so that he did *gather* the meaning of "mensa" from what I said". Could this man be properly said to have *told* his friend what "mensa" meant? That he *couldn't* is indicated by the word "gather". But what if instead of saying "meant the same as "tompa" ", he had said *meant* "tompa", would "gather" be natural here? wouldn't it be more natural to say "so that he understood what I said, though I had thought it was nonsense, & what I said happened to be true"?

There seems no contradiction in saying: "He asked me what "mensa" meant; but I didn't tell him. I only told him that "mensa" meant the same as "τράπεζα", feeling pretty sure he wouldn't know what "τράπεζα" meant. But it turned out that he did know what "τράπεζα" meant, so that he was able to gather from what I said that "mensa" meant table, though I hadn't told him so".

This seems like: "I didn't tell him that he was illegitimate. I only told him that his father's present wife wasn't his mother, thinking he'd suppose that his father was married to his mother before he married his present wife. But he happened to know that his father had married his present wife 3 years before he was born; & that was how he discovered he was illegitimate. I didn't tell him."

The question then arises: Why is it correct to say in case (1), I didn't tell him what "mensa" meant? I did tell him, with regard to a word which he in fact understood (= knew what it meant) that "mensa" meant the same as that word meant. What more than this would have been required to make it true that I *did* tell him what "mensa" meant? I can only see 2 possible answers: (1) that I should have *intended* to create in him the extra belief, over & above the belief that the first word meant the same as the second, which he would have had about the first word if he had understood the second: this is an intention I might have had, in a case in which he didn't in fact understand either word, & in that case we should say I told him, but he didn't *understand me*; (2) that I should have believed he would understand the 2nd word: if I believed he wouldn't, I could hardly have had the *intention* mentioned under (1), since if I had that intention I should certainly choose a word which I thought he would understand. A person who wanted to tell the meaning would certainly choose a word which he thought would be understood—though he might be very careless about it—at least, he would reject any word which he thought wouldn't be understood, though he might not think positively with regard to the word he used that it *would be* understood. But from the fact that I say that 2 words mean the same, & believe you understand the second, it by no means follows that I'm telling you what the first means: I may, if I believe you understand both, be merely giving you an instance of synonyms. But suppose I believe you *don't* understand the first & do understand the second, must I, when I tell you that the first means the same as the second, be *telling you the meaning of* the first—or at least saying that so & so is the meaning (I may be lying or mistaken)? I *think* this is sufficient, without mentioning intention.

No: it's not sufficient—a necessary condition is that *I* should understand the second word.

Several cases must be distinguished:—

Suppose I tell him that "mensa" means the same as "τράπεζα", without myself understanding either word.

In that case, certainly, it's correct to say "I didn't tell him what "mensa" means; I couldn't, because I didn't know: all I

told him was that it had the same meaning as τράπεζα—whatever
that might be". But there's a catch about this. I could have told
him *that* "mensa" meant so & so, *without* knowing what it meant.
E.g. I could have *said* " "Mensa" means chair" just guessing or
making a mistake. I could have given him *an* answer to his question, without knowing whether the answer was correct or not.
What we need to know is what is necess. to entitle us to use the
words "I gave an answer to his question". And it is necess. that *I*
should have understood the *second* word I used: it is not sufficient
that *he* should have: since though, if he does & he believes me, he
will have been led to believe that "mensa" means so & so, the
prop. that it did mean that was *not* the one I was making. But
isn't it one which my words *meant*?

Suppose a parrot has been taught to say "My name's Nancy".
When it says these words, is it saying that its name is Nancy?
Yes & No. *Yes*, if all that's meant is that it said *some* words which
meant that its name was Nancy; & it's not incorrect to use "It
said that its name was Nancy" in such a way that all the *parrot
need have done* to make the prop. expressed by these words true is
to have said in a particular way[1] the words "My name is Nancy".
But it's not the case that the words (a) "She said her name was
Nancy" *mean the same as* (b) "She said the words "My name is
Nancy" " since (b) could be understood by a person who didn't
understand the word "name" or the sentential form "——'s
name is ——", whereas (a) couldn't. How can this be, if that (b) is
true is sufficient to justify us in asserting (a)? It is because when
we say (a), we are using the words "her name was Nancy" to
express a prop.; & because the words "My name is Nancy"
mean that the speaker's name is Nancy. It is true that *all the parrot
need have done* is to say the words; but it's also necessary that the
words it used should *mean* that its name is Nancy. *We* are not
asserting that the words it used mean this nor are we asserting
that it used the words "My name is Nancy"; our assertion would
be true even if it had said "Mon nom est Nancy" or "Mein Name
ist Nancy": we are asserting that it used *some* words which have a
certain meaning; & since "My name is Nancy" are words which
have that meaning, the fact that she said those words together
with the fact that they have that meaning is a sufficient though

[1] If the parrot had said "If my name's Nancy, it begins with an "N" ", she
wouldn't have said her name was Nancy.

not a necessary condition for the truth of our prop. "She said her name was Nancy" means "She uttered *some* words which meant that her name was Nancy"; and that this is true does not follow from the fact that she said the words "My name is Nancy", but only from this fact *together with* the fact that the uttering of those words by any speaker have the meaning that the name of the speaker in question is Nancy. (It doesn't follow from this!)

But the answer is *No*, if we so use "She said her name was Nancy" that a necess. condition for its truth is that she should not only have used some words which mean that her name was, but should *have understood* those words. The parrot doesn't understand the words it uses. Do we use (a) in this manner? I doubt it. If there is such a usage, there must be a usage of "She said her name was Nancy" such that "She said her name was Nancy, but she hadn't the least idea what the words she was using meant" would be a contradiction. But is there one? I feel doubtful if there is. There is no contradiction in: "He said the words "The moon is round", but he wasn't saying that the moon is round, although the words "the moon is round" mean that the moon is round". But this may be merely because, in order to justify "He said that the moon is round", some words which mean that it is must be uttered *in a particular way* or *context*. Suppose a man repeats the line "Our birth is but a sleep & a forgetting": we can quite well say "He wasn't saying that our birth *is* so, he was only repeating a well-known line which means that it is". If I say "The sentence "The moon is round" begins with a "t" " I am not saying that the moon is round, though I am saying the words "the moon is round". Also if I say "It's not the case that the moon is round". If I say "If it's snowing, I shan't go out", I am not saying that it's snowing, though I am uttering the words. There's no contradiction in: "I said the words "it's snowing" but I wasn't saying that it was snowing."

But all this doesn't shew that there's any sense of "say" such that for it to be true that he *said* that it was snowing, it is necessary that he should have not only uttered words which meant that, but understood them. And I doubt if there is.

But suppose I say the words " "Mensa" means chair", it doesn't follow that I am saying (= asserting) that "Mensa" does mean chair. And I want to say, that I'm not saying so unless I *understand* "chair". But *this won't do*. The case of the parrot shews it won't.

⟨"Saying" does not always mean "asserting". Dickens "says" that Mrs Bardell was discovered in Pickwick's arms; but we should not say he *asserts* this except ironically.⟩

5

GIVE A DEFINITION

I used this expression (in *Phil. of Russell*, p. 183)[1], & used it so that a man will be "giving a def." of *x*, if he makes an assertion or statement about *x* *which can properly be called a def. of the meaning of x* (p. 184). It is therefore possible to give a definition, without giving it *to* anybody: e.g. you may have *given* a def. by writing it in a MS. which nobody ever saw.

But what sort of assertion or statement about *x* can be properly called a *def.*? You must have *uttered or written* a sentence ⟨No: in Dicts. this is not done. There is a convention that words which follow the word to be defined, after a full stop, express a definition of the "catchword"⟩ in which *x* *need* not be a constituent, but *can* be if used autonymously ⟨*x* *need* not *directly*; but must, I think, *indirectly*—i.e. you must have already explained that you are using so & so as a name for *x*, e.g. I'm going to call p ⊃ q "(1)", and the assertion you make must be to the effect that *x* means so & so. But you might say: I'm going to call *the* sentence immediately preceding this "(1)"; & here *x* is *not* a constituent even in the sentence you use to explain what you are going to use as a name for it⟩; you must have uttered or written it in such a way that you can be properly said to be *making an assertion* by its means—e.g. not merely uttered it as one of the clauses in an if . . . then . . . sentence, or have preceded it by "it's not the case that", or by "it's doubtful that", or "Is it the case that . . . ?" . . . — & either (1) you must be *using* it in such a way that if another person, who did not understand *x*, understood by it what you *mean* by it & believed you were right, he would be believing with regard to *one particular meaning* that *x* had *that* meaning (which is quite different from merely "understanding" *x*): thus, you may be giving a def. of *x*, even though *the words you use* are being *mis*used by you—i.e. haven't got the meaning with which you are using them—don't mean what you mean by them: in which case you can properly be said to have *asserted not* what *you* meant by them, but

---

[1] ["Russell's 'Theory of Descriptions' ", in P. A. Schilpp (ed.), *The Philosophy of Bertrand Russell* (Evanston and Chicago, 1944). Reprinted in G. E. Moore, *Philosophical Papers* (London, 1959).]

what they do mean; or (2) the sentence you use actually has a meaning, such that any one who understood it, & believed what it meant, would be believing with regard to *one particular meaning* that it had that meaning: *this* is the sense in which a parrot might "give a definition", without understanding the sentence, & in which you would be giving one if what you meant by the sentence was what it means.

(1) is to allow that you may have "given a def.", but expressed it badly or incorrectly.

But now what needs to be explained is what is meant by saying "believe with regard to *a particular meaning* that *x* has that meaning".

We must note that people don't say that a French–English dict. *gives definitions of* or *defines* the French words of which it *gives* (here again not *to* anyone) an English translation: *translation* is *not* a kind of definition. Ought (1) & (2) to have been modified to make this plain? Also in a *dict.* there are no *sentences* saying either " "mot" means the same as "word" " or " 'mot' *means* word".

Instead of asking "What does "lexicon" mean?", a man may ask "What's a lexicon?": both are perfectly good (correct) ways of asking for the meaning of a word. Suppose the answer is "A dictionary". A child who hasn't the least idea what "dictionary" means, i.e. doesn't understand the word, won't understand this answer. Yet the person who makes it has *given an explanation* of the meaning of "lexicon".

Now a person who doesn't understand either "lexicon" or "dictionary" may quite well understand the sentence (statement ? you are said not to understand a "statement", if you know that a given sentence was meant to convey a statement, but don't understand the sentence) " "Lexicon" has the same meaning as "dictionary" ", since the proper meaning of this is " "L." & "D." both mean something or other, & what they mean is the same". A person who has told you this, has *not* told you what either means (I may *tell* a person that so & so is the case, when in fact it is not the case). What must he have done, in order to have told you what "Lexicon" means?

Either (1) he must have used some form of expression, e.g. " 'Lexicon' means dictionary", which *properly* has a meaning such that its meaning can't be understood except by someone who *understands* every word which follows "lexicon" & also understands the whole phrase (this is the sense in which a parrot might tell it to you)[1]; *or* he must have used some form of expression by which *he* meant what is properly meant by an expression of the last kind, although it hasn't properly got that meaning (this covers the case of people who wrongly use " "lexicon" means what is meant by "dictionary" " to *include* " 'Lexicon' means dictionary"); *or* he must use some expression of kind (1) & mean by it what it does mean (this case is covered by (1)).

Suppose you say: (1) " 'Lexicon' means 'dictionary' ", or (2) "A lexicon is a dictionary", or (3) " 'Lexicon' means what is meant by 'dictionary' ". Nobody understands (1) or (2), unless he understands "*dictionary*"; & even if (1) & (2) *include* (3), a person who believes them is believing something about "Lexicon" which he is *not* believing, if he is *only* believing (3).

(3) is like "x has for father the man who is father of y". A man who tells you that is not telling you who was the father of x; though if you happen to know who was father of y, you can *infer* who was father of x.

---

[1] ⟨A person is not said to understand "dictionary", if he only understands its use as a name for itself. What is called "using" as distinct from "mentioning" *can be defined* as any sort of use which can only be *understood* by a person who understands or misunderstands the word in question. (?)⟩

6

SENTENCES AND PROPOSITIONS

If a statement can't be *properly said to be* a definition, does it follow that it's *not* a definition? If the moon can't be properly said to be round, does it follow that it's not round? If the word "round" can't be properly applied *to the shape* of the moon, does it follow that the moon isn't round?

It is certain that the moon might have been round, & that yet there might have been *no proper way of saying* that it was; that therefore the sentence "The moon is round" might not have been a proper way of saying so.

From the prop. that the moon is round, it does not follow that the sentence "the moon is round" expresses *any* true prop.; *nothing* follows about the *sentence* "the moon is round" or about any word or sentence whatever.

From (a) "The moon can be properly said to be round" it seems to follow that (b) the moon *is* round. (b) does follow from (a), but (a) does not follow from (b).

"It's *not* the case that (a)" will then mean: The 2 props. (b) the moon is round & (c) the sentence "the moon is round" means that the moon is round, are not *both* true. Hence from "It's not the case that (a)" not-(b) does not follow. But from not-(a) together with (c), ∼ (b) *does* follow.

(c) ' "The moon is round" *is* a proper way of saying that the moon is round'; & from *this* prop. together with (b) "the moon is round" there does follow (a) "The moon *can be properly said* to be round". Hence from ∼ (a) there follows ∼ (both (c) & (b)); & hence from ∼ (a) & (c), there follows ∼ (b).

7

THE LIAR

As W. says 3.332,[1] no sentence can (possibly) be contained in itself.

This is a good example of a necessary prop. The general prop. from which it would seem to follow is: No whole can possibly be identical with a mere part of itself. y is a mere (proper) part of $x \rightarrow x \neq y$.

In order that a sentence should be a proper part of any sentence, the latter sentence must have a proper part which is not a proper part of the former, from which it follows that the 2 can't be identical.

But it does not follow from this that a sentence cannot "say" (= be used to say) something about itself.

E.g. "This sentence, which I am now uttering (or writing), began with a T".

W. says it *does* follow that no *prop.* can say anything about itself.

Why not?

A prop. *can*, because it always does, say of itself that it is true, because (p) . "p is true" means the same as "p".

But a prop. can't say of itself that it is *false*.

Try this prop.:

"The prop. expressed by *this* sentence which I am now writing is false"

= "There is a prop., & only one, which both (a) is expressed by *this* sentence which I am now writing & (b) is false".

The 2 different sentences just written down do seem to express a prop. & to express the same prop.

The use of "this" in them, though it seems to be demonstrative, seems to differ from most demonst. uses of "this", in that in most cases that to which a demonst. "this" refers is something neither identical with nor contained in the sentence which contains the "this", and the sentence which contains it can be properly said to have no meaning at all *by itself*, & nobody can understand its meaning unless he knows what the outside thing is to which the

[1] [L. Wittgenstein, *Tractatus Logico-Philosophicus* (London, 1922).]

"this" refers. In this case the "this" does not refer to any outside thing, & hence it cannot be said, for this reason, that the sentences have no meaning *by themselves*. But of course the "I" does refer to something outside the sentences, & hence it can still be said that they have no meaning by themselves: in order to understand them it is necessary to know *who* is uttering them. And also the "now" & the present tense refer to something outside. Hence both sentences have a different meaning on each occasion of their utterance.

Now suppose I write up on a blackboard:

"The sentence, of which these words form a part, begins with a T".

Anybody can understand this, & see that what it means is true.

But suppose I write:

(1) "This prop. is false" (or "This sentence is false").

The natural thing to say is: *Which* prop.? You haven't mentioned any prop. Your words are meaningless.

Suppose I answer: What I meant was: (2) *The* prop. expressed by this sentence is false; & therefore my words are *not* meaningless.

In that case, what my words mean is: The prop. "There is a prop. wh. is the only one expressed by this sentence & which is false" is true.

Since $p = p$ is true.

But, if the only prop. expressed by this sentence is the prop. "There is a prop. which is the only one expressed by this sentence & which is false" this prop. can't be true unless it's also true that it is false; since it asserts that the only prop. expressed is false & this *is* the only prop. expressed.

Consider the prop. A. "There is a prop. which (a) is the only one expressed by this sentence, & (b) is false".

A is *in fact* the only prop. expressed by this sentence.

Hence, unless A is false, A can't be true: for there can be no prop. satisfying both (a) & (b).

A, however, does not *assert* that A is the only prop. expressed by the sentence used to express it.

Hence *if* the prop. meant by the *sentence* (1) is A, then from prop. (1) its own falsehood does *not* follow: its falsehood follows only from prop. (1) *together with* the prop. B. that prop. (1) is the only prop. expressed by sent. (1).

The prop. "A is false" can't be identical with the prop. "A". Is this Wittg.'s point?

When people say: If (1) is false it is true, & if true it is false; their statement is false, if they mean that "(1) is false" *entails* "(1) is true" & that "(1) is true" *entails* "(1) is false". Neither entailment holds. B is required in both cases.

8

WORDS AND THEIR MEANING

It is obvious, with regard to any word whatever, that it might not have meant what it does mean; there is no contradiction in the supposition of its having a different meaning. "Tiger" might have meant what, in fact, "lion" means or what "penny" means; "hot" might have meant what "cold" means, or what "square" means. It is perfectly conceivable that this should have been the case.

But now consider the prop.: 'Tiger' means what it does mean. This says 2 things: (1) 'Tiger' has a meaning & (2) the tautology: There is no meaning, which "tiger" has & also does not have.

But what then is meant by: (3) "Tiger" might not have meant what it does mean?

It would seem that it ought to mean: The prop. " 'Tiger' means what it does mean" might have been false; and (4) this would mean that the *conjunction* of (1) & (2) might have been false, i.e. that there's no impossibility in the supposition that they should not *both* have been true: i.e. that the supposition that they're not both true is not a self-contradictory prop. And it really is perfectly possible that (1) & (2) should not *both* have been true, since it is possible that (1) should not.

9

ENTAILMENT

(1) "(p . q) entails r" certainly does not entail (2) "p entails (q entails r)", for *all* values of p, q & r.

But, suppose p, q & r are all *necess*. props.: doesn't (1) entail (2) for all values of p, q & r which are *necess*. props.?

Let us take as value of p (α) "there were 4 $\rightarrow$ there were > 3", of q (β) "there were $> 3 \rightarrow$ there were > 2", of r (γ) "there were 4 $\rightarrow$ there were > 2".

Then $(\alpha) + (\beta) \rightarrow (\gamma)$; but does (α) *entail* that (β) entails (γ)? I think certainly not.

Is every prop. of the form "p entails q" *necess*., if true? i.e. if p does entail q, is it a contradiction to say "p does not entail q"?

(1) "p & (p $\supset$ q)" entails q.

Is the denial of this (1) self-contradictory?

(2) p . (p $\supset$ q) . $\sim$ q is, of course, a contradiction: that it is follows from (1). But that the denial of (1) is also a contradiction is not so clear.

Yet the statement that (2) is *not* a contrad. does seem to be self-contradictory; or rather that it is a contrad. seems to be an internal property of it.

(2) $= p . \sim (p . \sim q) . \sim q = p . \sim q . \sim (p . \sim q)$. But is a person who says that this is *not* a contradiction, contradicting himself? He is saying something which is necessarily false, but that doesn't seem to be the same thing.

Does ' "p & (p $\supset$ q)" entails q' entail "p entails ("p $\supset$ q" entails q)"?

Certainly not.

Let p be "I'm sitting down" & q be "it's not raining".

Then "p $\supset$ q" = It's not the case both that I am sitting down & that it is raining; & this prop. certainly does *not* entail "it's not raining"; & hence it can't follow from the truth of p that it *does* entail it.

Can we say: If (2) I'm sitting down, then if (1) it's not the case both that I'm sitting down & that it's raining it follows that (3) it's not raining?

Certainly we can; but this doesn't mean that from (2) it follows that (3) follows from (1). It only means that from (1) & (2) there follows (3).

From (1) "It's not the case both that (3) I'm sitting down & that (5) it's raining" there seems to follow (6) "If I'm sitting down (4) it's not raining".

But whereas (1) follows from "I'm not sitting down", (6) doesn't; therefore (6) doesn't follow from (1).

What is the case is that from (1) & (3), (4) follows.

It *seems* as if we can say: If (3) & (5) are not both true, it follows that *if* (3) *is true* (5) *is false* & also that *if* (5) *is true* (3) *is false*: and that these 2 things are not the same, although each follows from the other.

If you know that (3) & (5) are not both true, & *don't know* that (3) is false nor yet that (5) is false, you can infer with certainty that *if* (3) *is true* (5) *is false*, & that *if* (5) *is true* (3) *is false*. But if you do know that (3) is false, you can't correctly infer from (1) that if (3) is true, (5) is false; nor, if you know that (5) is false, can you correctly infer from (1) that if (5) is true, (3) is false.

Perhaps the solution is this: what follows from (1) is *not* "If (3) is true, (5) is false", but "if (3) is true *too*, then (5) is false".

10

"TRUE" AND "FACT"

It is a fact that the moon is round = *It is true that* the moon is round = The moon is round = That the moon is round *is a fact* = That the moon is round *is true* = That the moon is round *is a true prop.*

The prop. that the moon is round *is true* = The moon is round, but ≠ *The prop. that* the moon is round *is a fact* (but = That *the prop. that* the moon is round *is true is a fact*).

Similarly

I know that the moon is round ≠ I know *the prop. that* the moon is round = I know that *the prop. that* the moon is round *is true* = I know *the fact* that the moon is round.

Similarly

It is the case that the moon is round = *It is true that* the moon is round = The moon is round, but ≠ *The prop. that* the moon is round *is the case.*

11

THAT "SEE" IS USED IN DIFFERENT SENSES

(1) A. I see the moon.

    B. Do you see the whole of it?

    A. No: part of it is hidden by a cloud ("by the leaves of a tree", etc.).

(2) A. I see the moon.

    B. Do you see the whole of it?

    A. Well; it's only a crescent, and I *see* the whole of *that*. But I don't *see* the part of its surface which is in shadow.

(3) A. I see the moon.

    B. Do you see the whole of it?

    A. Yes; it's full moon, & no part of it is hidden by a cloud or anything else. But, of course, I don't see every *part* of it; and I only see one *side* of it.

"I see the moon" is so used that what it expresses will be true, in any of the 3 different cases. And "the moon" in "I see the moon" is used in exactly the same way as in "The moon is a solid body, approximately spherical, shining only by reflected light, & much smaller than the earth & than Venus".

Now consider:

(4) "The moon always turns the same *side* or face to the earth; so that the *side* of the moon which we *see* from the earth is always the same: we never *see* that *side* of it which is always turned away from the earth".

Is "see" used in the same way here in (4) as in (1), (2) & (3)? I try to prove later that it is *not*.

"There is a side of the moon which we never see" does entail "There is a part of the moon which we never see" but *not* "We never see the whole of the moon" because "Yes" is answer to (3).

In the case of any opaque object, that you are seeing *it* entails that you are *seeing some* part of its surface; but that you are seeing some part of its surface does not entail that you are seeing it—if the part is very small, we should often rightly say "Well; I see a little bit of your arm, but I can hardly say that I'm seeing your arm."

I think that the difference between the use of "see" in "I *see* the moon" & "I *see* part of the surface of the moon", is *like* the difference between "I see a shade of red which is nearer to orange than to purple (violet?)" & "I see a speck or spot or line or patch (not necessarily sharply outlined) which is of a shade of red nearer orange than purple". *Only*, in this latter case, each prop. entails the other, &, therefore, since the meaning of "this shade of colour" is certainly not identical with the meaning of "a speck or spot or line or patch which *is* this colour", it follows that "see" stands for a different relation in the 2 cases.

In the case of a physical line which is red, you can, of course, see that line without seeing any shade of red at all, e.g. if you are colour-blind. It is only in the case of a *sense-datum* which is red that you cannot see it without seeing some shade of red. The physical line will *be* of some shade, but when you see it you don't *see* that shade. You can't see the property "would look so & so in such circumstances".

"I see the moon." This use of "see" is certainly to be defined in terms of *another* use of "see" which I call "directly see". That prop. asserts that I stand to *the moon* in a certain relation; and there is a certain relation expressed by "see" in which I do stand to any part of the moon's surface which I am "seeing", & in which I do not stand to any part which I am *not* "seeing", & in which I certainly do *not* stand to *the moon*. *Is* this certain?

When I see a crescent moon, I *directly* see a crescent-shaped sense-datum, & it is of this sense-datum that I am speaking when I point & say "There's the moon". Of this crescent-shaped sense-datum it seems I can say with truth: "That is the lighted part of that part of the surface of the moon which faces the earth". But it seems I can also say of the same sense-datum: "*That* is the moon". But the moon is certainly not identical with any lighted part of its surface. Hence, if both of these things can be said with truth, "is" must be being used differently in the 2 cases.

Let us call the side of a half-crown, on which there is or was (it may have been effaced) a likeness of the king or queen's head, "its head", & the other side "its tail". And let us also so use these expressions that, if a half-crown were sliced in two, so as to form 2 thinner discs, on one of which was *the* likeness of a head (= *the* likeness which was on the half-crown), & on the other the coat of arms, it would no longer be correct to say that the side of that disc on which the likeness was, was the "head" of a *half-crown*: only that it had *once been* the head of a half-crown, but was so no longer. In other words let us call a metal surface the "head" of a half-crown only so long as it actually is part of the surface of a half-crown; so that the prop. with regard to a metal surface that it *is* the "head" of a half-crown, entails that it is at the moment part of the surface of a half-crown, not merely that it was so once.

Then, this being understood, we so use "see", that from the fact that the head of a half-crown is being *seen*, it *follows* that a half-crown is being *seen*; although from the fact that a half-crown is being *seen* it by no means follows that the head of that (or any) half-crown is being seen. On the other hand from the fact that a half-crown is being tossed, or is in somebody's pocket, it *does* follow that the head of that half-crown is being tossed (or is in that person's pocket).

Yet "half-crown" is being used in exactly the same *sense* when we say "I see a half-crown" & when we say "He's tossing a half-crown" or "I have a half-crown in my pocket".

There is *some* relation, though *not* one which can be properly expressed by "see", such that from "I see a half-crown" it *follows* that I have *that* relation to the head of a half-crown, & to the head of the half-crown in question.

Now suppose I see a half-crown (only one), & also see its head; & suppose I am not seeing it double, but have only a single "image" of it. There is then only one among all the things I am "directly seeing" at the moment (only one of my visual sense-data) which could possibly be identical with the half-crown in question, & only one which could possibly be identical with the head of the half-crown in question; & the one which could possibly be identical with the half-crown is the *same* as that which could possibly be identical with its head. But the half-crown is *not* identical with its head: ∴ *either* the half-crown *or* its head is *not directly seen*. But both are certainly *seen*. It remains possible that neither is *directly seen*.

But now: Is the relation between me & a half-crown which I express by (1) "I see that half-crown", different from that between me & the head of that half-crown which I express by (2) "I see the head of that half-crown"?

If, in either case, the relation expressed by "see" is that which I call "directly see", the 2 relations are certainly different, for they can't both be directly seen. But how if neither relation is what I call "directly see"?

In the case of any opaque object, x, there are certain conditions (*one* or more) such that you can properly be said to be "seeing" x, *if & only if* you are *seeing* a part of the surface of x which satisfies those conditions. The prop. that you are seeing x both entails & is entailed by the prop. that you are seeing a part of the surface of x which satisfies the conditions in question; and, if we express the conditions in question by "ϕ", I think it can be rightly said that "he is seeing x" is short for "he is seeing a part of the surface of x which satisfies the conditions (or condition) ϕ". But in the case of 2 opaque objects, the moon & the planet Venus, the conditions in question are, I think, different in one respect from what they are in the case of most objects. In the case of most objects there is, I think, *only one condition* which a part of the surface of a solid object need satisfy, in order that the prop. that you are seeing a part of the surface of that object which satisfies it should entail & be entailed by the prop. that you are seeing the object in question. The condition is one which can be expressed by saying that the part of the surface of x in question must be a *considerable* part of its surface, where "considerable" means the same as "more than a little bit" of the surface; & I think what is meant is that the part of the surface in question must be a *fairly large* fraction of the whole surface (it certainly need not be as much as a half).

⟨No: this is not so: another condition is that you should be seeing part of the boundary of the object. Suppose you have a black framework with a round hole cut in it of a diameter just smaller than that of a half-crown, & place it over a half-crown in such a way that you can't see any part of the edge of the half-crown. I think we should hesitate to say that you are seeing the half-crown; we should be inclined to say you are *only* seeing a part of it, & that even though the part of its surface you are seeing is a *larger* proportion of the whole, than in cases where we should say you are seeing the half-crown, e.g. where half its upper surface is concealed by another half-crown overlapping it. So, too, when you're so close to a wall that you can't see any part of its boundary: you're inclined to say that you're *not* seeing the wall, only a part of it. So, too, perhaps, when we say "You can't see the wood for the trees". In order to see *a wood*, you must see part at least of its boundary.⟩

Of course "fairly large" is vague; but then so is "seeing" an opaque object. There are border-line cases, in which it's doubtful whether it's right to say you were "seeing" an object or not. If you only see a little bit of a person's arm, you would say "I can't say that I saw his arm; I only saw a little bit of it". But there is *no answer* to the question *how large* a fraction of the surface of his arm you must see in order to be entitled to say "I saw his arm". There are many different cases in which you would say: "I don't know whether I can properly be said to have seen his arm, though I did see a good bit of it". Usage has fixed, for many cases, that in those cases you do express the facts correctly by saying "I saw his arm"; and it has also fixed, for many cases, that in those cases you express the facts correctly by saying "I did not see his arm"; but for many cases it has not fixed that either the one or the other expresses the facts correctly: just as it hasn't fixed that it is correct to express the facts by saying "The dog did go round the goat" nor yet to express them by "He did not go round the goat". In the case of most opaque objects, it seems we can say that whether you saw the object or *only a bit* of it, depends on the proportion between the size of the surface or the sum of the surfaces you did see to the whole surface of the object; but usage has not fixed *precisely how large* a proportion the surface or bits of surface seen must bear to the whole surface for you to say correctly that you saw the object.

⟨*No:* it does not depend *only* on this: it is a necessary condition that you should see a good part of the *boundary* of the object—in many cases, at all events. *Perhaps* not when, e.g., you see a house in a wood from a distance.⟩

The peculiarity in the case of the moon, & of Venus seen through a telescope, is that whether you *saw* the moon (or Venus) or not does not seem to depend *only* on the proportion which the part of its surface seen bears to its whole surface, nor on this together with the seeing of a boundary. The moon & Venus are almost (?) unique among objects in having regular phases. And I think usage has fixed that when you see *a crescent moon, however* thin the crescent may be, you can be rightly said to be *seeing the moon* (& so with a crescent Venus through a telescope), in spite of the fact that the proportion of the moon's surface which you are seeing is considerably smaller than when, e.g., half a full moon is covered by a cloud.

But I don't think all this is necessary to prove the point that the sense in which you can be said to "*see*" part of the surface of an opaque object (e.g. "see" the head of a half-crown) is different from that in which you are said to "see" an opaque object.

Proof.

A. Any prop. of the form (1) "*x* is an opaque object, & S is seeing *x*" entails the corresponding prop. of the form "S is *seeing* part of the surface of *x*".

B. But *no* prop. of the form (2) "*x* is part of the surface of an opaque object, & S is *seeing x*" entails the corresponding prop. of the form "S is *seeing* part of the surface of *x*". Perhaps, it is more correct to say that there *is* no corresponding prop. of this latter form; since it is meaningless to talk of part of the surface of a surface.

But if in props. of form (2) "seeing" did mean the same as in props. of form (1), every prop. of form (2) *would* entail a prop. of form "S is *seeing* part of the surface of *x*".

It is tempting to say

C. *Part* of what you are saying about an opaque object when you say that you are seeing it, is that you are seeing part of its surface;

whereas obviously no part of what you are saying of a surface when you say that you are seeing *it*, is the absurdity that you are seeing part of *its* surface. But C does not *follow* from A; since if it did it would follow that part of what you are saying of an object when you say it is a cube is that it has 12 edges: which is *not* the case (Langford). Nevertheless C may be true; & I think it is. And if part of what you are saying when you say "I see the moon" is "I see part of the surface of the moon"; it will be obvious that the first "see" had a different meaning from the second, since certainly no part of what you say when you say "I see part of the surface of the moon" is "I see part of the surface of part of the surface of the moon".

(1) "I see this half-crown" entails (2) "I see part of the surface of this half-crown".

But (2) "I see part of the surface of this half-crown" does not entail "I see part of the surface of part of the surface of this half-crown".

Does not this prove that the use of "see" is different in the 2 cases?

But let us consider the fact that (1) "I see a shade of red" is *logically equivalent* to (2) "I see a speck, or a spot, or a line, or a patch or etc. which is of a shade of red" (all these words used in the sense-given sense).

Since "a shade of red" does not mean the same as "a speck, or a spot, or a line or a patch etc. which is of a shade of red", it follows that "see" is used differently in (1) & in (2).

But since each of (1) & (2) entails the other, we cannot say that either use of "see" is definable in terms of the other, whereas we can say that "see" as used of an opaque object *is* definable in terms of "see" as used of part of the surface of an opaque object, since "I see part of the surface of a half-crown" does *not* entail "I see a half-crown".

For this reason the sense of "see" in which we see opaque objects can't be the sense which I call "directly see"; since this latter is not definable in terms of any other sense of "see".

Can the sense of "see" in which we see parts of the surfaces of opaque objects be identical with the sense which I call "directly see"?

What are the objections to saying so?

In order to state some of them, it is necessary to distinguish *two* senses of "being red" etc., "being square" etc., "being loud" or "high in pitch" etc., one of which I propose to call the sense-given sense.

To say of the cover of a book that it *is* bright red seems to mean that it would *look bright red* under certain circumstances; that it is "square" that it *would look square* under certain circs.; to say that a physical sound is "loud" that it would *sound loud* under certain circs., etc.

⟨The same physical sound may be loud *in one place* & *soft* in another; as a rule it *gets softer* the further you are from the place where it is made. It is loud *in a given place*, if to people very near that place it would *sound* loud, provided they weren't deaf or had wool in their ears, etc. As to whether, when an amplifier is used, the sound produced by the amplifier is the *same* sound as that produced by, e.g., the person who speaks into it, I don't think usage is fixed: it's not wrong to say it is, nor to say it isn't. Hence we can't say a sound is only loud if it would sound so to a person near the place where it's produced. And we certainly can't say it's only soft if it would sound so to a person near the place where it is produced: sounds which wouldn't *are* soft in other places.⟩

These are the physical senses of "being red", "being square", "being loud", etc.

But there is another sense: in cases (1) & (2) that in which an after-image seen with closed eyes *is* red or *square*; & in case (3) that in which a *subjective sound* is loud.

In the case of a c.e.[1] after-image there is no sense in saying that it would look red under cert. circs., but doesn't look red now. The sense in which such an image *is* red is one in which that it is red can be *seen*, & such that an after-image wh. *is* red, can't be seen unless some shade of the colour red is seen; whereas one cannot *see* that the cover of a book is red, in the physical sense, if that means that it *would* look red, whenever certain conditions were fulfilled. One can, indeed, often make sure that the conditions are fulfilled & then *see* that it looks red to *you*; but it is doubtful whether one can ever be properly said to *see* that the conditions are fulfilled, e.g. that one's sight is normal; & even if one could, one can't see that it would look red to anyone under those [conditions], which is a thing which cannot be known except as a consequence of past experience.

⟨A physical surface which *is* red (e.g. the cover of a book) can be seen by a person who is not seeing any shade of the colour red. So too a physical surface which *is* square or circular, can be seen by a person who is not seeing the *shape* "square" or the shape "circular". But it does look as if you can be said to *see* that a coin is circular, even when it doesn't *look* circular to you; much more, when it *does* look circular to you. So too we should certainly say, we can *see* that a tie is red, in *some* cases where it looks red.⟩

One can't, then, distinguish (1) "is red" in physical sense from (2) "is red" in sense-given sense, by saying that in sense (1) one can never *see* that a thing is red, whereas in sense (2) one can.

I think the distinction is this:

"is red" (2) is such that it is impossible to see a thing which *is* red in that sense, without seeing some shade of the colour red.

[1] [closed eyes.]

⟨But this knocks on the head the possibility that a physical surface can *be* in sense (2) *both* of the colour it looks to you & of the colour it looks to me.⟩

"is red" (1) is such that it is quite possible to see a surface which *is* red in that sense, without seeing any shade of the colour red.

And it is to be noted that the sense of "looks red" in which "is red" (1) = *would look red* to anyone under conditions ϕ, is one in which a thing can't *look red* to anyone, unless he is seeing some shade of the colour red. When a person *sees* that a surface is circular or square in sense (1), it need not look square or circular to him in *this* sense (there may be another in which it must). But in the case of colours, I think a person can't be said to see, e.g., "that surface is red", unless it *looks red* to him. But, in the case both of colours & shapes, it is the case that you can see a thing which *is* of such a shape or colour in sense (1), without *seeing* that shape or any shade of that colour, & therefore without its *looking to be* of that shape or colour in the fundamental sense of *look*, in which a thing can't look to you to be of a certain shape or colour, unless you *see* that shape [or colour].

We can only distinguish (2) & (1) by saying that (2) is the sense in which one can say of an after-image seen with closed eyes that it *is* of such & such a colour; & by saying that there are no conditions such that, in order to be sure that it *is red* in this sense, we have to be sure that it would *look red* to anyone under those conditions. An after-image may gradually change in colour, e.g. become fainter; & hence there is no contradiction in supposing that one which started by being red, might become yellow. And hence also there is no contradiction in saying of one which is red *now*, but has lasted for some time: this after-image might have become yellow by now—might, therefore, have been yellow now, though in fact it is red. Hence also of one which has lasted some time & which started red, there is no contradiction in saying that it might have started yellow—might, therefore, have been yellow at a time when, in fact, it was red. But to say *at the moment it starts* of one which starts red, that it might have been yellow at that time, is self-contradictory. Yet it's not easy to say clearly why. It clearly isn't self-contradictory to say of it later on that it might have been yellow at starting. But at the moment of starting there is no means of *specifying which after-image you mean* except as *this red* one? Of course, there might have been a yellow one *instead of* a red one in the place where the red one is: but then it wouldn't have been the *same* image. Later on it has meaning to say "*This* image might have been yellow when it started": but then you can identify the image as *the one you* are seeing now, with its colour. Of an image which is red *at a given time* t_1 it is self-contradictory to say *at that time* that it isn't red; though there is no contradiction in saying of *the same image* at an earlier or a later time that it *won't be* or *wasn't* red at t_1: it certainly *might* not be red at t_1, & *might not have been* red at t_1. But though it's self-contradictory to say at t_1 of an image which is red at t_1, that *it isn't red*; it's *not* self-contradictory to say of it that it *might not have been red* at t_1. To say of it that *it might not* is not to say that there is no contradiction in "This isn't red"; but only that there would have been no contradiction in saying of *it* in the past "This won't be red at t_1", & that there would be none in saying of *it* in the future "This wasn't red at t_1".

Similarly "I don't exist now" or "This doesn't exist now" are self-contradictory. But "I might not have existed now (at t_1)" or "This mightn't" are not, because what they mean is merely that there would have been no contradiction in my saying of myself in the past "I shan't exist at t_1", & will be no contradiction in my saying of myself in the future "I didn't exist at t_1". No-one could, of course, have said of "this" in the past "this won't exist at t_1" unless this did exist at the past moment in question; nor could anyone say of "this" in the future "this didn't exist at t_1" unless "this" exists at the future moment in question.

12

"MAKES NO SENSE" AND "TRUE"

' "Go away" is true' makes no sense.

That this prop. is true depends partly on the use of the expressions "Go away" (or any other imperative) & "true"; & that they are used in the way in question is a contingent & empirical prop. These expressions *might* have been used in such a way that the sentence did make sense: e.g. if "Go away" were used to mean "I shall go away" or "You will go away"; or if "is true" were used to mean "is a command".

But it does not *say* anything about the use of imperatives & "true": it only *says* something about the whole *sentence*; and, though it's true that the whole sentence *might* have made sense, it's not true that it could have made sense, *if* the expression "Go away" & "is true" were used in the way they are used. That, when so used, the whole sentence *can't* make sense is true & is not an empirical or contingent prop. And when we say that the whole sentence doesn't make sense, our reason for saying so is that, if these expressions are used in a certain way, it *can't* make sense, & that they are, in fact, used in this way.

Now it may be said that ' "You ought to go away" is true' also doesn't make sense; on the ground that a person who says the words "You ought to go away" is, if he's using them in the ordinary way, not *asserting* anything. The mere fact that an indicative form of expression is used does not shew that it makes sense to add before it "It's true that" or "It's false that". If a person who says "You oughtn't to do that" or "You oughtn't to have done that", is not *making any assertion*, then it will make no sense to say that what he said was true or was false: in one sense of "said" he won't have *said* anything; he will only have given a command. It is only when sentences are used in such a way that by using them a person may be making an *assertion*, that it makes sense to add "it's true that".

But how about "He believes that you ought to go away"? It has to be said that here "believes" is used in such a way that *what* is said to be believed *can't* be true or false: that therefore the generalisation that anything which is believed is a prop. is a mere mistake. A prop. is something which can be *asserted*.

13

RUSSELL'S VIEW IN "EXTERNAL WORLD"[1]

He implies that when we say, e.g. of a coin at which we point, "This coin is circular", this is not true, but something else, which he tries to give, is.

In lecturing I used to urge that he obviously doesn't mean "whenever anybody says", but only "whenever anybody says *truly*"; & that hence he contradicts himself if he says it isn't true.

Similarly I said that I was contradicting myself in what I said about "Pickwickian" senses: for I say that if by saying A. "That coin is circular", I mean only something of the form "If so & so had happened in the past, I should be having a circular sensible which was a sensible of the same thing as this sensible", (a) I should be using "circular" in A in an outrageously Pickwickian sense, i.e. *not* in the sense in which we do use it; but I say also (b) the coin certainly is circular & (c) the *only* sense in which it is so *may* be this Pickwickian sense, which is *not* that in which we use the word. The contradiction is "That coin is circular, in the ordinary sense: but the only sense in which it is circular *may* be one which isn't ordinary".

I could have avoided contradiction, if, instead of saying, "The *only* thing that is true of a coin, *when it is circular*, is the complicated prop. which is not what we mean by saying that it is", I had said "The *only* thing that is true of a coin, *when every ordinary person would agree that it is circular*, is the complicated prop. which is *not* what they mean by saying it is circular". This would imply that *whenever* any ordinary person says a physical object is circular, he is saying something false; *not* only when he makes a mistake about its shape.

So we can make Russell avoid contradiction by saying that instead of meaning "whenever anybody says *truly*" he means "whenever any ordinary person would *say* that a person who says so is right".

What is the objection to this? What the reason for saying that whenever any ordinary man would *say* that a person who says so is right, then the person who says so *is* right?

[1] [B. Russell, *Our Knowledge of the External World* (London, 1914).]

331

R. must say that a person who points & says "That's a man" is [saying] one of those things which are always false.

But if so any prop. of the form "any ordinary *man* would in this case say. . . " must be always false; whereas it's only if it's true that his prop. can be.

14

"IF . . . THEN"

The 4 possibilities (1) p . q
             (2) p . ~ q
             (3) ~ p . q
             (4) ~ p . ~ q
are mutually incompatible; & hence ~ (2) follows from (1), also
from (3), also from (4). It follows from (1) & (3) because from q;
from (3) & (4) because from ~ p; hence from (3) for 2 reasons,—
both because from ~ p & also because from q.

Now "if p is true, q is true" does, *in general, not* follow from
~ p, & hence cannot be identical with or logically equivalent to
~ (2) in its commonest usage.

Also, in general, it does not follow from q: "if your uncle comes
tomorrow, you will have a present", does not follow from the
mere fact that you do get a present: you may get one, even if he
doesn't come, & the fact that you do has no tendency to shew that
"if he comes, you will" was true: though, if the prediction were
"if he comes, he will *bring* you a present", the case is different
because he can't *bring* one without coming: that he brings one
does prove that *both* p & q were true; and, when *both* p & q are
true, we should be apt to say "That shews you were right"; though
we *might* say "It was only an accident: you had no reason for what
you said: what you *meant* was not true". And quite certainly that
p & q are both true is not, *in general*, sufficient to entitle one to
say "If p, q".

But are there *any* cases in which ~ (2) *does* follow (a) from ~ p,
(b) from q?

(a) Keynes & Johnson both give instances of a *special* idiom, in
the case of which this *seems* to be true. K. says[1] they are "unusual"
(262), "not typical hypotheticals" (263); & instances "If what you
say is true, I'm a Dutchman", "I'm hanged if I know what you
mean". He says "the *force* of the props." is to deny the antecedent,
i.e. to say "What you say is not true", "I don't know what you
mean". We *can* say (Lewy says not) they are merely emphatic
ways of denying p; & in that case they are *identical* with ~ p —

---

[1] [J. N. Keynes, *Formal Logic*, 4th edition (London, 1906).]

don't merely *follow* from it; & are not therefore identical with or equiv. to $\sim$ (2), since though $\sim$ (2) follows from $\sim$ p, $\sim$ p does not follow from $\sim$ (2).

J. (I. p. 41)[1] repeats from K. the example "If that boy comes back, I'll eat my head", & adds others, e.g. "If you jump over that hedge, I'll give you a thousand pounds": and seems to say that there are cases where the "implicative form of prop. is introduced in *the* paradoxical manner" which consists in so using "if p, then q" that it follows from $\sim$ p (& also follows from q). He says of these cases that they "are always interpreted as expressing the speaker's intention to *deny the implicans*". Does this mean the same as to say that they are actually used as a way of denying the *implicans*, i.e. as another way of saying $\sim$ p? J. says lower down that the speaker uses such a phrase to "express his denial of the implicans", saying that when he does so "he tacitly expects the hearer to supplement his statement with a *tollendo tollens*".

Now, if in these cases, "If p, then q" is merely another way of saying $\sim$ p, then it is *not* merely another way of saying $\sim$ (2); since $\sim$ (2) does *not* entail $\sim$ p.

But according to Lewy, it is not *merely* another way of saying $\sim$ p, since it says also "p is as certainly false as q". And certainly $\sim$ (p . $\sim$ q) does *not* say this. Also that p is as certainly false as q, does not follow from $\sim$ p.

(b) K. & J. both seem to say that *sometimes* "if p, then q" follows from q. K. gives as instance "If he can't act, at any rate he can sing", saying that this is merely "an emphatic way of declaring the truth of the consequent". By saying that "here again the hypothetical is merely assertoric", he means again that it $= \sim$ (p . $\sim$ q), i.e. "It's not the case both that he can't act & that he can't sing". But if it is merely an emphatic way of saying q, it is *not* equivalent to $\sim$ (p . $\sim$ q), since though this follows from q, q does not follow from it. Can we here say again that it is equivalent *neither* to q nor to $\sim$ (p . $\sim$ q), since it is asserting "That he can sing is as certainly true as that he can't act"?

J. gives 4 examples (p. 41) one of which is "If Britain is a tiny island, the sun never sets on the British Empire". This seems to be an idiom in which "if" = "even if", or "even though"; & J.

[1] [W. E. Johnson, *Logic*, Part I (Cambridge, 1921).]

says of this usage that "such phrases are always interpreted as expressing the *speaker's* intention to *affirm the implicate*". Yet they don't *merely* affirm the implicate; & even if they did though $\sim(p \, . \, \sim q)$ would follow from them, they would not be equivalent to it.

NOTEBOOK VIII

(Begun at end of 1947)

1

ETHICS

Sometimes "x was intrinsically good" = "x was an experience worth having for its own sake" = "it was an intrinsically good thing that S had that experience".

But with this meaning: "It was an intrinsically good thing that S_1 had that experience, & that S_2 had this other one" is meaningless.

What does "intrinsically good" mean in this second case?

We sometimes use "It was a good thing that p" in such a sense that "It was a good thing that p, *because* if p hadn't been the case, q wouldn't have been" *may* be true, i.e. has meaning & is not self-contradictory.

2

"EITHER . . . OR . . ."

Does "Either p or q" *ever* = $\sim (\sim p \, . \, \sim q)$, i.e. *ever* = p v q?

(1) "He's either in China or Japan."
(a) This *can* be contradicted by: "Perhaps he's in neither."
(b) *More important.* If it merely meant "He's not in neither", this would be proved true by "He is in China", or by "He is in Japan".

But neither of these is sufficient to prove it true. Besides "He is in China" you need "And if he hadn't been, he would have been in Japan". And besides "He is in Japan", you need "And if he hadn't been he would have been in China".

I.e. "He's either in China or Japan" ≠ "At least one of the 2 is true", but says also "If $\sim$ p, then q" & "If $\sim$ q, then p".

(2) "I either sowed pansies or violets here."
(a) *Can* be contradicted by: It's possible you sowed stocks.
(b) If it meant $\sim (\sim p \, . \, \sim q)$ it would be proved true by "I sowed pansies" or "I sowed violets".

But *neither* is sufficient. Besides "I sowed pansies" you need "If I hadn't it would have been violets"; & similarly for "I sowed violets".

(3) Either he won't come at all, or else he'll bring his wife.
(a) *Can* be contradicted by: It's possible he'll come without her.
(b) If it = $\sim$ (he will come . he won't bring her), his not coming would prove it true: but it doesn't. You require also "If he had come, he would have brought her".

Nor does his bringing her prove it true. You require also: If he hadn't brought her, he wouldn't have come at all.

If it's Wednesday, it's either Tuesday or Wedn.
This isn't true.
What's true is: If it's Wednesday, one at least of the pair is true.

340

If it's Wednesday, then if it's not Wednesday it's Tuesday, is absurd. But "it's either Tu. or Wed." entails "if it's not Wed. it's Tu."

If p is false, then if *p is true*, q is true, is always absurd.

But If p is false, then $\sim (p . \sim q)$ is perfectly true: hence $\sim (p . \sim q)$ does *not* mean the same as "if p, then q".

"P ENTAILS Q" DOES NOT ENTAIL
"P CONTAINS Q"

"There's nothing which both is a man & is not mortal (p), & There are some men (q)" entails "There are some mortal men (r)" = "There are some things which are both men & mortal".

Is r, in this case, *contained in* p . q?

p . q is not a conjunction such that r is one of its conjuncts: if it were, what would the other be?

Similarly "This is scarlet" is not a conjunction in which "This is red" is one of the conjuncts.

4

ADJECTIVES AND SUBSTANTIVES

"Elastic" is an adjective & is not a substantive: I *know* this quite well, yet I don't know what I mean by saying it is an adjective.

So "elasticity" is a substantive & not an adjective: I *know* this is so, yet I don't know what it means to say so.

"Red", "white", "blue" are *both* adjectives & subst.—adjectives when used in some ways, substantives when used in others.

But don't "elastic" & "elasticity" *mean* exactly the same thing, though one is an adjective, the other not? "Possess elasticity" means the same as "is elastic".

INTERNAL RELATIONS

Suppose A is being used as a *logical proper name* for one absolutely specific colour & B for another, & that A is darker than B.

Then "darker than B" is an *internal* relational property of A: it's imposs. that A should not have had that property.

In *Philos. Studies*[1] I analyse this into: (x) . x is not darker than B entails x ≠ A: i.e. *any* prop. of the form "C is not darker than B" entails C ≠ A.

Is "A is not darker than B" of the form "C is not darker than B"? If so, this is to say that "A is not darker than B" entails A ≠ A.

But I don't think this analysis is correct.

I implied also that "A is darker than B" & "C is not darker than B" together entail A ≠ C: & certainly (x, y, z) : . x is darker than z . y is not darker than z : entails: x ≠ y.

This man has no wart on his nose, but Oliver Cromwell had a wart on his nose, therefore this fellow isn't Oliver Cromwell.

What does "A couldn't have failed to be darker than B" mean?

Does it mean: "His trousers were of colour A & his tie of colour B" entails "His trousers were darker than his tie", & so in all other cases?

This is certainly true:

(1) "His trousers were of A, his tie of B" does, *by itself*, entail (2) "His trousers were darker than his tie".

I.e. you do not need to *add* to (1) the premiss: & A is darker than B, to get the result. Any more than to "There are 2 dots in this circle" you need to add "2 is a number" in order to get "There are some number of dots in this circle".

Also

Is the relational property of a whole to one of its parts which consists in its having that for a part an "internal" relation?

I cut my nails yesterday: ∴ yesterday my right thumb-nail had a part which it has not got to-day: ∴ it can exist without that part,

---

[1] [G. E. Moore, *Philosophical Studies* (London, 1922).]

i.e. the having that part is not an internal relational property of my thumb-nail. But wasn't it an internal relational property of "my thumb-nail as it was yesterday"—of that *phase* of my thumb-nail? What does this mean? A thing can *change* by losing parts which it had before, & by acquiring parts which it didn't have.

6

"IF P HAD BEEN TRUE,
Q WOULD HAVE BEEN TRUE"

(Jan. 9, 1948)

I have long been puzzled by the fact that the prop. (C) "Hitler's invasion of Poland & Britain's last declaration of war on Germany took place in the same month" seems to entail (A) "If the month in wh. H. invaded *had been* July, the month in wh. B. last declared war on G. *would have been* July" *in a sense*, though it certainly does *not* entail (B) "If H. had invaded in July, B. would have declared in July". I say "in a sense" because the words of A *might* be properly used to mean B. What is the difference between the 2 senses of A? B is a *causal prop.*, whereas C certainly does not entail any causal prop., & therefore the sense of the words of A which it does entail cannot be B.

It seems very difficult to express the difference between the 2 senses of the words of A quite unambiguously in ordinary language.

The sense in wh. A *is* entailed by C can perhaps be put:

(D) "If it could have been said with truth of the invasion wh. H. actually made "This invasion is taking place in July", it would also have been possible to say with truth of B.'s last declaration "This declaration is being delivered in July" ".

But even this is still perhaps ambiguous, since it is not perhaps quite clear that it asserts that H. did actually invade Poland once & only once.

Do we say the same thing as D, making this point clearer, by saying:

(D$_1$) There was one month & only one of which it was true *both* (1) that H. invaded Poland in it *&* (2) that if the prop. that it was July had been true, then the prop. that B.'s declaration took place in July would also have been true. I.e. in symbols ($\exists$ x, y) . H. invaded in x & no other . B. declared war in y & no other . if it had been true that x was July, it would also have been true that y was July.

We should say D$_1$ only when both (1) we know (or are perfectly convinced) that H.'s invasion was *not* in July & (2) *we had previously thought or someone had suggested that it was in July*. (This explains why we incline to say that (2) means "If it had turned out that".)

On other occasions we use "if p had been true . . ." not only when we are perfectly convinced that p was not true, but also when we are uncertain that p is true but are certain that q is. We do this in arguing in favour of p. "This, which he did do, is just what he would have done, if he had done the murder". (Montague on Detective stories.)

On the other hand B is, in symbols, of the form

If it had been true that $((\exists x) . x$ was H.'s only invasion of Poland . x took place in July), then it would also have been true that B.'s last declaration occurred in July.

C, in symbols, is of the form

$(\exists x, y, m) . x$ was H.'s only invasion of Poland . y was Britain's last declaration . m was a month . x & y both took place in m.

Wherever we are asserting that there *was* one & only one thing of a certain description, this assertion must fall *outside* the "if" clause, as it does in (D_1).

Similarly when we are asserting that there were people there.

Thus: Suppose all the people there voted "Yes"; Smith was not there, & we know that if he had been, he would have voted "No".

This is the case, where Ramsey says (p. 249)[1]: we can say both "If Smith was there, he must have voted "Yes" " & (1) "If Smith had been there, he would have voted "No" ".

But, if we know Smith wasn't there, we can also say, can't we?

(2) $(\exists \alpha)$: such that α is not null . such that all members of α & only members of α were there . & such that if Smith had been a member of α, it would have been true of him that he voted "Yes".

(2) does not say the same as (3) "If S. had been there, he would have voted "Yes" ", for one reason bec. (3) does not assert that anyone was there, but for another bec., though (3) does follow from (2), (2) would not follow even from the conjunction of (3) with "$(\exists \alpha)$: such that α is not null . α contains all who were there & only those", since to get (2), you need "All who were there voted "Yes" " which is not entailed by (3): (3) might quite well be true even if all that were there voted No.

The phrase in (2) "it would have been true of him that he voted "Yes" ", seems, at first sight, as if it ought to mean the same as

[1] [F. P. Ramsey, *The Foundations of Mathematics* (London, 1931).]

"he would have voted "Yes" "; yet it is doubtful if we could rightly use the latter phrase in this case, since it suggests its use in (3), which is a *causal* prop. (as Ramsey says "such being his nature": perhaps better "because of the opinions which he holds" —we have learned that in the past he has held certain opinions, & we believe that the holding of those opinions in the past was due to something in him which would also cause him to vote "Yes"), whereas (2) is not. Can one not say of (2) that it is merely another way of saying (4) "All who were there did vote "Yes" "? Not quite; for though (2) follows from (4), (4) does not follow from (2), but only from the corresponding universal prop.: ($\exists \alpha$) of which it is true that it has members; that everybody who was there was a member & nobody else was; & that (x) . if x had been a member of α, it would have been true of x that he voted Yes. You can't mention anybody of whom you can't say that if he had been a member of α, it would have been true of him that he voted "Yes"; for, if you could, that person would be a person who, though a member of α, did not vote "Yes".

But is this so? From a prop. of the form "x was a member of α" it does not *follow* that x voted "Yes". People who were there *might* have voted "No". From their being there, it doesn't *follow* that they didn't: only from the conjunction of "x was there" with (4).

We do, however, say "If it had . . . it would have" in cases where the consequent doesn't *follow* from the antecedent, but only from *antecedent together with* (in conjunction with) some "fact or law": e.g. if A had been in this drawer, B would have been (so Ramsey, p. 248), which we should say *follows* from "A & B were both in same drawer".

Take "All the books in shelf A were green", or "All the people here last night were Englishmen".

It's absurd to produce a book bound in red, & to say "If this had been in shelf A, it would have been bound in green". We *can* say "*Since* it isn't green, it can't have been in shelf A". And similarly it's absurd to say of Lewy: "If L. had been here last night, he would have been an Englishman". We should say "Since he's not an Englishman, he can't have been here last night".

But can't we say: "If it had turned out that this was in shelf A, it would have turned out that this was bound in green"?

It's absurd to say "If L. had been here last night, he would have been an Englishman" & even to say "If L. was here last night, he must be an Englishman". Why? since "If he was there, he must have voted "Yes"" is *not* absurd. It's not absurd to ask "Is Lewy an Englishman?" What is the difference between the 2 cases, between "Everybody who was there voted "Yes"" & "Everybody who was here last night was an Englishman"? Again "If this book came from shelf A, it must be bound in green" or "If it had come, it would have been" seem both absurd. Why? ⟨No: *both* not absurd for blind man, 2nd not absurd for anyone.⟩

(1) From "All here were Englishmen" & "Lewy was here" there follows "Lewy is English". ∴ "L. is not English" → ∼ both (All were Eng. . Lewy was here).

(2) So too ("All on shelf A are ALWAYS green" *&* "This was on shelf A") → "This *was* green". ∴ This was *never* green → ∼ both ("All on shelf A are *always*" & "This one was").

(3) Or take "At the moment all on shelf A are green" & "My copy of Orly Farm is on A" → "My copy of O.F. is green". This allows "If my copy of O.F. is on shelf A, it must be green", which is not absurd, provided I don't know whether my copy is on shelf A or not, nor yet whether it is green or not. But does it justify "If my copy had been on A, it would have been green"?

⟨Yes, it does in the sense: If my copy had been identical with one of the books that were there (& somebody might have thought it was), it would have been green—which *follows* from "All that were there were green"; not in the causal sense that being put in that shelf would have changed its colour.⟩

So too (2) allows: "If *this* was ever on shelf A, it must have been at some time bound in green", wh. is not absurd, provided I don't know whether it was ever on shelf A or not, nor whether it was ever green or not.

A blind man might quite well say of a staring red book, which he had in his hand but of which of course he couldn't see the colour, "If this book came from shelf A, it must be bound in green". He would say so, if he'd been told it came from shelf A, but didn't feel quite certain he could trust his informant; but he must have trusted a previous informant that all the book on shelf A were green. His present informant may have made a mistake & thought he took it from shelf A, when in fact he took it from shelf B. In such a case the informant would say "No; it isn't green, it's bright red". And the blind man would say: "Then it can't have come from shelf A, *for if it had, it would have been green*". If his present informant still insisted that it did, he might be led to conclude that his previous informant was wrong; & that therefore he was wrong in saying "if it had, it would have been green". Why is it *not* absurd for a blind man to say this, whereas for a man who saw that the book was staring red, it would be absurd? Or perhaps it wouldn't be absurd for the man who did see it was staring red to say so? He might say so in order to support his conclusion that it didn't come from shelf A, & that an informant who said it did was wrong.

It is, of course, sensible to say "If it had come from A, it would have been green" where it is *not* sensible to say "If it came from A, it is (or "must be") green". This is the difference between the blind & the seeing man: the *blind* man can sensibly (under different circumstances) say both—first the latter, then (on being informed that it's bright red) the former. But the seeing man, at a time when he saw it was red, could not possibly say "If it came from A, it must be green" (in the dark, he might), but could say "If it had come from A, it would have been green".

But what is the analysis of this "If it had . . . it would have . . ."? It is not a causal assertion—not an assertion that the book would have *changed its colour*, like "If it had been painted all over with green paint, it would have been green". Doesn't it really say, not, as it seems to, that this particular book would have been green, but something like "If *the* book I have in my hand had come from A, it would have been a green book?"

This would be: $(\exists x) . x$ is the only book in my hand . if x had come from A, x would have been green. And this won't do!

How about: If I had had in my hand a book from A, it would have been green. This is true enough & follows from "all the books in A are green". And then I can infer: Since this book isn't green, it isn't from A.

I think this is perhaps all we mean by "If this book had come from shelf A, it would have been green". *Any* book that had come from shelf A would have been green.

"If this book had been from shelf A, it would have been green" may be used in 2 ways:

(1) it may imply: I know it isn't green: & can then be used as an argument for "it didn't come from A"

(2) it may imply "I know it is green", then being = If it had come from A, green is just what it would have been: as part of an argument in favour of "it came from A". In this case it implies: I don't know for certain (*independently?*) that it did come from A (Montague's case).

But now about Lewy:

[It] is all right [to say]

(1) If Lewy was there, it can't be true that all that were there were English.

So is: (2) If L. had been there, it wouldn't have been true that all were English.

(2) implies: I know that all were English: & is an argument to prove Lewy wasn't there.

(1) implies: I don't know whether he was or not, nor whether all were English or not.

Why can't you say: If L. had been there, he would have been English, just as you *can* say "If this book had been from shelf A, it would have been green"?

Because you *can* say: *Any* book from shelf A would have been green, but *can't* say: Anybody who was there would have been English?

And *why* can you say the first, but not the second?

Why can't you say: If Lewy was there, he is English, while you can say (a blind man can, or any man in the dark) "If this book came from shelf A, it is green"?

It looks as if since "All books on shelf A are green" justifies the latter, "Everybody there was English" *ought* to justify the former.

And again "Everybody there voted Yes" does justify "If Lewy was there, he voted Yes"; why then does not "Everybody there was English" justify "If Lewy was there, he is English"?

Suppose a person who doesn't know (independently?) whether Lewy is English or not. The mere knowledge that "All that were there were English" won't justify him in saying "If Lewy was there, he is English". But "None but English *could* be there— none but English were allowed in", *would* justify "If L. was there, he must be English". Like "Only holders of tickets were admitted", wh. would justify "If Lewy was there, he must have had a ticket". "Only holders of tickets were allowed in" is *causal* =

The failure to have a ticket would have caused any one to be denied admittance.

"As a matter of fact, only white men were there" is very different from "Only white men were admitted". Both allow "If he was there, he must be white"; but the 2nd only allows "If he had been there, it would have proved him to be a white man" (*not* "he *would* have been a white man").

Is it true that we are only entitled to say (can only say with truth) "If it *is* true that p, it *is* also true that q", in cases in which on discovering that $\sim p$, we should still be entitled to say "If *it had been* true that p, it would have been true that q"?

This *seems* to be disproved by

(1) "If Hitler's invasion was in July, B.'s declaration was in July" & by (2) "If S. was there, he must have voted "Yes" ",

since (3) "If Hitler had invaded in July, B. would have declared in July"

& (4) "If S. had been there, he would have voted "Yes" "

may quite well be false; i.e. though (1) & (2) are true, yet (3) & (4) may be false.

7

JOHNSON

Conjunctive & enumerative "and" (p. 28).[1]

"Cats mew and dogs bark" is a single prop. formed by the conjunction of "cats mew" *and* "dogs bark". Here the 2nd "and" is enumerative. The whole prop. is *not* a conjunction, as is "This is round & hard". Similarly " "Cats mew" & "dogs bark" are 2 props." *is not a conjunction* ⟨Isn't it equivalent to: " "Cats mew" is a prop. *and* "dogs bark" is a prop.", which *is* a conjunction?⟩; whereas "Cats mew & dogs bark" is. But when J. says (p. 122) "the substantival items constituting the denotation are united merely by the enumerative "and" ", this is not true of "Moore *and* Russell are both members of the class "Fellows of Trinity" ", since this = "Moore is a Fellow & Russell is"—a conjunction. It *is* true of "Nick & Tim form the class "Moore's sons" ", since we can't say "Nick forms the class & Tim forms it": yet it is identical with the conjunction "Nick is one of Moore's sons, T. is another, & there are no others".

[1] [W. E. Johnson, *Logic*, Part I (Cambridge, 1921).]

8

[NO TITLE]

It seems doubtful whether you can say "From "It froze last night, but the ice doesn't bear today" you *can infer* "It froze last night" ". This doesn't seem a matter of *inference*. Can you even say "From "It froze last night, but the ice doesn't bear today" it *follows* (would follow) that it froze last night"? Yet it seems you can say: "From "It didn't freeze last night" it *follows* that the 2 props. "It did freeze last night" and "The ice doesn't bear today" are not both true". And can't you even say that from "It didn't freeze last night" you *can infer* that the prop. made yesterday "The 2 props. "It will freeze tonight" & "The ice won't bear tomorrow" are not both true" was true? That the person who said that those 2 props. were not both true, was right? But perhaps you can say that from "The 2 props. "It froze last night" & "The ice doesn't bear today" are both true" you *can infer* that it froze last night; & this perhaps because you *can* say that from "The prop. "It froze last night" is true" you can *infer* that "it froze last night", & vice versa.

Can you say that the sentence "It froze last night" & the sentences "It's true that it froze last night" or "The prop. that it froze last night is true" are *merely* different ways of saying the same thing? Perh. *sometimes* they are; but *sometimes* not, for it seems as if, sometimes, when you use "true" you are thinking of a property which belongs to many props. but *not* to others, & in thinking "It froze last night" you certainly needn't be doing this. I.e. in Lewy's language (*Mind*, July /46) [it seems] that *sometimes* the prop. "It's true that it froze last night" *contains a concept* which "it froze last night" does not contain. A man (or dog?) who knows it is freezing, need not be familiar with the concept "true". But what seems quite certain is that, in any case, i.e. whether the 2 expressions are, in a particular case, merely different ways of saying the same thing or not, it is *always* right to say that *if* it froze last night it follows that it's *true* that it did & that the prop. that it did is true, & vice versa. *What* property are you thinking of when you think "Some props. are *true*, others not"? I think very likely "People are sometimes right in their assertions

354

& beliefs, sometimes wrong—Some of their ideas are true, others false", i.e. of the property which belongs to a person's *idea*, when he has a true idea. But of course you are not thinking "Somebody *has* the idea that it froze last night, & that idea is true"; but, perhaps, something like "If anybody were to think that it did, he would be right—that would be an instance of having a true idea".

How about "It froze last night" & "It's not the case that it's not the case that it froze last night" or "It's false that it's false that . . ."? Here I think we must say that these are not *merely* different ways of saying the same thing: in one case you have the concept of negation or falsity, in the other not: & you certainly can say that *each* follows from the other: If it froze last night it follows that it's not the case that it's not the case that it froze last night. But you can't say: If it froze last night it *follows* that it froze last night.

What is a prop.? If nobody had ever made *false* statements or had *false* beliefs, should we ever have come upon the idea of a prop.? *Perhaps* we should: it might have been sufficient to notice that when so & so is the case, *x* may not *know* that it is: *knowing* that it is involves *conceiving the prop.* that it is, something *not* involved in the fact that it's freezing, in spite of the fact that if it's freezing *the prop.* that it is must be *true*, i.e. that *if* anybody *had* conceived that it is, he would have been right.

A man certainly can "*assert*" "You ought not to have done that" & *think* (= believe) that he ought not to fight. Does it *follow* that "You ought not" or "I ought not" is a prop.? If so, what is expressed by such sentences must be capable of being true or false—must *be* either the one or the other. But it may be said that "assert" & "think" don't mean the same here as in other cases; & that from the fact that a man asserts "You ought not" or thinks that you ought not it doesn't follow that what he says is either true or false; but hasn't he made a prop., a statement?

9

PROPOSITIONS AND SENTENCES

There are many English sentences, which, though they make good sense, if used by themselves in certain circumstances, yet are of such a form that if you were to write or utter before them the words "I believe that . . ." or the words "I know that . . .", the whole sentences thus constructed *would make no sense*. E.g. "Go away", "Please, don't whistle", "Is it raining?", "Which of your sons is the taller?". The sentences "I believe that go away", "I know that please, don't whistle", "I believe that is it raining", "I know that which of your 2 sons is the taller", all *make no sense* (& one could say "aren't sentences"), if the expressions of which they are composed are being used in accordance with good English usage. Of course, these expressions *could* be so used that these sentences did make sense: e.g. in (3), if "is it raining" were used as we now use "it is raining", (3) would make perfect sense; or if "I believe that" were used as we now use "I have just uttered the words" or "I have just asked the question". But (3) doesn't make sense (one *could* say "is not a sentence at all") if the 2 expressions "I believe that" & "is it raining" are both being used in accordance with good English usage. And similarly in the other 3 cases.

But there are plenty of sentences, making sense by themselves under suitable circumstances, which are also such that if you add before them the words "I believe that" or "I know that", then, *either* with the one addition *or* with the other, the whole sentence thus formed also makes good sense; & there are some such that though the addition of "I believe that" does not give a sense-ful sentence, the addition of "I know that" does. "I believe that I've got a very bad pain" perhaps makes no sense, because if you have there can be no mistake about it; but "I *know* that I have", under certain circumstances, certainly does make sense. Let us call all sentences such that the adding before them of "I believe that" or "I think that" makes good sense, & also sentences such that the adding before them of "I know that" does so, "*declarative* sentences". It is to be noticed that, with this meaning, the main verb of a declarative sentence need not be in the indicative mood:

"I believe that, if it had frozen last night, the ice would have borne today", makes good sense, but "would have borne" is not in the indicative mood. But it is not *only* sentences such that the adding before them of these words makes good sense that I wish to call "declarative". "I *think* that I believe that numbers are classes of classes, but I'm not sure I do" does make sense; & so, in answer to "Do you believe my story?" it may make sense to say "I *think* I do, but I'm not quite sure I do". But it is doubtful whether "I think that I think that I believe they are" makes any sense at all; & still more doubtful whether "I think that I think that I think that I believe they are" does so. But I want to call any sentence beginning with "I think that", which makes sense, a "declarative" sentence, & it is certain that there are some of these which are such that the addition before them of "I think that" or "I know that" does *not* make sense. So also any sentence which begins with "I know that" & which makes sense is to be a "declarative" sentence; although there are *some* of these such that neither the addition of "I know that" before them nor that of "I think that" does make sense. E.g. "I know that I know that I've got a pain" perhaps makes sense, &, if it does, "I think that I know that I know that I've got a pain" will also make sense; & hence both of these will be declarative sentences: but do "I know that I know that I know that I've got a pain" or "I know that I think that I know that I know that I've got a pain" make any? In any case we can find *some* beginning with "I know that" & *some* beginning with "I think that", such that the addition before them either of "I know that" or "I think that" makes no sense.

I propose therefore to use "declarative" in such a way that an *English* sentence will be "declarative", if & only if it *either* (1) begins with "I know that" or "I think that" & makes sense *or* (2) is such that when it is immediately preceded *either* by "I know that" *or* by "I think that" the whole makes sense. How about "I'm certain that", "I'm sure that", "I feel sure that", "It's certain that"? All such sentences, *if* they make sense, are certainly "declarative". But isn't it the case that whenever they do, the addition of "I think that" before them *also* makes sense, so that they come under (2)? No: "I think I'm sure that I've got a bad pain" is very doubtful.

Let us then correct our def. to: An Eng. sentence is "declarative" if & only if *both* it makes sense, when the words & syntax are used in accordance with good English usage, & also *either* (1) begins with "I know that", "I think that", "I feel sure that", "It's certain that" or any other of the Eng. phrases which mean the same as one of these *or* (2) is such that the sentence formed by adding one of these before it makes sense.

10

SENTENCES AND PROPOSITIONS

How is the sentence "It is raining" related to the prop. "It is raining"? What is the difference between them?

(1) The words (or sentence) "He said it *was* raining" obviously don't mean the same as the words "He said the words 'It *was* raining' ". A man may quite well have said it was raining without saying those words; & he may quite well have said those words without saying that it was raining. That he should have done the latter is neither a necessary nor a sufficient condition for his having done the former.

(2) It may be suggested that they do mean the same as "He said the words "It *is* raining" ". But in order that he should have said it was raining it is certainly not *necessary* that he should have said these words: he may have used words in another language which mean the same. E.g. suppose a German comes in & says to me "Es regnet", & some-one who doesn't understand German asks me "What did he say?", it is quite correct for me to answer "He said it was raining".

This is the fact which, I think, Ramsey tried to meet by saying that a prop. is a class of sentences, grouped together as having the same meaning. I.e. to have said it was raining, it is only necess. for him to have uttered *some* sentence having the same meaning as "It is raining".

This is *necessary*; but is it sufficient?

⟨What Ramsey says (p. 33)[1] is that any two *symbols* (of a certain kind) which express agreement & disagreement with the same sets of possibilities, will be called by him "instances of the same prop.". But adds that they are *instances* of a certain prop. "*just as*" all the "the"'s on a page are instances of the word "the"; though, whereas the "the"'s are instances *of the same word* owing to their physical similarity, the symbols are instances *of the same prop.* because they have *the same sense* (= "express agreement & disagr. etc".)

Can it be "just as"? Of each "the" we can say "This is the word "the" " or "This is a "the" ". Acc. to Ramsey we can say

---

[1] [F. P. Ramsey, *The Foundations of Mathematics* (London, 1931).]

similarly of each symbol, e.g. "p ⊃ q", "This is the prop. "p ⊃ q" "; but we can't say "This is *a* prop. "p ⊃ q" ". But of each *instance* of the symbol "p ⊃ q" we can say "This is the symbol "p ⊃ q" ". But if we say "This is the prop. "p ⊃ q" " it is not of the instances of the symbol, nor of the symbol, that we are saying that it is that prop.⟩

(3) Wisdom has pointed out that there is this difference between the meaning of (a) "He said it was raining" & (b) "He uttered or wrote some sentence that had the same meaning as "it is raining" "; namely that a person does not understand the sentence (a), unless he understands "it was raining" (or "it is raining"?)—let us say understands "raining", whereas a man may understand (b) without having the least idea what "raining" or any word equivalent to it means.

This is certainly important; but what does it shew?

It is important to notice that a man does not understand "He *made the statement* that the sun is larger than the moon", unless he understands "the sun is larger than the moon", i.e. "statement" ≠ "sentence"; just as also "he asserted the *prop.* that the sun is larger than the moon" is not understood unless the same is understood. Now Wisdom, p. 436[1], says that the *factual claim* made by "he uttered the sentence "Sun larger than moon" " is nevertheless the same as that made by "He stated that sun is larger than moon". But it is not: the latter means at least this "He uttered or wrote some sentence which *means* that the sun is larger than the moon". In this sense a parrot who has been taught to say "The sun is larger than the moon" *can* be said to have *stated* that the sun is larger than the moon, or *said* that it is, though he attached no meaning to his words. But, of course, it is not incorrect for a man who murmurs "The curfew tolls the knell . . ." to protest: I wasn't *saying* that the curfew tolls, I was only repeating a line of poetry.

But what *is* a prop.?

We have only said that "He asserted the prop. "p" " does not mean the same as "He uttered (or wrote) the sentence "p" or some equivalent", & that it means in addition "he uttered a sentence which means p". That sentence "p" means p is an empirical prop. But of course a man who says that the sun is

---

[1] [J. Wisdom, "Metaphysics and Verification (I)", *Mind*, vol. XLVII (1938). Reprinted in J. Wisdom, *Philosophy and Psycho-analysis* (Oxford, 1953).]

larger than the moon is not saying anything about the sentence
"p". Are we, when we say he said that? Are we saying something
about the sentence we use, i.e. that he uttered *some* sentence that
had the same meaning? If so, we are also *mentioning* the meaning,
because we understand our own sentence. We are saying, He
uttered some sentence which had *this* meaning. But, if so, we need
not be saying anything about the sentence we use. We are
implying something about it.

CAN YOU "HEAR" A PROPOSITION?

Morris[1] said "You can only hear a sentence". But when you say "I heard today that S. is dead", you are not saying that you heard the sentence "S. is dead".

In this 2nd use of "heard", "I heard that p" = I heard *some* sentence which meant p, *and* p. I.e. if S. isn't dead, I didn't hear that he is. But perh. it *can* be used = simply "I heard some sentence which meant p".

But this won't quite do. I must not only have heard some sentence which *meant* p, I must (1) have heard somebody *assert* that p & (2) I must also not *know* that $\sim$ p . I heard today that S. is dead, but I don't know whether it's true, is not self-contradictory. But isn't "I heard today that S. is dead, but he isn't"? Anybody who knew that S. wasn't dead, wouldn't say "I heard that S. is dead", but e.g. "I heard *a rumour* that S. is dead", or "a false rumour".

One important point is that the sentence "I heard that S. is dead" can't be understood by anyone who doesn't understand "S. is dead", whereas "I heard the sentence "S. is dead" " can. And so can (a) "I heard somebody make an assertion, which he expressed by a sentence which meant the same as the sentence "S. is dead" "; for there is no *contradiction* in adding "but I haven't the least idea what "S. is dead" means", although it is very unlikely anyone would say (a) unless he *did* know what "S. is dead" meant.

---

[1] [Lazerowitz ?]

NOTEBOOK IX

[1948–1953]

1

ANALYSIS (July/48)

Plato (*Laws*, 895 D) says that 2 different questions may be asked about anything whatever (περὶ τὸ ὂν ἅπαν). We ask one of these questions when we *give* (προτείνεσθαι) the name of the reality (ὄν, οὐσίαν) in question (& we can only do this, if it happens to have a name: P. has implied that every "reality" has a name, which is, of course, untrue) & ask what is the λόγος of that reality, & we ask the other when we *give* (προτείνεσθαι) the λόγος of the reality in question & ask what is its name. He has previously insisted that any reality (οὐσία) on the one hand, the λόγος of that reality on the other, & its name on the third hand, are three different things.

He goes on to illustrate by taking the name "ἄρτιος" & the λόγος "ἀριθμὸς διαιρούμενος εἰς ἴσα δύο μέρη", & asking whether it isn't the same ὄν which we "προσαγορεύομεν", both when we are *given* this λόγος & answer the question what is the name of the reality whose λόγος it is, & when we are *given* its name & answer the question what the λόγος of the thing so named is.

Now it seems that that for which "ἄρτιος" is a name is the property or concept which we are attributing to 2, & to 4, & to 6 etc. when we say that each of these is an *even* number; and when Plato says that the λόγος of this property is "number which *is being divided* into 2 equal parts", it seems clear he is making 2 mistakes. (1) If we say that 4 is "even", we are not saying that it *is* being divided at all—only, perhaps, that it is *divisible*: certainly if it is even, a number must be *divisible*. But (2) though it must be *divisible*, it is not true that it is divisible *into 2 equal parts*. ⟨Leibniz also made this mistake: Frege, *Grundlagen*, p. 14 quotes from him "Eine gerade Zahl kann in zwei gleiche Theile getheilt werden".⟩ A cake or a piece of paper can be divided into 2 equal parts; but when the number 4 is divided by 2 it is not divided into 2 equal parts. To say that it is divisible by 2 is to say that there is some integral (or cardinal) number—(one & one only (?))—such that the product of this number & 2 is 4: in this case 4 is the product of 2 into *itself*, not into "another 2"; but in the case of 6, the number such that 6 is a product of it & 2, is, of

365

course, *another* number, namely 3. With this def of "even", i.e. "divisible by 2", it is not in accordance with ordinary language to say that 2 itself is "even"; since it is not in accordance with ord. lang. to say that 2 can be *multiplied* by 1. But mathematicians & logicians, of course, would say that 2 itself is the *product* of 2 & 1, & that 2 is a *factor* in itself, just as they so use "part" that any whole can be said to be a "part" of itself, i.e. use "x is a part of y" = x is *either* identical with y *or* a part of y.

Possibly, however, by "divisible into 2 equal parts", Plato means "a *sum* of 2 equal parts". And, of course, 2 persons is a *sum* of one person & one *other* person ⟨Of course, not in same sense (which is *the* proper one) in which 3 is *the sum* of 1 & 2⟩; but the number "2" is not the sum of 2 "ones"; it is the sum of 1 added to *itself*. And of course no even number is the sum of 2 *equal* numbers, since no *2* numbers can be equal to one another, though mathematicians would say that any number was equal *to itself*. No *number* is divisible into 2 equal parts; although any collection, whose number is an even number, is divisible into 2 collections, *equal* to one another in the sense that they have the *same* number of members.

"is a sum of 2 equal parts" → "is divisible into 2 equal parts", but not *vice versa*, since e.g. a spatial or temporal whole is *not* a sum of any parts, but entails that any parts which "make it up" should be spatially or temporally continuous.

As for *numbers* "x is divisible by 2" = "There is some integral number y such that x is the number resulting from adding y to itself" = $(\exists y) . x = y + y$, except that the latter description certainly applies to 2 itself as well as to all other even numbers, whereas in ordinary language we should not say that 2 is divisible by 2.

$$((\exists y) . x = 2 \times y) = (\exists y) . x = y + y.$$

What does Plato mean by the "λόγος" of the reality of which "ἄρτιος" is the name? If he had known English, I think he would certainly have recognised that "even" & "ἄρτιος" were 2 different *names*, though names of the same reality, but I think he would have been inclined to say that "ἀριθμὸς δίχα διαιρούμενος" & "number divisible by 2" were the *same λόγος*, not 2 different ones: i.e. by λόγος he means, not *an expression*, but what it expresses. But in all probability, except in the case of "names", he had not distinguished clearly between an expression & what it expresses.

But if the λόγος of "even" (the property, not the word) is not the expression "ἀριθμὸς δίχα διαιρούμενος", but what this expresses, how does the λόγος differ from the reality of which it is the λόγος?

I think the answer is: In no way. Plato's assertion that the λόγος differs from the οὐσία may be due to his seeing that the *expression* of the λόγος differs from the οὐσία, & *not* seeing that he does not really mean by λόγος any expression. But it is perh. partly due to the fact that it seems a person can *understand* the name "ἄρτιος", without knowing that any even number must be divisible by 2. Juliet, in using dice, knows quite well that 2, 4 & 6 "*are even numbers*" & that 1, 3 & 5 are not; but it may be doubted whether she *knows* that 2, 4 & 6 are all numbers which can be got by adding a number to itself (= divisible by 2), & hence whether when she *says* they are even, she *means* by this that they can be got in this way. What does she mean? Does she merely *apply* the word "even" to them, & not mean anything? Or does she mean merely that they are all *called* "even"—that the name "even" applies to them? Is the test (necess., or suff., or both?) that she *understands* "even" merely that she applies it to those numbers, & those only, to which it does apply? She might do this without *meaning* anything by the word: by chance? This would be excluded by a sufficient variety of tests; but would it follow that she *meant* anything by it? It is not by chance that she applies "James" rightly to James; but does it follow that she *means* anything by "James"? She certainly uses it as a name, but that is different. She *applies* it to the *same* person on different occasions, though he *looks* different on diff. occasions. But with "even" she *applies* it to different numbers; & hence, if she doesn't do it by chance (& she doesn't) does it follow that she *means* something by it? She doesn't use it as a *proper name* for anything as she does "James". It is tempting to say that she applies it correctly to different even numbers because she *feels* some respect in which they are similar to one another & *not* to odd numbers. Could it be that she *feels* that each is a sum of some number added to itself, although, even when she understands this phrase, she could not be sure that that is what she feels? Can we say that she does attach meaning to "even", but no *definite* meaning?

If you add any number to itself once only, the number you thus get—a sum—is also the product of 2 & the number in

question. $1 + 1 = 1 \times 2, 2 + 2 = 2 \times 2, 3 + 3 = 3 \times 2,$
$4 + 4 = 4 \times 2$, etc.

Can we say that "even" *means* (1) "number to be obtained by adding some number to itself"

or *means* (2) "number to be obtained by multiplying some number by 2"

or *means* (3) "number divisible by 2 without remainder".

If we say (3) 2 itself is not an even number, though of every other even number (3) is true.

But (1) & (2) are *necessarily* true of every even number. Are (1) & (2) merely the *same* thing in different words? If we say "even" *means* (1), does it follow that "even" does *not* mean (2)?

And, in order to give the meaning of "even", is it necessary to refer to any process by which a number *is obtained*?—any *operation*?

That $2 = 1 + 1$ does not mean "2 can be *obtained* by adding 1 to itself".

Perhaps the ultimate def. of "even" is as follows:—

6 is an even number = In the case of every set of things A, which contains 6 *members* & no more, there are 2 other mutually exclusive sets, containing *the same number* of members as one another, & such that every member of either set is a member of A & every member of A is a member of one or other of them.

⟨But this def. won't do for "2 is an *even* number", since in this case there are not 2 mutually exclusive "*sets*", having the required property. One thing can't be said to be a *set* of things: we so use "set" that there must be more than one in a set.⟩

What is meant by "2 is an *even number*"?

$(\exists n) . n + n = 2$. Perhaps we need to explain that this means: There is a *cardinal* (or integral) number, n, such that $n + n = 2$.

But this needs further explanation of how the signs "+" & "=" are being used.

Our formula does *not* mean (as Plato seems to suppose) that 2 is divisible into 2 equal *parts*.

Can we suppose that it says something about any collection, in which the number of items is 2 & no more? e.g. $(\exists x, y) . x \neq y .$ x is an item . y is an item . nothing except x & y is an item. Here again we can't say *properly* that each item in the collection is a "part" of the collection: it is a *member*: nor would there be any sense in saying that one item was "*equal to*" the other. Of a collection of 4 items we *can* say that it *includes* (*not* "has for members") 2 other collections, of 2 items each, & that each of any 2 such is *equal* to the other, in the sense that it contains (has for members) *the same number* of items. And when one collection is *included* in another, we do often speak of it as a *part* of that other: e.g. *part* of the crowd went off down High St.; but we should scarcely speak of *one* member of the crowd as "part" of it.

Sophocles & Shakespeare form a collection, which has 2 members & 2 only. One of the members spoke Gk., the other English; & we *could* say that the *number* of members of this collection wh. spoke Gk. was *the same* as the number wh. spoke English, i.e. 1 in each case. (We could also say that the number of members of it which spoke German was 0, bec. neither of them did.) What *number* of members of such & such a collection did so & so? = How *many* members of such & such did so & so? And to this: "only one", or "none" are perfectly proper answers. I.e. 0 & 1 are, *in one sense*, "numbers"—i.e. are proper answers to the question "How many?"

Soph. is *a* member of this collection, & he is *only one* member of it—not the *only* member of it, nor yet *more than one* member of it.

People *say* this class also *includes* (not has for members) the 2 sub-classes "things identical with Soph." & "things identical with Shaks.", each of which has only one member, & neither of which is identical with that member.

2

NUMBERS

N. has only one child $= (\exists x) . x$ is a child of N. and $(x, y) . y \neq x . \supset . y$ is *not* a child of N.

Let $\phi x = x$ is a child of N.

Then "N. has only one child" $= (\exists x) : \phi x . (y) . y \neq x . \supset . \sim \phi y$.

Now the expression obtained by substituting a variable for ϕ in this expression, expresses a function of ϕ: we could call this function, in English, "applies to one & only one thing"; and we can call this function a property (Eigenschaft) of ϕ. (Frege, p. 59).[1]

Why should we not say that this function *is* the number 1? It is a property which belongs not only to ϕ but to all concepts which apply to one & only one thing.

Similarly "Venus has no moons" $= \sim (\exists x) . x$ is a moon of Venus, & if we here substitute a variable for "is a moon of Venus", we obtain an expression which expresses a property of the Begriff "being a moon of Venus"; & why should we not say that this property *is* the number 0? Why should we not say that the property of "applying to nothing" *is* the number 0? F., p. 67, gives $(x) . x$ is *not* a moon of Venus.

Any 2 concepts each of which applies to one thing & one thing only, can be said to apply to the *same number* of things; i.e. the answer to the question "how many things does this apply to" is "One". And similarly in the case of any 2 concepts, each of which applies to nothing, they can be said to apply to the *same number*, since in the case of each the answer to the question "how many things does this apply to", will be the same, viz. "None".

F., p. 68 says that though we have explained the sense of "the number 1 *kommt zu*" & "the number 0 *kommt zu*", we can't in these Begriffe distinguish 0 & 1 as "independent, recognizable objects".

Now, understanding ϕ as above, to say that the number 1 "kommt zu" ϕ is *logically equivalent* to saying "$\sim (x) . \sim \phi x$ *and* $(x, y) . \phi x . \phi y . \supset . x = y$" (F., p. 67) which again is *logically equivalent* to $(\exists x) : \phi x . (y) . y \neq x . \supset . \sim \phi y$.

F. uses the curious expression "The number 1 *kommt zu* the

---

[1] [G. Frege, *Die Grundlagen der Arithmetik* (Breslau, 1884). Eng. trans. (by J. L. Austin) *The Foundations of Arithmetic* (Oxford, 1950).]

Begriff ϕ" to mean only "I is *a* number which belongs to ϕ".
From the mere fact that $\sim(x) \sim \phi x$ & that also $(x, y) . \phi x . \phi y$.
$\supset . x = y$, it does not follow that no *other* number also belongs to ϕ?

He also gives the expression: 'The number $(n + 1)$ kommt zu
the Begriff F, if there is an object a which falls under F & is
such that the number n kommt zu the Begriff "falling under F
but not a" ', as an attempt to *explain* (erklären) the relation of the
immediate successor of a number to that number.

He says this last won't do as a *definition*, because we don't
know what is meant by "the number *n* kommt zu the Begriff G".

He says that by this *explanation* together with that of "I kommt
zu", we can say what is meant by (es bedeute)

"the number $1 + 1$ kommt zu the Begriff F"

i.e. it means "There is an object, a, which falls under F, & is
such that the number I kommt zu the Begriff "falling under F
but not a" ".

But he says our explanations don't suffice to shew (1) that
Julius Caesar is not a number, or (2) that if a & b both "kommen
zu" F, a must be identical with b: that all we have done is to
explain the meanings of "I kommt zu" & "o kommt zu", but
that this is not enough to explain "I" & "o". "I" is only a *part*
of "I kommt zu"; & therefore you must not say that "o" & "I"
are *properties* (Eigenschaft) of Begriffe, though "I kommt zu"
is a property of certain Begriffe.

He goes on to say that in "The number of moons of Jupiter *is*
4", "is" = "is the same as"; & then strangely enough, that this
assertion is an assertion about the *expression* "the number of the
moons of Jupiter" & the *word* "4"—namely that the expression
& the word "bezeichnen" the same object. If this latter prop. were
true, then "the number of moons of the earth is I" could not
possibly be logically equivalent to "$(\exists x) : x$ is a moon of the
earth . $(y) . y \neq x . \supset . y$ is *not* a moon of the earth" since this
neither entails nor is entailed by any prop. about the word "I" &
the expression "the number of moons of the earth"; although it
does both entail & is entailed by "the number of moons of the
earth is the number I". He compares it with "Columbus was the
discoverer of America" which is certainly equivalent to "Columbus
& nobody else discovered America", & which is certainly not
equivalent to any prop. whatever about the *word* "Columbus" &
the *expression* "the discoverer of A.".

3

ANALYTIC

Frege (*Grundlagen*, p. 4)[1] says that a truth is analytic if, in order to prove it, one needs only (1) "the universal logical laws" & (2) "definitions". He does *not* say that a truth is analytic *only* if this condition is satisfied. And he adds that you must "also take account of the props. on which the *reliability* (Zulässigkeit) of a def. rests". How "take account" of these? & what *are* these?

On p. IX he has already said that any enquiry into the *justification* (Berechtigung) of a def. must be *logical*; and talks of "the logical justification (?, here Rechtfertigung)" of defs. But he goes on to add that defs. must "bewähren sich" by "their fruitfulness"—"by the possibility of conducting proofs by their means"; but also says that you have not strictly proved anything, if the defs. you use in the proof are only "justified" (gerechtfertigt) by the fact that you haven't come upon any contradiction. What *does* he think "justifies" a def.?

On p. 76 he proposes, as a *def.* (what of ?), the following
Let the sentence "The st. line *a* is parallel to the st. line *b*"
have the same meaning as
"The direction (Richtung) of *a* is the same (gleich) as that of *b*".
He next calls this an "explanation" (Erklärung).

⟨This is by no means the only way in which we use "direction". E.g. if a person looks in a direction parallel to that in which I am looking, we can say that he is *not* looking in the same direction as I am: there is (1) one sense of *direction* in which "look in that direction" is a command not complied with unless you are looking towards (= in the direction of) some object towards which the commander is pointing & (2) another sense in which a person is looking in the same direction as you are if he is looking in *the same direction* along the same straight line: e.g. if a person is in a straight line between me & the pole-star, or I am in a straight line between him & the pole-star, & we are both looking in the direction of the pole-star, we are looking in the same direction.⟩

[1] [G. Frege, *Die Grundlagen der Arithmetik* (Breslau, 1884). Eng. trans. (by J. L. Austin) *The Foundations of Arithmetic* (Oxford, 1950).]

He then says that the "known laws of identity (Gleichheit)" are "as analytic truths developed from the concept itself", & adopts Leibniz's *def.* of identity "Eadem sunt, quorum unum potest substitui alteri salva veritate"—calling this also an "explanation". He explains further (77 top) that he understands L. to mean "*universally* substitutable", & says that all the laws of identity are *contained* in universal substitutability.

Now no *substitution* can occur unless that which is substituted is *different* from that for which it is substituted. L.'s rule therefore can only be a rule for deciding when 2 *different* things are the same: & they never are. It looks as if what he was thinking of must be a rule for deciding when 2 different *expressions* have the same *meaning, or* have the same *denotation*: which? "The author of Wav." has not the same meaning as "The author of Marmion", but it is right to say "The a. of W. was identical with the a. of M.", or that the 2 phrases *denote* the same person. But "the a. of W." is not *universally* substitutable for "the a. of M." *salva veritate*; e.g. in " 'The a. of W. did not compose W.' is self-contradictory". Is the expression "1 + 1" *universally* substitutable *s.v.* for "2"? Perhaps, yet Frege says (Vol. I, p. 7)[1] that "2"" & "2 + 2" have a different *Sinn*, though the same *Bedeutung*, & though he would certainly say $2^2 = 2 + 2$. (He says, Vol. II p. 254[1] "Die Identität (Gleichheit) ist eine so bestimmt gegebene Beziehung, dass nicht abzusehen ist . . .". But is it? Certainly not, if it means what L. says.) Would he say that Sinn of "1 + 1", is different from that of "2"?

On p. 21[2] he takes as *proof* that geometrical Axioms are "synthetic" that they are "independent of one another & of the logical "Urgesetzen" ".

[1] [G. Frege, *Grundgesetze der Arithmetik*, vol. I (Jena, 1893), vol. II (Jena, 1903).]
[2] [*Grundlagen der Arithmetik*.]

4

PROPOSITIONS

Suppose I say of a particular person at a particular time "He said it was raining", using these words to say so.

Nobody can understand these words of mine unless he understands the words "it was raining"; whereas if I had used the words "He said the words "It is raining" " a person who did not know what "it is raining" means would have understood my words perfectly well.

"He said it was raining" means the same as "He asserted *the prop. that* it was raining", whereas "He said the words "It is raining" " says nothing about *the prop. that* it was raining, but only about the *sentence* "It is raining". If Ramsey (p. 33)[1] were right that every instance of the words "It is raining" is an instance also of *the prop.* "it is raining", in the same sense of "instance", it would (surely?) follow that in saying "He said the words "It is raining" " I was saying something about *the prop.* "it is raining"; whereas we so use prop. that, in saying this, I could not be said to have said anything about *the prop.*, unless, in order to understand my words, it was necessary for a person to understand the words "It is raining"; and this is not the case. I.e. it is *not* true that every instance of *the words* "It is raining" is also *in the same sense* an instance of *the prop.* "it is raining"; since in "He said the words "It is raining" " (on *each* occasion), from the fact that you have uttered an instance of the words "it is raining" it follows that you have said something about *the words* "it is raining", whereas it does *not* follow from this fact that you have said anything about *the prop.* "it is raining".

"He said it was raining" *entails* that he uttered or wrote, etc., *some* set of words which meant that it was raining: we can, therefore, say that in making this prop. we are saying something about *words*, but we are not saying anything about any particular words.

But though that he should have uttered or written, etc., some set of words wh. meant it was raining is a *necess.* condition for its being true that he said it was raining, it is not a *sufficient* condition:

[1] [F. P. Ramsey, *The Foundations of Mathematics* (London, 1931).]

e.g. suppose he said the words "Consider the sentence "It's raining" ""—it certainly does not follow from this that he said it was raining.

And for *believing* that it's raining or *finding* that it's raining, it's *neither* necess. nor sufficient that he should have *used* in any way any set of words which meant it was raining—not even images of such a set?

Every prop. about sentences (words) in general is a prop. about instances of sentences (words); & every prop. about a particular sentence (word) is a prop. about instances of it.

If there were no instances of them there would be no words or sentences.

But *it is not true* that every prop. about any particular prop. is a prop. about instances of a sentence.

It is *not true* that every prop. about props. in general is a prop. about instances of sentences.

It is *not true* that if there were no instances of sentences there would be no props.; since, even if there had never been any sentences, some props. might have been true & others false, since "the prop. that the sun is shining is true" = "the sun is shining".

What *is* true is that if there were no instances of sentences, no prop. could be *asserted*—there would be no *asserted* props.

But it is not true that if there were no instances of sentences no prop. could *be believed*, nor yet that no prop. could *be true*, nor yet that no prop. could be *false*.

Every prop. which is true, except props. about sentences, *could* have been true, even if there had been no sentences: from the fact that it's true that the sun is shining it doesn't follow that there are any sentences, since if the sun *is* shining, it follows that it's true that it is, & obviously does not follow that there are any sentences.

Again every prop. which is false, except props. which entail the existence of sentences, could have been false, even if there had been no sentences: from the fact that it's false that it's raining, it does not follow that there are any sentences, since that it's false that it's raining follows from (perhaps, is identical with) the fact that it's *not* raining (in this neighbourhood now), & from the fact that it's not raining now it obviously does not follow that there are any sentences. We couldn't *say* that it's not raining now, unless there were sentences; but from the fact that it's not it doesn't follow that we can *say* that it's not.

I understand what Ramsey means by a printed *instance* of the word "the": by all the *instances* of "the" on a page, he means what we should usually call all the "the"s on a page. But he is wrong when he says that they are instances of the same word on account of their physical similarity: it is not owing to physical similarity that "THE" & "the" are both instances of the word "the", but because, owing to *conventions* for writing down sounds, they both are ways of writing the same sound; & we must add to "the same sound", the clause "when used with a particular meaning or set of meanings"—those conveyed by "the" as distinguished from "thee". ("The" has a different meaning in "*the* whale" from that which it has in "*the* author of W.")

⟨There is no reason whatever to say that "THE" is more physically similar to "the" than to "THEE"; yet the first 2 *are* instances of the word "the", & the last is not.⟩

Am I right when I say that every prop. about the word "the" is a prop. about instances of it?

What sort of props. *do* we make about words?

1. This is the word "the" (pointing at a printed, written, etc. symbol).

2. The word "the" begins with a "t".

3. The word "the" occurs 20 times on this page.

1. would only be spoken, & is in part telling you how the written symbol is pronounced; & in this case the prop. you are making is a prop. about sounds similar to the one you are making: you are saying "this symbol is pronounced in *this* sort of way"—where you give a specimen of *the sort*.

Is this an "autonymous" use of the sound? Is one using the *instance* or *token* as a name for the *sort* or type to which it belongs? or is one using the *sort* or *type* as a name for itself?

By a *name* I think we always mean a *type*, i.e. we never use an *instance* or *token* as a name of anything; but to say that we are using the type as a *name* for itself is to say that we are using an *instance*—we mustn't say as a *name*, but in that way which is such that to use the *type* as a name for itself *means* the same as using a *token* of it in the nameless way in question. You can't use the *type* at all, except by using a *token* of it.

⟨If I say "this "the" is written with an unusually long stroke to the "t" "; then, of course, I am making a prop. about *that instance or token*; but I am not using that token as a name for itself: any more than when I point at a person & say "That is the Mayor" or "That person has a very long nose", I am using the person pointed at as a name for himself.⟩

When I say " "the" begins with a "t" " I am not merely saying that the instance or token in question begins with a "t": I am saying that *all* "the"s begin with a "t"—that *every* instance does. When I write again now " "the" begins with a t", I am both (1) writing the *same sentence* over again & (2) making the *same* prop. a second time; and I should not be doing this if on the first occasion I were saying of the instance of "the" which is fourth from the left in the [seventh] line above this that *it* began with a t. Whenever I am called "Moore" it is *the same* name which is being used for me; & it would not be if on any occasion the *token* or *instance* were being used as a name for me. And when I use "Moore" as a name for the name "Moore", it is equally true that it is not the token which I am using as a name—though I *am* using the token in a nameless way, such that to use the type as a name for itself is the same thing as to use some token of it in that nameless way.

5

"THE EPIMENIDES"

Epimenides, who was himself a male Cretan, used the words "Κρῆτες ἀεὶ ψεῦσται" to make *some* statement, which these Greek words could, without clear misuse, be used to express. *One* statement which they could, without clear misuse, be used to express is "Every statement, without exception, which is ever made by a male Cretan is a lie". I do not think they could, without misuse, be used to mean what "Male Cretans are always liars" would mean in English, i.e. "Every male Cretan, without exception, is a liar": I do not think ἀεί is ever used in this particular way in which "always" is sometimes used in English. In any case, I think it is quite certain that E. was not using them in either of these two ways. I think we should get nearer to what he meant by saying he meant "Male Cretans constantly tell lies"—where "constantly", as is usually the case in English, does *not* mean that *every* statement they make is a lie, but only that they very very often—habitually—make statements that are lies. But if he had been asked: Do you mean that this is true of *all* male Cretans, without exception? I think he would certainly have answered: "No, I don't; of course, there are exceptions; I myself, for instance, am an exception". So that I think we should come nearest to what he actually meant by: "There are very few exceptions to the rule that male Cretans constantly lie" or (what comes to the same thing): "If ever you meet a male Cretan, you will rarely be wrong in assuming that he is an habitual liar".

But the proposition that a male Cretan had made *this* statement would not have even *seemed* to entail any consequences of the smallest interest to philosophers. The proposition which *has* seemed to entail interesting philosophical consequences is the prop. that a male Cretan made the statement "Every statement, without exception, made by a male Cretan, is *false*". For from the *conjunction* of the two props. (1) that a male Cretan made this statement & (2) that this statement was TRUE, i.e. that every statement without exception made by a male Cretan at that time, really was false, there does *seem* to follow inevitably a contradiction, viz. that the statement in question was *both* true & false:

for if it is true *both* that every statement made by a male Cretan at that time was false, and *also* that a male Cretan at that time made this statement itself, it *seems* to follow that that statement of his was false; i.e. from the assumption that that statement was true, *conjoined with* the assumption that a male Cretan made it, it seems to follow that that statement was false; while it *also* quite obviously follows that it was true. But it is impossible that one & the same statement should be *both* false *and* true. Hence it seems to follow that it can't be true *both* that the statement was true *and* that a male Cretan made it. And hence if a male Cretan *did* make it (as seems certainly possible), it *must* have been false. It *seems*, in short, that from the hypothesis that E., or any other Cretan, made the statement "All statements made by Cretans are false" it would follow quite conclusively that this statement *must* itself have been false: it *must* have been the case that at least one statement made by a Cretan was true: since it is self-contradictory to suppose both (1) that a Cretan made the statement, & (2) that it was true. Hence one or other of these conjuncts must be false; i.e. if we suppose (1) true, (2) must be false; whereas, if we suppose (2) true, (1) must be false: i.e. if (2) is true, it is imposs. that a Cretan should ever have stated that it was—a queer result!

We thus *seem* to get a result, which is a little paradoxical; namely that a statement, which might possibly have been true, if made by anyone but a Cretan, cannot possibly be true, if made by a Cretan. Or, to put the paradox in a different way: that, if it were true that every statement, without exception, made by a Cretan is false, it would be impossible that any Cretan should ever make this statement. Isn't it strange, perhaps incredible, that there should be any statement whatever, such that from the supposition that it is true, it follows that it is impossible that any person of a particular class should assert that proposition? I fancy, however, that many philosophers have supposed, falsely, that *another* paradox follows or *seems* to follow from the premises —viz. that the statement (1) "Every statement made by a Cretan is false" is itself such that if true, it must be false, & cannot therefore possibly be true. But careful inspection shews that this conclusion does not even *seem* to follow: all that even *seems* to follow is that the 2 statements (1), & the additional statement (2) "A Cretan made the statement (1)" cannot *both* be true; it does not even *seem* to follow that (1) *by itself* entails a contradiction. It *seems*

evident that if (1) is true, & if also any Cretan states that (1), then
(1) must be both true & false; but it does not even *seem* evident
that (1) itself must be self-contradictory, whether stated by a
Cretan or not. If (1) is true, it does *seem* to follow that *either*
Epimenides never stated that (1) *or* E. was not a Cretan; & also
that no Cretan ever stated that (1): and this is surprising enough.
But it does not even *seem* to follow that from the mere hypothesis
that (1) is true it follows that (1) is false. I think many philosophers fail to distinguish clearly between the two very different
props. (a) "(1), if true, must also be false" & (b) "(1), if true *and*
stated by a Cretan, must also be false". (a) would be a more
surprising, more paradoxical, prop. than (b). It would be more
surprising that (1) by itself should entail a contradiction than that
the conjunction of (1) with "A Cretan asserted (1)" should entail
one.

Philosophers *also*, in dealing with this subject, seem often
to speak as if there were no difference between the statement
"Every statement made by a Cretan is false" & "Every statement
made by a Cretan *is a lie*". And it may be admitted that nowadays
many people often use "lie" as if it were a synonym for "false
statement". I think, however, it is still right to say that this is a
misuse of "lie": e.g. it is not recognised in Shorter O.E.D.,
which gives for "lie" "false statement *made with intent to
deceive*". In any case, even if *one* proper use of "lie" is "false
statement", there is *a* well-established use such that by no means
all false statements are "lies". E.g. it is not self-contradictory to
say: "What he said was false, but he wasn't lying, for he fully
believed that it was true". In this, correct, use of "lie", in order
that a false statement should be a lie, it is essential that the person
who made it should have known or believed it to be false, &
perhaps also that he should have *wished* that those who heard or
read it should believe it to be true (= had the intention of
deceiving). (It is perhaps worth noticing that there is an even
greater difference between "false *prop.*" & "lie", than between
"false statement" & "lie". Nothing can be either a lie or (perhaps?)
a false *statement*, unless someone has *asserted* it: but many props.
are false, which no one has asserted: e.g. from the prop. that it is
false that the moon was larger than the sun 40 million years
ago, it by no means follows that anybody has ever asserted that
the moon was then larger. It is, of course, true that any prop.

might be asserted & is therefore a *possible* statement; but any prop. which has never been asserted *is* not a statement ⟨Is this true?⟩ & *a fortiori* is not a lie, although it may quite well be false.)

Again it is commonly assumed that even if (as is certain) a false statement need not be a lie, yet it *is* necessary that a lie should be false: and the Shorter O.E.D. implies that nothing can be a lie unless it is false. But it may be doubted whether this is correct. It is not clearly self-contradictory to say: "What he said happened to be true, but nevertheless he was lying when he said it, for he fully believed it to be false & yet wished to persuade others that it was true". And hence I think we may say that from the prop. that a given statement was a lie, it does not follow that it was false. If so, then, when R. (p. 60)[1] asks of Epimenides' supposed statement that every statement made by a Cretan was a lie: "was this a lie?", & supposes that if it was, "a contradiction" *seems* to result, he is quite mistaken in thinking that any contradiction even *seems* to result. For though, if the statement was true, it follows that it was also a lie, it by no means follows that it was also false. That E.'s statement was a lie is by no means incompatible with the supposition that it was *not* false: even if it was not false, it was a lie, provided E. believed it was false & nevertheless wished his hearers or readers to believe it true; for he then *wished* to deceive them, though, if they believed him, they would not actually have been deceived but would have been believing something true.

In the case of Epimen., then, a *contradiction* only results from the *conjunction* of the 2 props. (1) Every statement, without exception, made by a Cretan is false, & (2) One statement made by a Cretan is (1). From this conjunction it *seems* to follow that (1) is *both* true & false. I.e. in this case it is from the conjunction of (2) with the premiss that (1) *is true*, that it follows that (1) is both false & true. From the conjunction of (2) with the premiss that (1) is *false*, no contradiction follows. Russ., however, p. 60, speaks as if *the same contradiction* in another & simpler form "is afforded by the man who says "I am lying" "; adding "if he is lying, he is speaking the truth, & vice versa".

He is, of course, here assuming, as before, and as the O.E.D. assumes (a false assumption in my view), that it is impossible

---

[1] [A. N. Whitehead and B. Russell, *Principia Mathematica*, vol. I, 2nd ed. (Cambridge, 1925).]

that the same statement should be both a lie & true; and, as before, a contradiction will even *seem* to result, only if "I am lying" really does entail "I am making a statement which is in fact false" & not merely "I am making a statement which I believe to be false". It is perhaps a feeling that this is so which leads R. later (p. 62) to make the ambiguous & obscure statement "When a man says "I am lying", *we may interpret his* statement as: "There is a prop. which I am affirming & which is false" ". Similarly Ramsey (p. 48)[1] says of "I am lying": "This we *should* analyse as "($\exists$ "p", p) : I am *saying* "p" . "p" means p . $\sim$ p". Quite certainly this is a *false* analysis of "I am lying"; but what is true is that "I am lying" only even *seems* to entail a contradiction, if it entails this, which would be a correct analysis of "I am making a false statement", if for "saying" we substitute "making a statement by uttering or writing".

In this case, however, a contradiction only *seems* to result, from the conjunction of the hypothesis (1) that a man is *stating* that he is making a false statement, with the hypothesis (2) that what he states is *false*; whereas in the Epimenides case, wh. Russ. calls *the same contradiction*, the appearance of contradiction only results from the conjunction of the hypothesis (1) that a Cretan is stating that every statement made by a Cretan is false, with the hypothesis (2) that his statement is *true*. Russ.'s statement that (it seems as if) "if he is lying, he is speaking the truth, & vice versa" is a sheer mistake. The fact is that from the hypothesis that his statement "I am making a false statement" is *false*, in conjunction with the hypothesis that he is making that statement, it *does* seem to follow that his statement is true; but *vice versa* not at all. From the conjunction of the hypothesis that he *is* making a false statement (i.e. that his statement that he is, is true) with the hypothesis that he is stating that he is, it does not even *seem* to follow that his statement "I am making a false statement" is *false*, i.e. that he is *not* making any false statement. R.'s assumption that *vice versa* holds or *seems* to hold is probably due to his failing to notice the difference between "I am making a false statement" & "I am making a false statement *in saying* this" which = "*This* statement is false" where "*this* statement" refers to the statement (if any) made by use of the *token* sentence, which is an instance of "This statement is false", which the man in

[1] [F. P. Ramsey, *The Foundations of Mathematics* (London, 1931).]

question is uttering or writing. It is perfectly possible that a person who says "I am making a false statement" should be *at the same time* making some *other* statement; e.g. a person who says this by word of mouth may at the same time be making a false statement in a letter; & in such a case it does not in the least follow from the hypothesis that his statement "I am making a false statement" is *true*, that *this* statement is also false: it only follows that he is making *some* false statement.

Now a man may certainly say *the words* "This statement is false"; but it seems clear that by so doing he cannot be making any statement at all, unless certain conditions are fulfilled. E.g. your tutor, in looking over your essay with you, may point to a sentence you have written, by the use of which you were making a statement, & say the words "This statement is false". His words do then express a statement—he is making a statement by their use: & his statement is that the statement you had made is false. The use of the word "this" which the tutor is then making is what W. E. Johnson calls the "demonstrative" use. Or suppose the use of "this" is what W. E. J. calls "referential", not demonstrative. E.g. I might write: "Russell says that if "I am lying" is true, it is a lie: but *this statement is false*". I am there really making a statement by my use of the words "this statement is false", viz. that Russell's statement is false. And another person, disagreeing with me, might point at my statement "This statement is false", & say of it "*This* statement is false"; & would then, by the use of these words, be really making a statement. But if by the words "This statement" the speaker or writer is referring to no statement other than that, *if any*, which he himself is making by his use of the words "This statement is false", then he is making *no statement at all* by the use of the words.—We might say: It is obvious that no statement can say of *itself* that it is false: no statement can be identical with the statement that it is false.

R.'s *vice versa* would then only hold if by "I am lying" he meant, *not* "I am making *some* false statement" but "*This* statement is false", where "this statement" refers to the statement, if any, which the speaker is expressing by saying "This statement is false". And the "solution" of the contradiction in that case is that by the use of this sentence *no* statement is expressed, though in other cases the words in question do express a statement. Suppose I write up on the blackboard the words "This statement is false",

& when asked "What statement are you referring to?" point at those words themselves, thus making clear that the use of "this" is not the referential use; it is then quite right to say that those words so used do not express *any prop.* at all; & therefore that in this case I am not pointing at a prop. or a statement but *only* at words. We can say of these words that with this use of "this statement" & the ordinary English use of "is false", *if* the words expressed any prop. at all, the prop. in question would be identical with its negation: hence they don't express *any* prop. It is not that they express a self-contradictory one, for they don't express any. The relation to contradiction is only that *if* they expressed a prop. at all, then from the hypothesis that the prop. in question was true it would follow that it was also false, & therefore that it was both true & false; & also from the hypothesis that it was false, it would follow that it was also true, & therefore both true & false.

6

LEWIS CARROLL'S PUZZLE

(*Mind*, 1894, p. 436)[1]

Uncle Joe says he can *prove* that, of the 3 barbers, A, B & C, C is certain to be at home when they reach the shop.

When he says he can *prove* it he means he can shew that it *follows logically* from certain known facts.

The known facts wh. he maintains do entail that C will be in are:—

(1) A, B & C are never *all out together* (bec., if they were, there'd be nobody to mind the shop)

(2) A never goes out without B.

And his argument is

(a) that from (1) it follows that *if C is out, then if A is out B is in*

(b) that from (2) it follows that if A is out B is out

(c) that from (a) & (b) conjoined it follows that, if C were out, it would be true both that if A is out B is in, & that if A is out B is out

(d) that "if A is out B is in" & "if A is out B is out" can't both be true—are incompatible

(e) that since both would be true if C were out, C can't be out. I.e. the argument proposes to shew that from (1) & (2), together with (3) "C is out", there follows a self-contradictory prop., viz. "If A is out B is in and also if A is out B is out."

Now, as L.C. knows perfectly well, there must be some fallacy in this argument, since (1) & (2) are quite consistent with the hypothesis that C is out & A & B both in. Uncle Jim says he doesn't see why this shouldn't be the case; and in fact nobody can see it, since it can be the case. L.C.'s question is: Where is the fallacy in the argument?

W. E. Johnson's reply is that "if p, then q" merely means "p ⊃ q" i.e. $\sim$(p . $\sim$q); and that hence (d) is false. And obviously $\sim$(p . $\sim$q) & $\sim$(p . q) are perfectly compatible; since both will be true if p is false; & p (in our case, "A is out") certainly may quite well be false, since "A is in" is not self-contradictory.

But this is certainly *not* the correct solution, since, even if in some cases "if p, q" means merely $\sim$(p . $\sim$q) (I know of no case

---

[1] [Lewis Carroll, "A Logical Paradox", *Mind*, vol. III, 1894.]

where it clearly does mean no more), it is certain that in our case "if A is out, B is out" is *not* being used merely to say "The 2 props. "A is out" & "B is not out" are not both true", since if it were, the discovery that A was in would prove it to be true. W.E.J. (*Mind*, 1892, p. 19)[1] makes an astounding mistake as to what is sufficient to justify his "interpretation" of "if p, q" as "$\sim$(p . $\sim$q)". He actually says that to justify it "it is only necessary to urge that the ordinary use of "if" must at least *include* the affirmation of the disjunctive (i.e. $\sim$(p . $\sim$q))". It certainly is true that every ordinary use of "if p, q" is such that *part* of what is affirmed is $\sim$(p . $\sim$q); & that hence what is affirmed can't be true unless $\sim$(p . $\sim$q) is true—the truth of $\sim$(p . $\sim$q) is a *necessary* condition for that of "if p, q". But in order to justify J.'s "interpretation" it would be necessary to shew, not merely that it was a necessary condition, but that it was a *sufficient* one. How can J. have supposed that it was "*only necessary*" to shew that it was a necessary condition?

But "if A is out, B is out" is ambiguous. It may mean (α) "If at any time A is out, then at that time B is out", i.e. it may be what Russell calls (most unfortunately) a *formal* implication, viz. "(t) . A out at t . $\supset$. B out at t", & what J. (followed by Keynes) calls (p. 17) a "conditional". J. (& Keynes) says (p. 17) that in a prop. of this form "the apparent consequent" has no "independent import". The fact is that "*at that time* B is out" or "B out at t" don't express a prop. *at all*. J. is quite right (p. 20) in saying that this is identical with the categorical prop. "Every time which is a time when A is out, is also a time when B is out", which is equivalent to the prop. "Every prop. of the form "$\sim$(A is out at this time . B *not* out at this time)" is true", unless perhaps it adds "And there is at least one time when A is out", i.e. = *whenever* A is out, B is out. (β) It may say of 2 props. that if the one is true, the other is true. E.g. "If A was out at 12 noon G.M.T. on Jan. 1, 1894, B was out at 12 noon G.M.T. on Jan. 1, 1894". It must be noted that the form of speech "If it's true that A is out (or was out), it's true that B is out (or was out)" is not unambiguous; it may still mean (α), (α) being something which does *not* say of 2 props. that if the one is true, the other is. How is one to explain unambiguously what one means by an assertion about 2 props.?

[1] [W. E. Johnson, "The Logical Calculus. I. General Principles", *Mind*, vol. I 1892.]

The question is the same as that of making clear what Russell means by a *material* implication, which is a statement about 2 props. of the form $\sim$(p . $\sim$q), as opposed to a *formal* implication, i.e. a prop. of the form (x) . ϕx $\supset$ χx, or $\sim$($\exists$ x) . ϕx . $\sim$$\chi$x, which does not assert of any 2 props. $\sim$(p . $\sim$q).

What if J. on Lewis Carroll (*Mind*, 1894, p. 583)[1] understands by "If A out, B out" not (β) but (α)? He then says that "If A out, B out" & "If A out, B in" are not incompatible. But "Whenever A is out, B is out" & "Whenever A is out, B is in", *are* incompatible. But, how about (a) "$\sim$($\exists$ t) . A out at t . B out at t", & (b) "$\sim$($\exists$ t) . A out at t . B in at t"? These are not incompatible; both will be true if "$\sim$($\exists$ t) . A out at t". "Whenever A is out, B is out" = "($\exists$ t) . A out at t . $\sim$($\exists$ t) . A out at t . B in at t", & this *is* incompatible with "($\exists$ t) . A out at t . $\sim$($\exists$ t) . A out at t . B out at t"; since (a) & (b) jointly *entail* "$\sim$($\exists$ t) . A out at t." But suppose J. was using "If A out, B in" = $\sim$($\exists$ t) . A out at t . B out at t = "A & B are *never* out together." How are we to understand his "*If C is out*, then if A is out B is in"? "Whenever C is out, A & B are *never* out together" is NONSENSE: "$\sim$($\exists$ t) . C out at t . $\sim$(A & B *never* out together *at t*)" is also nonsense. This shews that we must understand his "If C is out, then if A is out, B is in" as "$\sim$($\exists$ t) . C is out at t . A out at t . B out at t". *Or* as "$\sim$ (C out now . $\sim$ (if A out, B in))" = $\sim$ (C out now . $\sim$($\sim$A out now . $\sim$B in))) = $\sim$(C out now . A out now . $\sim$B in).

$\langle$Uncle Joe says: Whenever C is out, the hyp. "If A out, B in" is *in force*; meaning (a) "At any time at which C is out, *a* prop. of the form "If A is out now, B is in now" will be true", which is quite sensible. But it would *not* be sensible if we took "If A is out, B is in" to mean "At any time at which A is out, B is in". But what then does "if A is out, B is in" here mean? Does it mean simply $\sim$(A now out . B now out)? Do I want to suggest that (a) means "At any time at which C is out *and* A is out, B is in"? How does this differ from "At any time at which C is out, $\sim$(A out . B out)"?

The whole thing is to be something which follows from "Never (A out, B out, C out)".

I say that (a) is "sensible", & so it is. But does it *follow* from "Never (A out, B out, C out)" that it is *true*?$\rangle$

[1] [W. E. Johnson, "A Logical Paradox", *Mind*, vol. III, 1894.]

7

ANALYTIC PROPOSITIONS

Kant meant props. of the form "Every brother is male" (without existential import), i.e. of the form $\sim(\exists\, x)\,.\,x$ is a brother $.\,\sim$ (x is male); & he calls them "analytic" because every prop. of the form "x is both male & a sibling" *contains* or *includes* the *corresponding* prop. of the form "x is male" (he *says* the "predicate" is *contained* in the "subject", i.e. of the prop. "Every brother is male"—"male" is contained in "brother").

By no means every necessary prop. is of this form, i.e. is "analytic" in Kant's sense.

When can one prop. be properly said to *contain* another? So far as I can see p contains q, only where

(a) p is a conjunction & q one of the conjuncts, or a conjunction of some but not all the conjuncts;

(b) p is of the form A. $(\exists\, x)\,.\,\phi x\,.\,\chi x\ldots$; and, if we call the *corresponding* prop. of form $(\exists\, x)\,.\,\phi x$ or $(\exists\, x)\,.\,\chi x$, etc., a "factor" in any prop. of the form A, & call the prop. of form A in question the "product" of all its "factors", then q is one of the "factors" of p, or a "product" of some but not all its "factors".

With this def. of "contains" it is not true that whenever p *entails* $(\rightarrow)$q, then p *contains* q.

E.g. (1) $((p\,.\,q)\rightarrow p)\rightarrow(2)\,(\sim p\rightarrow\,\sim(p\,.\,q))$, & here though every prop. of form p . q *contains* the corresponding prop. of form "p" & also the corresponding prop. of form "q", it is *not* true that every prop. of form $\sim p$ *contains* every corresponding prop. of form $\sim(p\,.\,q)$; nor is it true that (1) *contains* (2).

⟨A prop. of form "$\sim p$" does not contain the prop. which is the product of its own negation with any other prop. you please; & yet $\sim p\rightarrow\,\sim(p\,.\,q)$ for all values of p & q.⟩

What relation must a necess. prop. have to this meaning of "contains", in order to be properly called "analytic"?

$\sim(\exists\, x)\,.\,x$ is both male & a sibling $.\,\sim$ (x is male) is both necess. & analytic. Why do we call it the latter? Because from the hypothesis that it was false, it would follow that a prop. of the form "x is male & a sibling, but not male" was true; &, if this were so, that the conjunction of a prop. which *contained* another prop. with the contradictory of the contained prop. was true.

8

CONDITIONAL SENTENCES

Sentences of the kind which, in grammars, are often called "conditional sentences", & which consist of two clauses, one of which is sometimes called the "antecedent" or "protasis", the other the "consequent" or "apodosis", are used to express props. of two very different kinds—kinds which Keynes (*Formal Logic*) proposed to distinguish by calling the one kind "hypotheticals" or "pure hypotheticals", the other "conditionals". How can we give a correct description of the difference between these two kinds of props.?

Very often a form of conditional sentence, which is used to express a prop. of the one kind, cannot be used to express a prop. of the other kind ("cannot", in accordance with the rules of the language in question: of course, it is logically possible it should be so used). But in some cases the very same sentence *can* be used to express either a prop. of the one kind or a prop. of the other; and perhaps the best way of explaining the difference between the 2 kinds of prop., is to start with examples of sentences which can be used in both ways & to point out the difference between their meaning when used in one way & when used in the other.

Here are two examples:

(a) If it's raining, there are clouds overhead.

(b) If you have one penny in one pocket & another in another, you have at least two pennies about you.

(a) A person who uttered this sentence, might be using it to mean (1) "If it's raining *here now*, there are clouds overhead *here now*" or (2) he might be using it to mean "*Whenever* it's raining in any place, there are clouds overhead in that place" or "If it's raining in a place, there are *always* clouds overhead there". (1) is of the kind Keynes calls "pure hypotheticals", (2) of the kind he calls "conditionals".

(b) Similarly a person who used (b), might (1b) be referring exclusively to the person to whom he was speaking & the time at which he was speaking, & saying of the 2 props. "You have one penny in one pocket & another in another at this moment" and "You have at least two pennies about you at this moment"

389

that they are related in a certain manner, or he might (2b), according to a well-known idiom, be using (b) to mean "A person (if any) who has at a given moment one penny in one pocket & another in another, *always* has, *at the moment in question*, at least 2 pennies about him".

How do (1) & (1b), on the one hand, differ from (2) & (2b) on the other?

Each of the first 2 states, with regard to some relation or other, that that relation holds between one prop., which it specifies, & another prop. which it also specifies; so that in this case the protasis-clause & the apodosis-clause, both of them, express props., & we can speak of one of these *props.* as the antecedent & the other as the consequent. But in (2) & (2b) the protasis-clause & the apodosis-clause do not express props. at all: the conditional sentence does *not* specify any pair of props. whatever, & assert of some relation or other that it holds between them. What do (2) & (2b) do? (2) gives a description which applies to many different pairs of props.—namely, the description of being a pair of which the one asserts with regard to a particular time & place that it is or was or will be raining at that time in that place, while the other asserts with *regard to the same time & place* that there are or were or will be clouds overhead at that time & place; and it says that in the case of *every* pair to which this descr. applies, it is not the case that the first of the pair is true & and the second false. And (2b) similarly gives a description which will apply to many different pairs, i.e. that of being a pair of which one member says of a given person that he has one penny in one pocket & another in another & the other says *of the same person* that he has at least 2 pennies about him; & says that in the case of every pair to which this descr. applies it is not the case that first is true, second false.

9

"IF . . . THEN"

What is the difference between "if p, q" & "p ⊃ q" in those cases, which are certainly the commonest & I doubt if there are *any* others, in which "if p, q" does *not* follow from ∼ p, nor from q, i.e. what, *besides* p ⊃ q, does "if p, q" say?

It is to be noticed that p ⊃ q, i.e. ∼ (p . ∼ q), follows from each of the 3 possibilities other than p . ∼ q, i.e. from p . q, from ∼ p . q, & from ∼ p . ∼ q; & we can say that it follows from p . q *because* q follows from p . q & p ⊃ q follows from q; & from ∼ p . q & ∼ p . ∼ q *because* ∼ p follows from each of them, & p ⊃ q follows from ∼ p.

And it is certain that a person who knew either of these 3 possibilities to be the case would be deceiving you if he said "if p, q".

If you asked him "How do you know that "if p, q"?" & he said "because I know ∼ p", or said "because I know q", we should say that it is *not* a good reason for saying "if p, q"—it doesn't shew that you know "if p, q"; whereas it would be a good reason for p ⊃ q.

There are 2 puzzles:—

(1) Does the occurrence of p . q prove you were right in saying "if p, then q"?

(2) It seems as if provided you *do know* that A & B are both in the same drawer, but *don't know* which, you will certainly be right to say (pointing) "If A is in this, B is"; though it would *not* be right for you to say this, if you did know they were both in this drawer.

But if from (1) "A & B are both in same" there *follows* (2) "If A is in this, so is B", then the latter must also *follow* from (3) "A & B are both in this" since (1) follows from (3); & it seems it doesn't.

By saying "If p, then q" you generally *imply* that you neither know that p nor that ∼ p, nor that q nor that ∼ q, & therefore that you don't know either that p . q, nor that ∼ p . q, nor that ∼ p. ∼ q. ("If p *had been* true, q *would have* been", often does imply "I know that ∼ p . ∼ q"). Can we say these things *follow* from "If p, then q", whereas they don't from p ⊃ q? Can we say that if it turned out that you did know that both p & q, then what you said, when you said "if p, then q" was *false*? I think not, though we might say you were not *justified* in saying it, because you would mislead people. "Was p true?" & "Was I justified in saying p?" may mean quite different things: e.g. I was not justified unless I *believed* p (was not justified, if I was lying), and although p was in fact true, I may have believed it wasn't. In this case, though p was true, I wasn't justified in saying it; & very often, conversely, I was justified in saying p, though p was false: as when Verrall told Browne that if he thought that "In the golden days" was a superb novel, he was quite right to say so.

Yet it seems obvious that from "A & B are both in the same drawer" there *follows* "If A is in *this* (the left-hand one), B is too", although from "A & B are both in this (the right-hand one)" there does *not* follow "If A is in *this* (the left-hand one), B is too".

⟨The fact seems to be that you can only say things (assert props.) of the form "If A is in *this*, B is so too", where you can assert truly several *different* props. of this form; and from "They are both in *some the same*" several *different* props. of this form *will* follow, whereas from "They are both in *this*" it is not true that several different props. of this form follow. That is to say "They are both in the same" is ambiguous—can be properly used with 2 different meanings, viz. (1) a meaning which follows from any prop. of form "They are both in this", but from which "If A is in this, B is too" does *not* follow; (2) a meaning from wh. "If A is in this, B is so too" *does* follow, but which does *not* follow from "They are both in this".⟩

10

LEWY ON ENTAILMENT

(March 3, 1949)

L. discovered following puzzle[1]:—

Let (α) = The sentence "Il n'y a pas de frère qui ne soit pas mâle" expresses the prop. that there's no creature which both is a brother & is *not* male & no other prop.; (β) = The prop. that there's no creature which is a brother & not male is a *necessary* prop.; (γ) = The prop. expressed by "Il n'y a pas de frère etc." is a *necessary* prop.

A. Then (α) & (γ) are both contingent props., & (β) *apparently* a necess. prop.

B. *Also* $(\alpha) + (\beta) \rightarrow (\gamma)$; and $(\alpha) + (\gamma) \rightarrow (\beta)$.

But it seems plausible to hold that C. since $(1)(\beta)$ is *necess.* & $(2)(\alpha) + (\beta)$ entail (γ), (α) *by itself* entails (γ).

But, if this were true, then both $(\alpha) + (\gamma) \rightarrow (\beta)$ & $(\alpha) \rightarrow (\gamma)$ would be true, & from the truth of both it would follow that $(\alpha) \rightarrow (\beta)$.

But it seems quite clear that (α) does *not* entail (β). What step in this argument, which seems to shew it does, can be wrong?

He says C is wrong. C seems plausible because *in some cases* where a contingent p + a necess. q entail an r, it *is* true that p *by itself* entails r: e.g. let p = "my tie is scarlet", q = "$\sim (\exists x) . x$ is scarlet . $\sim (x$ is red)", r = "my tie is red". Here from p, *by itself*, r does follow: q is not required as an additional premiss. What is the difference between this case & that of (α), (β), (γ)? He says the difference is that $\sim (\exists x) . x$ is scarlet . $\sim (x$ is red) is a principle of inference, *in accordance with which* you can infer "my tie is red" from "my tie is scarlet"; but (β) is *not* a principle of inference in accordance with which you can infer (γ) from (α). (γ) follows from $(\alpha) + (\beta)$, in accordance with the principle of the syllogism. But while (β) is a principle in accordance with which from "King George is a brother" you could infer "King G. is male", it obviously is not a *principle* which allows you to infer

[1] [Cf. C. Lewy, "Entailment", *Aristotelian Soc.*, *Supplementary Vol.* XXXII, 1958.]

(γ) from (α), but only a premise such that the conjunction of it with (α) entails (γ).

Another point

He says that though (α) *by itself* does not entail (γ), yet it is quite a correct use of language to say "It *follows* from (α) that (γ)"; so that we need to distinguish 2 different uses of "follows" (& "entails"), which may be distinguished by calling one "entails by itself" the other simply "entails".

Another example. (a) "Scarlet entails red" does not by itself entail (c) "Scarlet entails coloured", although (a) *together with* (b) "Red entails coloured" does entail (c) & although (b) is a necessary prop. (b) is a principle of inference which would allow you to infer from "My tie is red" "My tie is coloured"; but it is not a principle in accordance with which you are inferring when you infer (c) from (a).

Another point

The fact that (α) + (γ) entails (β) proves that 2 contingent props. may entail *a necessary one*, although 2 necess. props. cannot possibly entail a contingent.

⟨Only a necess. one of the peculiar sort which consists in a true assertion that a given prop. is necess.⟩

Another point

He says that one clear distinction between "entails" & "strictly implies" is this: for the truth of "p entails q" it is a necessary (though not sufficient) condition that there shd. be some prop. which *makes for (supports, is favourable to)* the truth both of p & of q, i.e. some prop. r, such that "r is favourable to p" *strictly implies* "r is favourable to q"; but this is not a necessary condition for the truth of "p strictly implies q".

March 5 (about his paper at Moral Science Club on Mar. 3)[1]

It is not true that, where p is necessary, p always (ever?) entails "p is necess."; and this can be proved by pointing out that "All siblings are male" supports or is favourable to "All brothers

---

[1] [Cf. C. Lewy, "Entailment and Necessary Propositions" in M. Black (ed.), *Philosophical Analysis* (Ithaca, New York, 1950).]

are male", but in no way supports or is favourable to "That all brothers are male is a necess. prop.". "All siblings are male" though false, *might* perfectly well have happened to be true.

Whereas, for all values of p, p entails "p *is true*", it is not the case that, for all values of p, p entails "p *is necessary*". Necess. props. are not identical with those which truly assert *an entailment*.

Consequently (1) "p is necess." can't always be expressed in terms of "entail", & (2) there is no special sense of "true", in which *only* necess. props. are true.

As to (1), I don't know whether this was exactly what he said, nor what his reasons were. He seemed to be assuming that p is necessary = ~ p entails each of 2 mutually contradictory props., as is often done.

I don't think it is true that (1) "All siblings are males" supports or is favourable to (2) "All male siblings are male". If it did, (2) would *follow* from (1) ⟨why⟩, as "All siblings that are chipmunks are male" does: but (2) doesn't follow from (1), nor would (2) be any more *likely* if (1) were true, than it is as a matter of fact, & is in spite of the fact that (1) is false.

Yet I think L.'s *conclusion* that (2) does not entail "(2) is necessary" is true. Necessity is an *internal* property of (2); & this means that (2) couldn't be the prop. it is without being necess., i.e. from the fact that (2) is (2) it follows that (2) is necess. But it doesn't in the least follow that "(2) is necess." follows from the fact that (2) is *true*. That (2) is *true* also follows from (2) is (2), i.e. truth is also an internal property of (2). But whereas "(2) is true" follows from "(2) is necessary", the converse entailment does not hold.

Similarly that it is about Socrates in an *internal* property of "Socrates was executed": that prop. couldn't be the prop. it is without being about Socrates. But that it is about Socr. doesn't follow from the fact that it's true.

⟨Is "All sibs. are male" in fact favourable to "All things that are both sibs. & male are male"? i.e. "~ (∃ x) . x is sib . ~ (x is male)" to "~ (∃ x) . x is sib . x is male . ~ (x is male)"? I doubt it. But yet from "~ (∃ x) . x is sib . ~ x is male" there *follows* such a prop. as ~ (∃ x) . x is sib . ~ x is male . x is a chipmunk, i.e. any prop., which could be expressed by a sentence of the form ~ (∃ x) . x is sib . ~ x is male . ϕx, & the prop, expressed by substituting "x is male" for "ϕx" seems only to be a particular instance of such a prop.⟩

11

SELF-CONTRADICTORY

It won't do to define a s.-c. prop., as one which is, or entails, the conjunction of some prop. with its negation; since there is an immense class of s.-c. props. of which this is not true.

Let us define:—

p is self-contradictory = p is *inconsistent with* the Law of Contr., i.e. with $\sim (\exists p) . p . \sim p$.

(p is inconsistent with q = p entails $\sim q$)

Props. of the form $(\exists x) . \phi x . \sim \phi x$, though they neither are, nor entail, the conjunction of any prop. with its negation, are self-contradictory in this sense, since every such prop. entails $(\exists p) . p . \sim p$. The same is true of any conjunction in which a prop. of this form is a conjunct.

But every prop. which is or entails the conjunction of a prop. with its negation, is also self-contr. in this sense, since every such conjunction entails $(\exists p) . p . \sim p$.

What name are we to give to props. which are *the negations of self-contrad. props.*?

They have been called "tautological", "identical", "analytic", "necessary"; but it is better to avoid (1), bec. Wittg. has given it a peculiar meaning; (2) is not a clear expression; as for (3), it is quite unnatural to call $\sim (\exists p) . p . \sim p$ "analytic", a name applied by Kant to props. of the form $\sim (\exists x) . \phi x . \chi x . \sim \chi x$ (e.g. every material thing is extended; every brother is male), not to props. of the form $\sim (\exists x) . \phi x . \sim \phi x$, since ϕx does not "contain" ϕx, whereas $\phi x . \chi x$ does "contain" χx.

They are props. of which the truth follows from the Law of Contr.

How about the prop. with regard to a given dark blue that it is darker than a given light blue? with regard to a given high note that it is higher than a given low note? etc., etc. Are the negations of such props. self-contradictory? Does the truth of the props. themselves *follow from the Law of Contr.*?

How about $\sim (\exists x) . x$ is scarlet $. \sim (x$ is red)? Does the truth of this follow from the Law of Contr.?

From $\sim (\exists x) . \phi x$ does there follow A. $\sim (\exists x) . \phi x . \sim \phi x$?

It seems as if it did; but, if so, it would also follow from $\sim (\exists\, x) . \sim \phi x$.

A can be said to be *of the form* $\sim (\exists\, x) . \phi x . \sim \psi x$, if one explains that one is so using this expression that a value of ψ may or may not be identical with a value of ϕ. In words: "It asserts either of some property that nothing both has it & is without it, or of some pair of properties that nothing has the one & not the other".

12

LAWS OF CONTRADICTION AND
EXCLUDED MIDDLE

Von Wright gives (Idea of Log. Truth, p. 1)[1] as *Principle* of Contr. "No prop. is true & false", & as *Principle* of Ex. Middle "Every prop. is true or false".

And as *Law* of Contr. (p. 5) "If p is a sentence, $\overline{p \& \overline{p}}$ is a Truth of Logic"; & as Law of Excl. Middle "If p is a sentence, $p \lor \overline{p}$ is a Truth of Logic".

What is the difference between the *Law* of Contr. & the *Principle* of Contr.?

Acc. to v. W. (p. 4) "a Truth of Logic" = "a logically true *sentence*", so that what *Law* is saying will be "Whatever sentence you substitute for "p" in "$\overline{p \& \overline{p}}$", the resulting *sentence* will be logically true". Let's substitute "It's raining". We get "$\overline{\text{It's raining} \& \overline{\text{It's raining}}}$". This, we are told, is a sentence & is logically true. But what on earth does it mean? This has been explained by (p. 2) "If p expresses a prop. then $\overline{p}$ expresses its negation" combined with "By the negation of a given prop. we understand that prop. which is true if & only if the given prop. is false". But the second half of this explanation won't do at all. How is it to be proved that there's *only* one prop. wh. is true if & only if "it is raining" is false? There certainly is *one*, viz. "It's false that it is raining", but what proof is there that there aren't many others? By "if & only if" there is, I think, certainly meant here "is entailed by & entails"; & certainly "It's true that it's false that it's raining" is both entailed by & entails "It's false that it's raining". But isn't the same true of "it's not raining" & "it's not the case that it's raining"? (It's an improper use of "entails" to say, as Popper would, that "It's false that it's raining" entails & is entailed by "It's false that it's raining". But "improper"? what if it is? It's not improper to say "If it's not raining, it's not raining"; & why shouldn't P. say he's using his expression as another way of saying this? "If it's not raining, it's not raining" seems to be

---

[1] [G. H. von Wright, "On the Idea of Logical Truth (I)", *Societas Scientiarum Fennica, Commentationes Physico-Mathematicae* XIV, 4 (1948). Reprinted in G. H. von Wright, *Logical Studies* (London, 1957).]

merely another way of saying "If it's not raining, it's not the case that it's not not raining", just as "If it's raining, it *is* raining" is another way of saying "If it's raining, it's not the case that it's not raining"; and it's perfectly proper to say that "It's raining" both entails & is entailed by "It's not the case that it's not raining".) Yes; it's perfectly proper & true to say "It's false that it's raining" both entails & is entailed by "It's not raining", & also "It's not the case that it's raining".

On the other hand, though you *can* say "It's false that it's raining" both entails & is entailed by "It's true that it's false that it's raining", you *can* also say that these 2 expressions express the same prop.

It is quite certain that a *sentence of the form* "x is a grandparent" is merely *short for* the corr. sentence of the form "x is a parent of a parent", and expresses exactly *the same prop*. But yet I think it's also correct to say that from any *prop.* of the form "x is a grandparent" there *follows* the corr. *prop.* of the form "x is a parent of a parent", & vice versa.

On the other hand, it seems that a sentence of the form "it's true that p" is *not* merely *short for* the corr. sentence of the form "it's not false that p", although the props. expressed do *mutually entail*. Can we say that the 2 sentences express exactly the same prop.? On the other hand, it does seem that "it's false that p" *is merely short for* "it's not true that p", and that *here* the 2 sentences do express exactly the same prop. (People say truly that to say of an expression e, "*e* isn't true" is not the same as to say of the same expression "*e* is false", since *expressions* may be meaningless, & therefore neither true nor false. But the sense of "false" in which *props.*, not sentences, are false, is such that the word "false", when used in that sense, *is* merely *short for* the expression "not true", if "true" is here used in the sense in wh. *props.*, not sentences, are said to be true.) The fundamental point seems to be that the relation of prop. $\sim$ p to p is different from that of prop. p to $\sim$ p: sentence p is *not* short for "$\sim (\sim p)$", though *prop.* p is equivalent to prop. $\sim (\sim p)$. Prop. $\sim$ p *contains* prop. p; but prop. p does not contain prop. $\sim$ p, though prop. $\sim (\sim p)$ does *contain* prop. $\sim$ p.

13

TIME

On Jan. 26, 1950, I said to von Wright that the prop. A. "It will be raining at 12 noon to-morrow" was identical with B. the prop. which at that date would be correctly expressed by "It is raining now"; and he agreed. But the 2 props. are *not* identical. One difference is that A is *about* an absolutely specific event which was happening at the moment when I said those words, whereas B is *not* about that event in the sense that that event is a constituent of it (the event might be the abs. specific event then occurring which was a using of those words by me; and that event was not only a constituent of the prop. I was *expressing* (I wasn't asserting it!) but *also* a constituent in the *expression I was using*: the words I uttered by themselves did not express a prop. at all: what expressed a prop. was (can one say?) the fact that they were uttered *then*, or (can one say?) the fact that the event in question *was* an uttering of those words). And another difference is that B is *about* some absolutely specific event occurring at noon on Jan. 27, whereas A is not, & *could not be*, *about* any such event in the sense that such an event was a constituent of it (it *could* be about such an event in the sense of containing an exclusive descr. of such an event, e.g. "at 12 noon tomorrow" *might* mean "simultaneously with the reaching of the mark at "12" by both hands of the . . . clock at Greenwich" where the exclusive descr. "the reaching by both hands, etc." is contained in the prop.). There is not only one but several props., which, at that date, might be correctly expressed by "It is raining now".

14

PROBABLE

C. I. Lewis (J. of P. XLV. 19, Sept. 9/48, in answer to Chisholm, p. 523)[1] says that in a case where 2 props. "R" & "S" are incompatible, " 'R' is highly prob." & " 'S' is highly prob." are not incompatible "bec. *in this form* (what does this mean?) they are incompletely stated & require the preface "Relative to P" or "Relative to "P & Q" " in order to be accurate statements of fact". ("In this form" says that the *sentence* "R is highly prob." expresses a *prop.* of the form "Relative to P, R is highly prob." & is therefore an incomplete way of stating this prop.)

Suppose we have a die so loaded that, regularly, in a series of 50 throws, 6 is thrown far more often than some number other than 6 is thrown, i.e. not only more often than *any* number other than 6 is thrown, in the sense "more often than 1, more often than 2, more often than 3, etc.", but "more often than a non-6 is thrown". Let "R" be the prop., with regard to a particular throw, "Some non-6 will be thrown" & "S" the prop., with regard to the same throw, "6 will be thrown". These 2 props. are incompatible; but so also are the props. "R is highly prob." & "S is highly prob.", since "p is highly prob." entails "p is more likely than not" and "it is more likely than not that some non-6 will be thrown this throw" is certainly incompatible with "it is more likely than not that 6 will be thrown this throw". Yet, if P be the prop. "This die is marked in the usual manner & is nearly a perfect cube" & Q the prop. "This die is loaded so as to give 6 far more often than a non-6", Lewis is right in saying that "relatively to P alone R is more likely than not", and "relatively to P *and* Q, S is more likely than not" are perfectly compatible. It follows that he's wrong in saying that "R is highly prob." is short for "Rel. to P alone R is highly prob." & "S is highly prob." short for "Rel. to P *and* Q S is highly prob.".

⟨Keynes (Chap. I) makes this same mistake wh. L. makes.⟩

p is highly prob. = it's *much* more likely than not that p.

The *absolute* use of "prob.", "highly prob.", "more likely than

[1] [C. I. Lewis, "Professor Chisholm and Empiricism", *The Journal of Philosophy*, vol. XLV, 1948.]

not", i.e. a use of these terms in sentences which are not of the form "*relatively to p*, q is prob.", etc. or of any form which has the same meaning (= is equivalent) is certainly extremely common, & prob. far more common than any other; and though in this usage, "q is highly prob." is not equivalent to any prop. of the form "relatively to p alone, q is highly prob.", yet Lewis is right in saying that the prediction "most likely a 6 won't turn up" *is justified* if "we know nothing about" this particular die being honest or loaded, but do know that in case of dies which are both properly marked & nearly perfect cubes a 6 turns up much less often than a non-6. But to say we are *justified* in thinking this does not mean that what we think is *true*, i.e. that it *is* most likely a non-6 will turn up: on the contrary, if there is somebody present who happens to know the die is so loaded that it turns up a 6 much more often than a non-6, & tells us so, we should say at once "Oh! then it's *not* most likely that a non-6 will turn up; we were wrong in thinking it was".

⟨Things which no-one in fact knows may be such that, owing to them, it is in fact likely or unlikely that p, provided they are such that the person who says p is likely or unlikely *easily might* have known these things. But that a thing which nobody can know, or which the speaker & his hearers couldn't easily know or have known, is incompatible with p, doesn't prevent its being true that p is prob. E.g. it's improb. that Churchill will die in the course of the next hour, just as it's not certain he is dead; but people near him may know he is at the last gasp & therefore that it's prob. he will; but this is a thing which *we here* couldn't easily have known.⟩

When L. says "On premise P alone, R is highly prob." & "On premise P & Q, ∼ R is highly probable" are not incompat. since *both are true*, this only means that a person who *knows nothing relevant except* P will be *justified in thinking* that R. is prob., although, if as a matter of fact Q is true as well, what he thinks will be false. It will be true that he is *justified in thinking that R. is prob.*, but not true that R is prob. It will be rational for him to believe R, though not true that R is prob. If p is prob. it is rational to believe p, but it may be rational to believe p where p is not prob. (as in case of loaded die).

Why does Keynes (& Lewis) make the mistake of thinking that "p is prob." is short for some prop. of form "on evidence q, p is prob."? Partly bec. "p is prob." *is* short for some such prop. as "I have evidence in favour of p, & none (or none so strong) in favour of $\sim$ p"; i.e. they overlook the difference between a prop. of form "On evidence q, p is prob." & "I have *some* evidence which makes it prob. that p, & none (or none so strong) that makes it prob. that $\sim$ p"? But NO; "It's not likely to rain in the next 5 mins." isn't short even for this. You have no right to say it unless you have evidence, and in fact you wouldn't; but that you have is no part of what you are saying: what you are saying is merely something as to what it's *reasonable to expect*—reasonable *also* to bet on.

15

McTAGGART ON TIME

McT. (*Nature of Existence*, II. 9) says that *positions in time*, "as time appears to us *prima facie*", are distinguished in 2 ways. (1) Of any two positions, one is *earlier* than the other. (2) Every position (says McT.) *is* either past, present, or future. But he should have said: "is *at any given time*".

He says the distinctions of kind (1) are "permanent", explaining what he means by "permanent", by saying "If M is ever earlier than N, it is always earlier". And that the distinctions of kind (2) are *not* "permanent", explaining this by "an event which is now (= at any time) present, was future, & will be past".

But is it true that, if M is ever earlier than N, it is always earlier?

"If M is *ever* earlier than N" = "if M is *at any time* earlier than N". Now Queen Anne's death *was* earlier than Marlborough's (merely another way of saying "Anne died before Marl."): that is true *now*; but it was not always true, e.g. in 55 B.C. it was true that Anne *would* die before M., but not true that she *did* die before M. The only thing that both *was* true in 55 B.C. & *is* true now is the prop. "Either A. *will* die before M., or A. *did* die before M., or A. *is* dying before M."; and this "*alternative*" (J.'s[1] phrase for "disjunctive") prop. certainly *is* true now, *was* true at every past moment, & *will be* true at every future. I.e. *this disjunctive prop.* is permanently true.

McT. is using "*is* ever earlier" as short for "*was* at any time earlier, *or* is now earlier, *or* will be at any time earlier". And this is not a correct usage, because a correct usage must be of a *sort* of event, not of a particular one.

⟨"If the milkman is ever earlier than the postman, I'll eat my hat" = "The milkman is *never* earlier" = "The milkman never has been earlier".⟩

I think he imagines that "either was at some time earlier, or is now earlier (= that other will come later), or will at some time be earlier" entails some prop. that could be expressed by "is earlier" where "is" is used *timelessly*, as it is said to be in "twice

2 *is* 4": but is there any such prop.? If there isn't, then he is using it as short for the disjunction, though he certainly doesn't know that he is.

"5 is a bigger number than 3" is said to be "*timelesly*" true; but we certainly can correctly say "is bigger now, always *was* bigger, & always *will be* bigger". But here this is a deduction from "is *necessarily* bigger".

16

[NO TITLE]

Let us use *"wrong"* = "morally wrong"[1] = action which the agent was under a moral obligation not to do; & "right" = *not* wrong.

And let us consider the view that whenever anyone asserts an action to be "wrong" in this sense, he is merely asserting that he personally has towards it at the moment of speaking a feeling of *moral disapprobation*; & let us use "disapproves of . . ." = "has towards . . . a feeling of moral disapp."; & let us so use "asserts an action to be wrong" that a man will be doing this not merely when the words he uses are of the form "x *is* wrong" but also when they are of the forms "x *would be* wrong", "x *was* wrong" & "x *would have been wrong*", but will be doing so *only* if he is using the word "wrong" in the sense of "morally wrong" & is using these expressions "*is* wrong", "*would be* wrong", "*was* wrong", & "*would have been* wrong" in their ordinary senses.

Let us call this view, view A.

The question we want to consider is whether, as I said,[1] from the conjunction of view A with the prop. (a) sometimes one man disapproves of a given action, & another does not even when he is thinking of or perceiving the action in question, it follows that the same action is sometimes *both* right & wrong; & whether the same conclusion also follows from the conjunction of view A with the prop. (b) sometimes the same man disapproves of a given action at one time & at another, when he considers it, does not.

Let us take as our given action Brutus' stabbing of Caesar & call this "X". Does it follow from the conjunction of A with (a') "Some people disapprove of X, & others, when they think of it, don't disapprove at all", that X was both right & wrong? Certainly not, for it doesn't even follow it was wrong; since,

---

[1] There are other uses, e.g. "I did just the wrong thing", when this follows from, e.g., "I screwed the button to the right, when I *ought* to have screwed it to the left". (N.B. "ought to" doesn't here mean that it was *morally* wrong of me to screw it to the right, that I was under a *moral obligation* to screw it to the left.) Similarly "he stuck the wrong end into the fire", "he wore his jacket wrong side out", and "you're wrong" = "you're mistaken".

[1] [In G. E. Moore, *Ethics* (London, 1912), pp. 89 ff.]

according to A, anybody who says it was wrong can only be saying that he himself disapproves of it; and whatever person you take, it can't follow from the mere fact that *some* disapprove of X, that *that* person does. Of course, if 2 different people each use "X was wrong" to mean "X occurred and *I* disapprove of X", they are, in one correct usage of the words "same sense", both using "X was wrong" *in the same sense* & that a sense which, if A is true, is *the* correct one; but nevertheless from the fact that what one of them says is true, it won't in the least follow that what the other says is true also.

And does it follow that X was wrong, from the conjunction of A with (b′) "Someone disapproved of X at one time, & at another, when he considered it, didn't at all disapprove"? Obviously not, for the same reason as before.

17

LOOKS

When a wall which is not bluish white, 'looks' bluish white to me (e.g. because I am wearing blue spectacles) I am certainly "directly seeing", i.e. "seeing" in the same sense in which I "see" an after-image with closed eyes, an expanse which *is* bluish white, and does not merely look so. Yet it is the surface of the wall which looks bluish white to me; and it is correct to say that the bluish white expanse which I directly see, *is* the surface of the wall. But the bluish white expanse which I directly see cannot be *identical* with the surface of the wall (the part of it which I am seeing). I.e. the "is" cannot here mean, as I thought, "is identical with". What does it mean?

When a ship on the sea, which is at a distance, "looks" small I am certainly directly seeing a sense-datum which *is* small; yet it is correct to say that this sense-datum *is* the part of the ship's surface which I am seeing, though this surface is *not* small.

18

FREE WILL

My will is free if & only if both (1) *if* I had *chosen* (or *decided*) to make a "voluntary movement" which I did not make, I should have made it; and (2) I *could* have *chosen* (or *decided*) to make it.

You *can* bicycle, even if you are tied to a chair in a locked room, so that you can't get a bicycle; you *can* speak English, even if you are so gagged that you can't utter a sound. What is meant in such cases by saying that you *can?*

Most people can't bicycle, unless they have learnt; and nobody can talk English, unless he has learnt.

But to say that you *can* bicycle at a given time, does not mean that you *could* at that time bicycle: e.g. if you were tied to a chair in a locked room, or if there were no bicycles then, though there had been in the past; you can't bicycle without a bicycle, even though you can bicycle.

We can (in general, perh. always) only act on external world (things outside our body) by means of *voluntary movements* of our body; and we can (in general) only produce *involuntary movements* of our body by means of *voluntary movements.*

What is a "voluntary movement"? When a bird flies away, that is a voluntary movement; but the bird doesn't "choose" to make it. And in general we don't *choose* our voluntary movements, or *decide* to make them. I think that, in general, we only talk of "choosing" or "deciding", when we have the idea of *not* making the movement, & *prefer* making it to not making it. The bird does not in general do this. Does it always "will" the movement? This is what is suggested by the name "voluntary". And perhaps *always* when we *make* a voluntary movement, we do "will" it, and this is what distinguishes our *making* it, from its *occurrence*; for it may occur without our *making* it. If so, a "voluntary movement", can be defined as a movement the willing of which is *in general sufficient* to produce it. It certainly is "in the control of the will" in some sense in which movements the willing of which is not *sufficient* to produce them are not, e.g. the beating of the heart. But a bird can *try* to fly—(you can *try* to move your arms, when

409

they are bound)—when its wings are broken; and trying is also a matter of the will. The *will* to make a voluntary movement, is, *in general*, sufficient to make it, but is sometimes only sufficient for you to *try* to make it. That the bird's *body* moves away, owing to its wings moving in a certain way, is not *all* we mean by saying *it flies* away: as Wittg. says, if *I raise* my arm, something else happens *beside* that *my* arm *is raised:* that *I raise* it is a *Handlung*, and this is what we mean by saying the raising is due to my *will*, though I neither *choose* nor *decide*. When I *choose* or *decide*, all that happens may be that I *try* to raise it.

INDEX OF PROPER NAMES

411

Printed in Great Britain by
Antony Rowe Ltd, Chippenham, Wiltshire

Also available in the series

KEY TEXTS

Descartes: A Study of his Philosophy
[1968]
Anthony Kenny
ISBN 1 85506 236 4   252pp

An Introduction to the Philosophy of History [1961]
W. H. Walsh
ISBN 1 85506 170 8   176pp

Of the Conduct of the Understanding
(from the *Posthumous Works*)
[1706]
John Locke
New Introduction by John V. Price
ISBN 1 85506 225 9   160pp

Essays on Suicide and the Immortality of the Soul [1783]
David Hume
New Introduction by John V. Price
ISBN 1 85506 167 8   132pp

Perception [1971]
Godfrey Vesey
ISBN 1 85506 161 9   114pp

Dreams of a Spirit-Seer [1900]
Immanuel Kant
ISBN 1 85506 158 9   176pp

Essays on some unsettled Questions of Political Economy [1844]
John Stuart Mill
ISBN 1 85506 160 0   172pp

Mental Acts [1971]
Peter Geach
ISBN 1 85506 161 9   114pp

Perpetual Peace
A Philosophical Essay [1903]
Immanuel Kant
ISBN 1 85506 159 7   218pp

Berkeley [1932]
G. Dawes Hicks
ISBN 1 85506 168 6   346pp

Kant's Introduction to Logic
And his Essay on the Mistaken Subtilty of the Four Figures [1885]
With a few notes by Coleridge
ISBN 1 85506 163 5   108pp

English Literature and Society in the Eighteenth Century [1904]
Leslie Stephen
ISBN 1 85506 217 8   230pp

Francis Hutcheson
His Life, Teaching and Position in the History of Philosophy [1900]
William Robert Scott
ISBN 1 85506 169 4   318pp

Sensationalism and Scientific Explanation [1963]
Peter Alexander
ISBN 1 85506 164 3   158pp

Kant on Education (Ueber Pädagogik) [1899]
Annette Churton (Translator)
ISBN 1 85506 165 1   146pp

All *Key Texts* publications are Demy 8vo (216 x 138mm)